Communication and Cross-Cultural Adaptation:
An Integrative Theory

INTERCOMMUNICATION SERIES

Series Editors

Howard Giles, *Department of Psychology, University of Bristol, Bristol BS8 1HH, U.K.*

Cheris Kramarae, *Department of Speech Communication, University of Illinois, Urbana, IL 61801, U.S.A.*

Editorial Advisory Board

William M. O'Barr, *Department of Anthropology, Duke University, Durham, NC 27706, U.S.A.*

Suzanne Romaine, *Merton College, Oxford University, Oxford, U.K.*

Rod Watson, *Department of Sociology, University of Manchester, Manchester, U.K.*

Other Books in the Series

Talk and Social Organisation
 GRAHAM BUTTON and JOHN R. E. LEE (eds)
Conversation: An Interdisciplinary Approach
 DEREK ROGER and PETER BULL (eds)
Communication and Simulation
 DAVID CROOKALL and DANNY SAUNDERS (eds)

Related Titles of Interest

Perspectives on Marital Interaction
 PATRICIA NOLLER and MARY-ANN FITZPATRICK
Afrikaner Dissidents: A Social Psychological Study of Identity and Dissent
 JOHA LOUW-POTGIETER

Please contact us for the latest information on all our book and journal publications:

Multilingual Matters Ltd,
Bank House, 8a Hill Road,
Clevedon, Avon BS21 7HH,
England

INTERCOMMUNICATION 2

Series Editors: Howard Giles & Cheris Kramarae

COMMUNICATION AND CROSS-CULTURAL ADAPTATION: AN INTEGRATIVE THEORY

Young Yun Kim

In celebration of human spirit that reaches for the unknown and embraces the unfamiliar

MULTILINGUAL MATTERS LTD
Clevedon • Philadelphia

Library of Congress Cataloguing in Publication Data

Kim, Young Yun.

Communication and cross-cultural adaptation.

Bibliography: p.
Includes indexes
1. Conversation — Cross-cultural studies.
2. Adjustment (Psychology) 3. Intercultural
communication.
I. Title.
HM258.K486 1988 302.2 88-5267
ISBN 0-905028-83-X
ISBN 0-905028-82-1 (pbk.)

British Library Cataloguing in Publication Data
Kim, Young Yun

Communication and cross-cultural
adaptation: an integrative theory.—

(Intercommunication series; 2)
1. Immigrants. Cross-cultural adaptation
I. Title II. Series
303.4′82

ISBN 0-905028-83-X
ISBN 0-905028-82-1 Pbk

Multilingual Matters Ltd,
Bank House, 8a Hill Road, & **242 Cherry Street,**
Clevedon, Avon BS21 7HH **Philadelphia, PA 19106–1906**
England. **U.S.A.**

Typeset by Editorial Enterprises, Devon
Printed and bound in Great Britain by Short Run Press, Exeter

Contents

List of figures

Preface

It was about a decade ago that my academic journey into the field of cross-cultural adaptation began. As a graduate student from Korea working on doctoral research in communication at Northwestern University, I was drawn to this inquiry by a deeply felt need to understand the cultural changes that I had experienced. What happens when individuals, born and raised in one culture, settle into a new culture? How do we cope with the uncertainties of the new environment? Why are some of us more successful than others in adapting to the changed life conditions?

I have engaged myself with these questions since then, and have become acquainted with the approaches of investigators in anthropology, communication, psychology, sociology and sociolinguistics. The field of cross-cultural adaptation can be overwhelming to many researchers due to its vastness, complexity and disjointedness. Although the field has benefitted from the richness and diversity of approaches, it suffers from the application of divergent disciplinary viewpoints by different investigators. Each conceptual model emphasises different aspects of the adaptation experiences. Employing labels such as 'acculturation', 'adjustment', 'assimilation' and 'integration', varied sets of factors are presented with only occasional cross-referencing. Often, researchers observe different 'independent' and 'dependent' variables without providing compelling theoretical reasons for doing so.

Recently, two anthologies have been published with an exclusive focus on the theme, cross-cultural adaptation. The first book, *Acculturation* (Padilla, 1980), presents articles that explore the dimensions and analyses of research findings on psychological experiences of immigrants. The second book, *Cross-cultural Adaption* (Y. Kim & Gudykunst, 1987), is a multidisciplinary anthology that presents current conceptualisations and research findings from anthropological, communication, and social psychological perspectives. These two publications have helped 'push' the field toward a greater integration of perspectives in describing and explaining the cross-cultural adaptation phenomenon.

The present volume follows these efforts to propose a single theoretical framework incorporating some of the major existing approaches. Based on a systems perspective and a communication focus, this theory utilises research findings across several disciplines. It thus explicates a set of constructs (and their empirical indicators) and interrelates them into an explanatory scheme linking personal and social communication patterns of individual immigrants and sojourners, their adaptive predisposition, and host environmental characteristics. In presenting this theory, divergent conceptualisations have been incorporated into a multidimensional model, with their respective 'places' clarified.

The present theory is claimed to be neither complete (in reflecting all existing theoretical perspectives) nor completed (in the sense of being 'finalised' in its form). Rather, it is offered as an up-to-date synthesis of viewpoints across disciplines based on a perspective broader than what has been available in the past. The theory reflects a belief that, to paint a realistic and useful picture of cross-cultural adaptation, we need to employ concepts at a higher level of abstraction and broaden our horizons to include as many different conceptual angles as possible.

I present this volume with a special joy of understanding my own adaptive metamorphosis. Responsibility for this book's content is solely mine, but several individuals have made important contributions to its making. I thank the Intercommunication Series editors, Howard Giles and Cheris Kramarae, for emphasising 'balanced INTERdisciplinary endeavors' of 'interdisciplinary souls'. They initially welcomed this book into the series, and have furnished me with encouragement and insightful comments. Five colleagues — Charles R. Berger, William B. Gudykunst, Michael W. Purdy, Brent D. Ruben and Stella Ting-Toomey — reviewed the manuscript at different stages of its completion and suggested many useful ideas. I also thank Gordon Craigo who gave so many of his hours for checking and rechecking of the drafts. My final appreciation goes to the publisher, Multilingual Matters, for its dedication to issues that interfuse many linguistic and cultural groups of the world.

Young Yun Kim

PART I

INTRODUCTION

1 CONTEXTS OF CROSS-CULTURAL ADAPTATION

You cannot step into the same river twice,
for fresh water is forever flowing towards you.
Heraclitus of Ephesus

Time and again, humans have demonstrated a remarkable capacity to cope with, and overcome, difficulties. Devastated by disastrous events such as war and natural calamities, people rise again and continue living under changed circumstances. Prisoners of war survive for many months and years under the most severe conditions. We readjust to life after the death of loved ones, and in the end deal with our own death. Many times we triumph over changes by coming out of hardship with a strengthened life force and a broadened and deepened understanding of self, others, and human conditions. In the words of Thayer (1975), 'Man [woman] is the most plastic of all earth's creatures' (p. 237).

Today, we are experiencing change in more dramatic ways than ever before, as has been articulated by Toffler (1970, 1980), Capra (1982), and others. Today's change is swift, fundamental, and unprecedented in scale, shaking even the most basic human conditions. It moves us to new technologies, new social structures, new values, new politics, and new human relations. Even in tribal and traditional societies, change has encroached upon nearly every stable pattern of life — cultural values, the structure and functions of the family, and the relations between generations. Toffler (1970) coined the term 'future shock' to describe the stress and disorientation to which many people are subjected in coping with too much change. The complexity, diversity, and rapid pace of change makes us 'strangers' in our own society. As Morrow (1985) has put it, 'Everyone is an immigrant in time, voyaging into the future' (p. 25).

Parallel to such technological-cultural change is the increasing movement of individuals from one society to another. More people are moving than ever before, crossing the cultural boundaries that separate the life patterns of peoples. In a single year, millions around the world relocate. In this human flow across national and cultural boundaries, there are diplomats and other intergovernmental agency employees, business men and women on international assignments, researchers working in cultures other than their own, professors and students attending conferences and academic institutions overseas, military personnel on foreign duty, and missionaries carrying out their religious services. Then there are the tens of millions of refugees and immigrants on the move across societal boundaries — in search of peace, freedom, security, and social, economic, or cultural betterment. (See Brislin, 1981; Dyal & Dyal, 1981; Furnham & Bochner, 1982; Taft, 1977 for more detailed discussions of various contexts of cross-cultural migration.)

Mass movements of individuals across cultural boundaries have been on the rise throughout the nineteenth and twentieth centuries. During the nineteenth century, impoverished workers, including many craftsmen and skilled workers displaced by advances in the technical division of labor, fled from Europe, flocking to the United States and colonies of the European powers. Between 1800 and 1914, net emigration from Europe was estimated at 50 million (Standing, 1984:15). In 1984 alone, more than half a million legal immigrants came to the United States, largely from Mexico, the Philippines, and Vietnam.

Today, about one-fourth the population of New York, San Francisco, and Los Angeles are foreign-born immigrants and their children. European countries, particularly England, France, Germany, and Austria, also have seen a large influx of Turkish, Portuguese, and Spanish migrant workers since the 1960's. Over three million non-whites are estimated to reside in France and about the same number in England. In Sweden, there are more than 100,000 Turks and slightly fewer Moroccans, and more recently Vietnamese, Cambodians, and Poles. As a result, one in eight people in Sweden is now foreign-born or the offspring of immigrants. In Germany, there are reportedly 175,000 Austrians, 109,000 Dutch, 602,000 Italians, 174,000 Spaniards, 106,000 Portuguese, 301,000 Greeks, 632,000 Yugoslavs, and a large unspecified number of Turks (cf. Foster & Stockley, 1984; Meznaric, 1984; Phizacklea, 1984).

In the 1970's, massive numbers of political and economic refugees moved from Southeast Asia and other places to various countries around the world. Over 50,000 Soviet Jews moved from the Soviet Union to Israel and the United States between 1970 and 1979. Approximately one million refugees — mostly from Southeast Asia, and some from the Soviet Union, Cuba, and Central and South American nations — arrived in the United States between 1975 and 1983 (Kerpin, 1984). In the African continent, there are reportedly close to 143,000 Banyarwanda living in Rwanda, Tanzania, and Uganda, and approximately four million Afghan refugees in Iran and Pakistan. One-fifth to one-fourth of Afghanistan's population is reported to live in exile. All in all, a total of 1,898,000 refugees entered and resettled in a country other than their own home country between 1975 and 1983 (US Committee for Refugees, 1984:4–9, 40).

The focus: adaptation of international migrants

Cross-cultural movement, indeed, has become a common place of our time. The pervasiveness of the movements of people across societies, along with the technological and social changes within societies, requires that we cope with numerous situations to which our previous experience simply does not apply. Learning to live with uncertainty has become one of the central challenges of our time. Regardless of the unique idiosyncrasies of individuals in their cross-cultural responses, many international migrants who travel in both time and geographical space experience an acute 'existential alertness', bringing a special significance to the term adaptation. Numerous people struggle to cope with the feelings of inadequacy and frustration in the changed environment: some resist change and fight for the old ways, others desperately try to 'go native', often experiencing a sense of failure and despair. Whether for a long or short term, international migration represents a situation where the newly arrived strangers are required to cope with substantial cultural change.

Of course, situations of international migration vary in the abruptness of the transition. For example, a sudden cultural transition was experienced by many Southeast Asian refugees after the Vietnam War. Due to the involuntary and traumatic nature of their departure, most had little chance to prepare themselves psychologically for life in the new country. Particularly during the initial resettlement phase, many suffered from a deep psychological dislocation and sense of loss (cf. Y. Kim, 1980). Even when the transition is voluntary, international migrants differ in their motivation to adapt to the new environment and to make the host society their 'second home'. (Hereinafter, the term 'immigrants' will refer to all long-term migrants including refugees, except when different migrant groups need to be identified separately.)

This motivation to adapt depends largely on the degree of permanence of the new residence. For immigrants, the move from their original culture to the host society is permanent, or is regarded as such at least initially. Although some may eventually return to their homeland, most immigrants are committed to the new society in the sense that it is now the setting for the conduct of their lives. Being full participants in that society for better or worse, they are unlikely to be able to segregate themselves from frequent contact with host nationals. Because of the necessity to make a living and attain social membership in the host society, most immigrants must be concerned with their relationship to the environment in a way similar to the native population.

For many short-term sojourners, on the other hand, contact with the new culture is only peripheral. Reasons for a sojourn in a new culture are often very pragmatic and specific — to pursue a vocation, to obtain a degree, or merely to enhance one's prestige in the eyes of the folks back home. This may require less overall commitment to the host cultural system (Taft, 1977:126). Foreign students, for example, can reduce their cultural adaptation to the bare minimum required to fulfill their role as a student and may confine their social contact to fellow students from their home country. A similar observation can be made about military personnel and their families in foreign countries, and about migrant workers as well.

Regardless of the specific situational demands, however, *all individuals in a changing and changed cultural environment share common adaptation experiences*. All are 'strangers' to their host society and cannot completely ignore the demands of the new life setting. To a greater or lesser extent, all must cope with a high level of uncertainty and unfamiliarity as they are in an ambivalent status. Temporarily at least, they are between two worlds — the familiar milieu of their original culture and their new locus in the host society. Many of the behavioral modes useful in the old setting may prove maladaptive in the new. As Schuetz (1944/1963) described:

> the cultural pattern of the approached group is to the stranger not a shelter but a field of adventure, not a matter of course but a questionable topic of investigation, not an instrument for disentangling problematic situations but a problematic situation itself and one hard to master. (p. 108)

Sooner or later, the immigrants and sojourners come to better structure, or make sense of, personally relevant situations in the host society. To handle the transactions of daily living requires the ability to detect similarities and differences between the surrounding host culture and the home culture. They gradually become acquainted with the aspects of living in the host culture: from maintaining basic survival necessities — physical safety and health — to working for their livelihood, developing relationships, and enjoying leisure activities. They become increasingly proficient in handling daily activities in the new culture, with improved skills to deal with situations they encounter.

Countless immigrants and sojourners, from the beginning of history, have adapted to a new and unfamiliar cultural environment. Some of them, of course, have not been so successful, have returned to their home cultures prematurely, or have found themselves with less than 'healthy' mental and social functioning. A few may never feel completely adequate, and in control of their lives, in the new culture. By and large, however, people learn to adequately manage their changed circumstances so that their daily life is not seriously impaired by their 'foreignness'. To this effect, numerous personal stories of various short-term and long-term experiences of adaptive change have been told. The following excerpts from the diary of a former American Peace Corps volunteer, Vicki Holmsten (in *Chicago Tribune*, May 27, 1978, Section 1, p. 10) succinctly testify to human resilience in the face of cross-cultural challenge.

> *December 12, 1975* — I am visiting the town that I have been assigned to — it's in the bush! A small town called Foequellie, it's about 27 miles and an hour of dirt roads out of Gbarnga, the Bong County capital. Here I am to spend the next two years. To be honest, I have a bad case of culture shock. Not much English spoken in town — the language is Kpelle, the people here mostly of the tribe of the same name. No electricity. Kerosene lamps and battery-run radios seem to be modern touches. The running water is provided by the houseboy who brings the buckets from the well.

> *January 5, 1976* — Why am I doing this? Why, why, why? We stayed in Monrovia long enough to shop for household necessities, then the members of our group took off for various parts of the country . . . . I move into a house in Foequellie and wait for school to begin.

> *February 19, 1976* — Rice, rice, rice. If I see another bowl of rice . . . We eat rice everyday.

> *March 17, 1976* — When you're sick you want to go home because there's nothing worse than being in a steamy jungle clearing when your entire body is hurting . . . . So you travel to the hospital where you will be shuffled through lines with crying babies, weary-eyed children, and

puffy-faced old ladies. Hours of waiting, waiting in lines that couldn't possibly make sense or lead to anything.

May 11, 1976 — What is it all for? I don't know. One of my students is dying. Life and death, the essence here. It's getting enough food to keep going and watching people die because there's no way to prevent it. I'm hurting very badly. Am I doing the right thing by being here? I know I'm not doing my best, I'm not even sure what that is anymore.

October 17, 1976 — I think I am only just now coming to terms with Africa. It is a very alive place. Life-giving and deadly at the same time. Life and death all out in the open, nothing muted or subtle. I am excited to be a part of it. I will never be African, but I am a part of it because I am investing myself in the future of the continent. One small part of Africa is mine, I am in one small part African.

January 16, 1977 — Eleven months to go. I'm sure now that I can do it. Positive feelings about being here. Good ideas about what to do in my teaching, the ability and self-confidence to implement them that are gradually coming with experience.

March 25, 1977 — Today I ate roasted termites. Not bad.

September 10, 1977 — I'm enjoying life here now. I finally belong, I'm accepted. I am at last Vicki Holmsten to the people of Foequellie, not the 'Peace Corps volunteer'. It's almost time for me to leave. I'm not sure I really want to.

September 25, 1977 — When I go to Monrovia, the first stop is always for hamburgers and ice cream. But if I'm there for more than two days, I get really hungry for my accustomed daily bowl of rice, and end up in a chop shop with an enormous serving of rice in front of me.

December 6, 1977 — I'm sad to be going home but nevertheless feel that the time is ripe. The school had a going away party for me Saturday night. It was absurdly perfect. People all over the house, palm wine, tear-jerking farewell speeches, appropriate exits and entrances at calculated moments. I was presented with a beautiful African country cloth robe — it is probably the most precious thing I will ever own. It's over now, time to pack up and go.

Personal accounts such as the above have been told by countless immigrants and sojourners all over the world — mostly among their families, friends and relatives. These stories provide endless illustrations of the remarkable ability of human beings to carry on life when completely estranged from the familiar environment of their home country. Thus we see today Nordics, Southern Europeans, Latin Americans, and Asiatics who have settled in New York, London, Paris, Montreal, and Sydney who eat the same food, wear the same kind of clothing, use the same style of furniture, and enjoy the same television program at the same hour. In rural Africa, blue-eyed Peace Corps volunteers and dark-skinned natives work on irrigation projects side-by-side. In Monterey Park, California, we have a Chinese-born woman as mayor, and her five-member city council includes two Hispanics and a Filipino-American.

Organisation of the book

There can be little dispute, among scientists and non-scientists alike, that cross-cultural adaptation takes place in individuals. Our present concern, therefore, is not *whether* individuals adapt, but *how*. This book is an attempt to describe and explain this issue, building on what has been previously articulated in various human-behavioral-social sciences about the cross-cultural adaptation process. (The term, human sciences, will be used throughout this book to represent all sciences of human behavior in social contexts.) It does so by *presenting an integrative, multidimensional theory that identifies patterns that are commonly and consistently present in the adaptation of individuals.* In this book, the term, adaptation, is used in a broad and general sense to refer to the internal transformation of an individual challenged by a new cultural environment in the direction of increasing fitness and compatibility in that environment. This working definition accommodates all other similar terms such as acculturation, assimilation, and adjustment that have been frequently used in different human science disciplines. (Details of the meaning of adaptation are discussed in Chapters 3 and 4.)

The proposed theory is based on the General Systems perspective that regards individual immigrants and sojourners as *open systems* interacting with a given cultural environment that is different from the home culture in which they were born and raised. The theory further views cross-cultural adaptation as a dynamic *communication* process. The individual and the host environment are considered to co-determine the course and outcome of the adaptation process through various communication activities. Within the open systems perspective and the communication focus, the theory integrates existing conceptualisations of cross-cultural adaptation as well as pertinent empirical findings in the human sciences including anthropology, communication, sociolinguistics, social psychology, sociology, psychiatry, and related disciplines. In addition, the theory attempts to forward a *general* description and explanation of the cross-cultural adaptation process, going beyond the uniqueness of individual experiences and circumstances. Key issues addressed in the proffered theory are:

(1) How do individuals adapt to a new, unfamiliar culture?
(2) What does it mean to be 'well-adapted' or 'poorly adapted' to a given cultural environment?
(3) Why do certain individuals display a greater adaptation than others? In other words, what are some of the crucial factors that facilitate or impede adaptation?
(4) How do the background characteristics of cultural strangers influence their adaptation to a new environment?
(5) How do the characteristics of a new environment influence the adaptation of cultural strangers?
(6) What patterns of adaptation do individuals go through over time in a new cultural environment?

These questions may sound simple, but the answers are not. For several decades, theoretical and research attempts have shed light on these questions, but our current understanding is still fragmentary, incomplete, and often confused. Chapter 2 reviews and analyses various existing approaches to cross-cultural adaptation to identify a number of problem areas in those approaches. This analysis will serve as the background against which a theory will be subsequently developed in Part II (Chapters 3–5). Details of the theoretical dimensions and constructs are presented in Part III (Chapters 6–9). From this theory, ideas for future research and practical concerns will be derived (Part IV, Chapters 10–11).

2 EXISTING APPROACHES: REVIEW AND ANALYSIS

> *The principal cause of stagnation and*
> *extinction is over-specialisation.*
> Arthur Koestler

The study of cross-cultural adaptation has been active primarily in the United States, a nation in which immigrants and ethnic diversity have always been a major reality and an issue of serious concern. Comparatively, immigrant adaptation studies have been more recent and less extensive in the academic traditions of European countries. Cross-cultural adaptation, because of its multiple facets and dimensions, has been viewed from several conceptual angles and measured in various categories (such as changes in economic condition, perception, attitude, behavioral patterns, linguistic proficiency and ethnic/cultural identity). Each of these categories, in turn, has included a number of elements that could be examined separately with varying degrees of scientific legitimacy. Social scientists today are far from being intellectually homogeneous in studying cross-cultural adaptation phenomena.

The literature related to cross-cultural adaptation has accumulated since the turn of the century. Today, the serious scholar of cross-cultural adaptation must study thousands of books and articles for a complete understanding of work in this area. The variety of literature and data sources makes it difficult for any one individual to gain familiarity with the whole body of literature across disciplinary boundaries. Although the field has benefited from the rich literature reporting the information and insights in cross-cultural adaptation phenomena, it has also suffered from increased specialisation, complexity, and, often, confusion resulting from the application of concepts, definitions, and methodologies peculiar to different disciplinary and ideological perspectives.

This chapter reviews and analyses the approaches that have been used in the human sciences to understand the cross-cultural adaptation process. Due to the diversity and complexity of the field, reviewing the entire field in an exhaustive manner is neither necessary nor useful for the present purpose. Instead, the overall trends and major approaches will be presented in terms of two levels of analysis — (1) the group-level approaches commonly observed in anthropological and sociological studies, and (2) the individual-level approaches predominant in communication, social psychology, sociolinguistics, and more recently in cultural anthropology and psychiatry. In addition, conceptual and methodological problems that are present in these approaches will be identified in terms of: (1) inconsistent use of critical concepts; (2) lack of cross-fertilisation between academic disciplines, particularly between the group-level studies in sociology and anthropology and the individual-level studies in communication and social psychology; (3) lack of cross-fertilisation between studies of long-term adaptation of immigrants and studies of short-term adaptation of temporary sojourners, and (4) the limited perspectives characterising cross-cultural adaptation as *either* a negative *or* a positive phenomenon.

Based on the review and analysis, the integrative, systems/communication approach taken in the proposed theory will be justified at the end of this chapter.

Group-level approaches

Scholars in anthropology and sociology have approached the field mainly on the level of immigrant (or ethnic) groups rather than on the level of individuals. Generally, anthropological studies have been primarily interested in describing the dynamics of cultural change in various societies (primarily 'primitive' cultures) resulting from continuous contact with another culture (primarily technically advanced cultures). In contrast, sociological studies have attempted to explain the socioeconomic and political dynamics between and among immigrant/ethnic and dominant groups within societies. Some of the uniformities traditionally observed in these two group-level approaches to cross-cultural adaptation are discussed below.

Anthropological approaches

Studies of cross-cultural adaptation have been traditional among American anthropologists since the 1930's. During the 1930's, the Social Science Research Council appointed a Subcommittee on Acculturation composed of three anthropologists — Robert Redfield, Ralph Linton, and Melville Herskovits — and charged it with the task of analysing and defining the parameters for this new field of inquiry within the domain of cultural anthropology (cf. Gordon, 1964). As the result, acculturation was formally adopted as a legitimate new area of study dealing with

> those phenomena which result when *groups* of individuals have different cultures and come into first-hand contact with subsequent changes in the original pattern of either or both *groups*. (Emphasis added. Redfield, Linton & Herskovits, 1936:149.)

Along this traditional line, Spicer (1968) defined acculturation as 'those changes set in motion by the coming together of *societies* with different cultural traditions' (emphasis added, p. 21).

As is evident in these definitions, the discipline of anthropology has treated acculturation primarily as a group phenomenon. In examining the acculturation of various groups, anthropological studies have often observed the importance of the presence of kin, friends and ethnic affiliates (Eames & Schwab, 1964; Mangin, 1960; Southall, 1961). These and other related aspects of urban ethnic enclaves have been viewed as key agencies facilitating the acculturation of new immigrants whereby they acquire the means for structuring their new environment and learn the behavior appropriate for the new environment. These resources for adaptation take the form of voluntary organisations and mutual aid groups (Banton, 1961; Little, 1957), providing the immigrant with moral and material support that ameliorates the shock of change.

Along with studies of ethnic communities and cultural groups, anthropologists have also approached immigrant acculturation by examining the 'ideal type' of personality or 'dominant' values and life patterns of a cultural group. The emphasis in these studies has been placed on assessing the learning and internalisation of new personality traits or new values by a cultural group as a replacement for those of the original culture. For example, Spindler (1955), in studying the acculturation patterns of Ojibwa and Menomini American-Indian cultures, focused on the change in the tribes' 'personality'-type characteristics as a result of contact with the dominant American culture. From this study, Spindler concluded:

there is a definable personality type characteristic of the least acculturated group which is appropriate to the patterning of the old
culture as it survives in the present and extends back into the past. It
also reveals that this personality type resembles that of the Ojibwa,
with whom the Menomini share a cultural fundament. It further shows
that significant changes away from this psychological base line have
occurred in the transitional segments of the continuum, and that these
changes appear to represent a breakdown of the native-oriented
personality structure. (p. 2)

Such anthropological focus on a normative value structure, however,
has failed to provide a consistent and concrete picture of American culture.
Hsu (1971), an anthropologist, points out the problem:

What do we mean when we say of an immigrant, 'He is Americanized'?
It seems clear that we do not have a precise idea as to what we mean
by 'Americanization', nor have anthropologists who deal with culture
contact and culture change helped in this regard . . . . How can we
gauge the extent of acculturation without a precise notion about the
culture to which the acculturated have supposedly acculturated
themselves? We cannot but agree that the picture is by no means clear.
We must develop a more precise idea on the notion of Americanization
to answer the question at all. (p. 111)

The difficulty of establishing an 'ideal type' seems inevitable when
one examines the empirical findings from sociological studies on American
value systems. In the area of marriage and family life, for example,
considerable variability has been found among different subgroups distinct
in socioeconomic status, ethnic traditions, religious preferences, and racial
ascriptions (Adams, 1971; Adams & Weirath, 1971; Winch & Spanier,
1974). Even when one accepts the general assumption that *the* American
culture is represented by those who are White, Anglo-Saxon, and
Protestant, differences in attitudes and values still exist among different age
groups and socioeconomic groups.

Sociological approaches

While the majority of anthropological studies have observed changes
in the culture of the target group itself, sociological studies have focused
primarily on issues pertaining to social stratification, that is, the hierarchical
classification of the members of society based on the unequal distribution
of resources, power, and prestige (Parrillo, 1966:80). Many sociological

studies have also investigated minority–majority relations focusing on the patterns and processes in which minority groups are integrated into the political, social, and economic structure of the host society (cf. Amersfoort, 1974/1982; Marrett & Leggon, 1979; Spiro, 1955).

Like anthropologists, sociological researchers generally treat individuals as abstract entities forming a social 'category', 'class', or 'strata'. M. Gordon (1964), for example, examined changes in the sociological meaning of ethnicity in the United States. He categorised social science definitions of assimilation into Anglo-conformity, melting pot, and pluralistic variants based on conditions of structural pluralism, ideological orientations, and psychological conditions. In this framework, Blacks, Jews, Catholics and White Protestants were analysed as American ethnic groups.

Similarly, Glazer & Moynihan (1975) analysed positions of ethnic groups in the United States in political salience, religion, community structure, assimilation, group identities, group relations, language demands, policy toward minorities and ethnic stratification. Recently, Blalock (1982) presented a theory of race and ethnic relations by focusing on social class conflicts, inequities, labor arrangements, power conflict and minority reactions, competition, discrimination, and segregation. Blalock's approach to ethnic relations combined attitudinal factors — such as hostility and intergroup tension that had been extensively investigated in social psychological studies of prejudice (e.g., Levine & Campbell, 1972) — with macrosocial studies of ethnic group discrimination. (See, also, Kinloch, 1974; Mason, 1970; Shibutani & Kwan, 1965, for other sociological studies of ethnicity and interethnic relations.)

These and other sociological studies of ethnicity and interethnic relations have proliferated in the United States during the past two decades. The political importance of ethnicity in the United States has made it a topic of both public and academic interest, generating enormous amounts of information about ethnic phenomena, structures, and processes (cf. Bentley, 1981:xi). The interest in ethnicity, however, extends well beyond the United States. In Canada, for example, Quebecois separatism and English–French bilingualism are still active social and political issues. Along this line, Berry, Kalin & Taylor (1976), for example, have investigated multiculturalism and ethnic attitudes in Canada.

In Europe, 'race' has also emerged as a political issue in recent nationalist campaigns, and the sociology of race relations has received increasing academic interest. In England, for example, there is a body of literature that constitutes a British sociology of immigration, and a number of different perspectives have emerged over the last twenty years. According to Phizacklea (1984), central attention has been placed on the negative significance attached to certain migrant groups (and their offspring) by the indigenous population. This perspective focuses on that component of the post-war migrant labor force drawn from ex-British colonies. Thus, British scholars have investigated the conflict relationship between class and race relations, and the extent to which the colonial 'immigrants' have been incorporated into the British class structure. Similar studies have been carried out in other European countries that have been receiving foreign immigrants (cf. Amersfoort, 1974/1982).

There are other sociological studies in which the main purpose is to record historical trends and developments of immigrant groups in various societies. Conroy & Miyakawa (1972), for example, studied assimilation and adaptation of Japanese-Americans focusing primarily on their peculiar economic and social success, and the intergenerational cultural and character differences between Issei (first-generation), Nisei (second-generation), and Sansei (third-generation) groups. Similarly, Bharati (1972) described demographic patterns, caste and marriage patterns, entrepreneurship, interpersonal relations, interethnic images, and the maintenance of beliefs and religious practices by Asians in East Africa.

Another sociological approach to immigrant adaptation has been the ethnographic study of immigrant communities. Gallo (1974), for example, conducted a participant-observation study of political alienation of Italian-Americans focusing on the perception of their political powerlessness and alienation from the American political system. Similarly, Gans (1962) studied the community life patterns and activities of Italian-Americans based on a qualitative, ethnographic analysis.

Assimilation versus pluralism

In both anthropological and sociological studies of cross-cultural adaptation, the main emphasis has been placed on immigrant groups rather than on individuals. Relatively little attention has been given to the pattern and process of adaptive change in individuals.

Further, studies conducted by American anthropologists and sociologists on the immigrant groups have often been influenced by the social philosophies (or ideologies) of a particular time period. Studies were often created and developed to fulfill an ideology (Postiglione, 1983:12). As such, they have appeared as successive ideological interpretations of the meaning of American history. At times, investigations of ethnicity appear to have been prompted less by scientific curiosity than by policy concerns (Bentley, 1981:xii). As Van den Berghe (1967) bluntly stated, 'social science theory [of ethnicity] is little more than a weathercock shifting with ideological winds' (p. 8). Because ethnicity has historically been a sensitive political issue, studies in this area have closely mirrored changes in the political environment. (See, also, Nagata, 1969, for a review of the literature.)

Historically in the United States, there has been a movement from a pole of assimilation to a pole of 'pluralism' (Postiglione, 1983:204). The perspective of assimilation is based on fundamental faith in the ideal that immigrants, given time, will ultimately change their original cultural traits to those of the American society. Such faith has stimulated social scientists to study how new immigrants blend into the 'melting pot' of American society. The melting-pot view of a coming-together of the 'best' traits of each culture became popularised by the Jewish immigrant Israel Zangwill's interpretation of it in his play *The Melting Pot*, first performed in 1908 (cf. Postiglione, 1983:16).

Reflecting the melting-pot view on the nature and direction of immigrant adaptation, M. Gordon (1964) conceptualised the adaptation process in terms of seven subprocesses of 'assimilation':

(1) cultural or behavioral assimilation,
(2) structural assimilation,
(3) material assimilation,
(4) identificational assimilation,
(5) attitude receptional assimilation,
(6) behavior receptional assimilation, and
(7) civic assimilation.

In this progressive model of assimilation, Gordon viewed acculturation as 'the first of the types of assimilation to occur when a minority group arrives on the scene' and 'may take place even when none of the other types of assimilation occurs simultaneously or later' (Gordon, 1964:71–81). Implicit in this assimilationist conceptualisation is the idea that incoming minority groups must, to some degree, strive to achieve all seven subprocesses of assimilation although the process may never be completed.

This vision of assimilation as the final goal of cross-cultural adaptation was first questioned when blacks challenged its validity through their Civil Rights Movement of the 1960's, preparing the way for a similar awakening among other ethnic groups. More recent challenges to the old melting-pot view have come from the 'new ethnicity' movement that began in the early 1970's in the United States. Michael Novak, author of *The Rise of the Unmeltable Ethnics* (1971), is exemplary in that he argued against cultural assimilation and advocated equal ethnicity for all. He described the feelings of alienation held by one large ethnic group, Poles, who were drawn to ethnic power movements in the competition for jobs, respect, and attention. In his subsequent article, Novak (1973) contended:

> There is no such thing as *homo Americanus*. There is no single culture here. We do not, in fact, have a culture at all — at least, not a highly developed one, whose symbols, images, and ideals all of us work out of and constantly mind afresh; such 'common culture' as even intellectuals have is more an ideal aspired to than a task accomplished. (p. 18)

The rise of ethnic movements has encouraged social scientists to focus on the ethnicity of immigrants and their communities rather than on assimilation. The cultural pluralist orientation emphasises the persistence of ethnicity as the basis of the continued importance of ethnic groups. Glazer & Moynihan (1963) noted that ethnicity pervades all spheres of life among ethnic individuals and groups. They rejected the melting-pot view, stating: 'The point about the melting pot is that it did not happen' (p. 290). Research in ethnic politics indicates a continued structure of ethnic relations and identification from one generation to another. Greeley (1974), Parenti (1967) & Wolfinger (1965), among others, found that 'ethnic' Americans possess political orientations different from those of 'non-ethnic' Americans as shown by respective voting patterns, and that ethnic voting patterns persist for many generations. (For more detailed accounts of the historical trends of social ideological development, see Feagin, 1984; Postiglione, 1983.)

Teske & Nelson (1974) took a more pluralistic perspective arguing that assimilation is a special case of changes that are involved in the acculturation process. *Acculturation*, according to Teske and Nelson, is (potentially) a bidirectional process and does *not* require changes in values within the acculturating group. *Assimilation*, however, is a unidirectional process (toward the dominant host culture only) and requires value changes within the assimilating group. Within this framework, Teske and Nelson defined acculturation according to eight characteristics: (1) a dynamic process that may involve (2) either groups or individuals in (3) direct contact situations between cultures. The changes that take place (4) can occur in one or both cultural groups and (5) changes in values may be involved. Acculturation does not require (6) a change in the reference group, (7) internal change, or (8) acceptance by the outside group or culture. When characteristics six, seven, and eight are present, assimilation is considered to have occurred.

These conceptualisations of acculturation and assimilation differ in their view on what the fundamental directionality of change *ought to be* in immigrant groups in the process of adapting to the host society. M. Gordon's assimilation model, for example, is focused on the adaptive change toward complete assimilation, but Teske and Nelson's acculturation model considers such assimilation as neither necessary nor inevitable.

Individual-level approaches

Along with the group approaches to cross-cultural adaptation in anthropology and sociology, some studies have examined the experiences of *individuals* adapting to the host society. By and large, these studies focus on strangers' *psychological reactions* and *social integration* while living in a new environment for varied lengths of time. These studies can be broadly grouped into two areas: (1) adaptation of long-term residents (such as immigrants and refugees living in another culture more or less permanently), and (2) adaptation of short-term sojourners (such as diplomats, international students, Peace Corps volunteers, and overseas employees of multinational corporations).

These studies have been conducted primarily by researchers in communication, social psychology, sociolinguistics, cultural anthropology, and psychiatry in the major countries receiving immigrants and sojourners, namely, the United States (e.g., Y. Kim, 1980; Padilla, 1980), Great Britain (e.g., Watson, 1977), Canada (e.g., Berry, 1975), and Australia (e.g., Taft, 1966). Typically, these studies have attempted to explain individual differences in the degree to which they adjust to the host cultural system. (For recent reviews of literature on short- and long-term cross-cultural adaptation, see Bochner, 1982; Brislin, 1981, Torbiorn, 1982.) Some of the key variables discussed in these studies are perception of and attitude toward the host society, level of satisfaction, patterns of interpersonal relationships, and host language competence.

Immigrant adaptation

Individual-level inquiries into long-term cross-cultural adaptation of immigrants have developed over the past three decades or so mainly in social psychology, and more recently in communication. Because of the relative newness of such inquiries, key concepts (such as acculturation and assimilation) from the 'older' fields of anthropology and sociology are used alongside new terms such as 'psychological acculturation' (Berry, 1975; Berry, Kim & Boski, 1987).

Unlike the traditional conceptualisations of acculturation and assimilation as primarily group-level phenomena, these more recent approaches view the same phenomena from the individual perspective. Acculturation, thus, is defined as 'the change in individuals whose primary learning has been in one culture and who take over traits from another culture' (Marden & Meyer, 1968:36), or as 'the process of cognitive, attitudinal and behavioral adaptation to the new cultural system' (Y. Kim, 1978a:199). Assimilation, on the other hand, is used to emphasise the process whereby immigrants become more similar to the native population as a result of interaction (Taft, 1957).

Overall, research of individual immigrants typically investigates their cross-cultural adaptation by identifying the key variables considered to influence the level of acculturation or adjustment. Variables and measurements in such studies, however, show little consistency across different researchers. For instance, Taft (1957) identified concepts such as attitudes, frames of reference, social motivation, ego involvement, beliefs, reference groups, role expectations, and role behavior as key aspects of immigrants' adaptation in the new culture (p. 142). Based on these variables, Taft delineated seven stages of 'assimilation', moving progressively from the 'cultural learning' stage to the 'congruence' stage. Each of these stages were conceptualised in two dimensions, internal and external. More recently, Taft (1977) presented a somewhat simplified schema in which adaptation is viewed to consist of four facets: 'cultural adjustment', 'national and ethnic identity', 'cultural competence' and 'role acculturation'.

On the other hand, Stonequist (1964) examined immigrant adaptation by focusing on an individual's inner strain or malaise, a feeling of isolation he refers to as 'marginality'. Along this line of conceptualisation, Shuval (1963) examined the nature of settlers into Israel in their early phase (first two years) of settlement. In doing so, acculturation was assessed by using three key variables: (1) acceptance of certain norms that immigrants perceived as representative of Israel, (2) seeking old-timers (rather than other immigrants) as sources of information and advice, and (3) general attitude toward the host population.

As in the sociological and anthropological approaches discussed earlier, implicit ideological positions in social psychological approaches to cross-cultural adaptation appear to have shifted from the earlier assimilationist view to the more recent pluralistic view. Taft (1957), for example, considered an eventual conversion of immigrants into the host culture as the 'end product' of the adaptation process. On the other hand, more recent researchers such as Berry (1980, 1984) have presented a pluralistic view by identifying assimilation as only one of several varieties of adaptive 'responses'. Berry (1984) proposed a fourfold model of acculturation based on two questions: (1) 'Are cultural identity and customs of value to be retained?' and (2) 'Are positive relations with the larger society of value, and to be sought?' By combining an individual's responses (yes, no) to these two questions, Berry and his associates identified four types of adaptation: 'integration', 'assimilation', 'rejection' and 'marginality'. Similarly, Stonequist (1964) viewed the process of cross-cultural adaptation of individual immigrants as following one of three major directions: (1) assimilation into the dominant group, (2) assimilation into the subordinate group, or (3) some form of accommodation between the two societies.

Another pluralistic psychological approach to acculturation by Padilla (1980) emphasised the significance of an immigrant's cultural awareness and ethnic loyalty. Cultural awareness, according to Padilla, refers to an individual's cultural heritage (language, history, foods) as well as the cultural heritage of the respondent's spouse and parents, language preference and use, cultural identification and preference, and social behavior orientation. Padilla also considered 'ethnic loyalty' (i.e., cultural pride and affiliation, perceived discrimination, and social behavior orientation) an important dimension of acculturation.

Important insights into individuals' communication behaviors in the host environment have been offered recently by social psychological and sociolinguistics researchers. Their theoretical focus is 'social identity', defined as

> that part of an individual's self-concept which derives from his [her] knowledge of his [her] membership in a social group (or groups) together with the value and emotional significance attached to that membership. (Tajfel, 1978b:63.)

With this focus, social identity theory (Tajfel & Turner, 1979; Turner, 1987) argues that individuals seek positive social identities in cross-cultural encounters, and that their communication behaviors are influenced by the salience of the interactants' group memberships and the 'threat' that such perception of group membership presents to one's social identity.

In this line of reasoning, language behavior has been given particularly detailed theoretical and research attention due to its crucial linkage with social identity (cf. Giles, 1977; Giles & Johnson, 1981). Individuals' second language competence, along with other factors, in interethnic situations has been explained by Giles and Johnson (1981, 1986) as negatively related to the strength of identification with their own ethnic group. In other words, immigrants or sojourners whose 'claim' of membership in their home culture is weaker are likely to develop a greater competence in the host language (cf. Mercer, Mead & Mears, 1979). Relatedly, research on 'ethnolinguistic vitality' has shown that the perceived strength or potency of the language of an ethnic group influences the degree to which its members will emphasise their ethnic identity in intercultural encounters (Giles, Bourhis & Taylor, 1977).

Another aspect of immigrant adaptation that has received substantial research attention in psychology and psychiatry is mental health. (See Dyal & Dyal, 1981, for a review.) This approach emphasises the clinical implications of adaptive experiences and the extent to which these experiences challenge the individual with new and unfamiliar psycho-social demands (Fabrega, 1969:318). The central consideration is that individuals living in these circumstances often experience severe psychological distress because the adaptive process leads to disruption in their customary life patterns. Besides experiencing psychological distress, immigrants, at least initially, are considered prone to impairment in their ability to manage varied social transactions (cf. Brower, 1980; Kinzie *et al.*, 1980; Williams & Westermeyer, 1986).

Sojourner adaptation

Studies of sojourners and their relatively short-term cross-cultural adaptation were stimulated by the post-Second World War boom in student exchanges and by the Peace Corps movement in the 1960's. For both groups, extensive literature describes the 'problems' of psychological well-being in encountering unfamiliar environmental demands during their sojourn overseas. A similar need arose in the private sector, with the increase in multinational trade during the post-war reconstruction period. Companies found that their overseas operations were being hampered because their staff were not effectively coping with unfamiliar social and business practices. Military personnel and experts engaged in technical assistance also experienced similar problems. (See Brislin, 1981; Furnham & Bochner, 1986; Landis & Brislin, 1983; Torbiorn, 1982; for extensive reviews of literature in this area.)

From studies of these diverse groups of sojourners, a number of theoretical and research issues have emerged. One of the concepts most extensively discussed and investigated in the field of cross-cultural adaptation is 'culture shock'. Because encounters with alien cultural environments present surprises and uncertainties (depending on the severity of cultural dislocation), the idea that entering a new culture is potentially a confusing and disorienting experience has been amply discussed, written about, and researched. Oberg (1960) first defined culture shock as the 'anxiety that results from losing all of our familiar signs and symbols of social intercourse' (p. 177).

Since Oberg, the concept of culture shock has been employed by many in various ways. Taft (1977), for instance, identified a number of common reactions to cultural dislocation:

(1) 'cultural fatigue' as manifested by irritability, insomnia, and other psychosomatic disorders;
(2) a sense of loss arising from being uprooted from one's familiar surroundings;
(3) rejection by the individual of members of the new society; and
(4) a feeling of impotence from being unable to competently deal with an unfamiliar environment.

J. Bennett (1977) expanded the meaning of this term and regarded it as part of the general 'transition shock', a natural consequence of a human organism's inability to interact with the new environment effectively. According to J. Bennett, transition shock occurs when individuals encounter

the loss of a partner in death or divorce; change of life-style related to passages; loss of a familiar frame of reference in an intercultural encounter; or, change of values associated with rapid social innovation. (p. 45)

(See Adler, 1975; Barna, 1976; Furnham, 1984; Furnham & Bochner, 1986; Torbiorn, 1982; for a more extensive review of literature on culture shock.)

The concept, culture shock, has been further extended recently to include 're-entry shock', the emotional and physiological difficulties an individual may experience on returning home from overseas. Adler (1981) and Gullahorn & Gullahorn (1963) have suggested that re-entry difficulties are likely to be more severe a short time after return than immediately on return to the home culture. (See Brein & David, 1971; Martin, 1984, 1985, for discussions of re-entry shock.)

Closely related to the studies of culture shock are studies of the trends in sojourners' psychological adjustment in a foreign cultural environment. Coelho (1958), in a study of Indian students in the United States, investigated how they perceived Americans and how these images affected their interactions with Americans. The Indian students' perception of Americans was found to be closely related to the extent to which they associated with Americans. Further, the students' perceptual patterns increased in complexity and refinement the longer the students stayed in the United States. Also, Selltiz and her associates (1963) investigated the attitudes and social relations of foreign students in the United States. They found that certain original characteristics of the students, along with certain conditions of their stay, strongly influenced the extent and nature of their association with citizens of the host country (p. 253).

Klineberg & Hull (1979), in their 11-country study of university exchange students, focused on the level of satisfaction as the indicator of adjustment. Their study concluded that prior foreign experiences and social contact with people local to the host culture were the two most important factors that enhanced the students' adjustment. More recently, Torbiorn (1982, 1987) presented a psychological model of 'subjective adjustment', with particular attention to the way individual sojourners are likely to respond to their surroundings and to their opportunities for achieving satisfaction in their new setting.

Many attempts have been made to identify the 'stages' of adjustment that individuals go through in a foreign environment. Oberg (1960), for instance, described four stages:

(1) a 'honeymoon' stage characterized by fascination, elation, and optimism;
(2) a stage of hostility and emotionally stereotyped attitudes toward the host society and increased association with fellow sojourners;
(3) a recovery stage characterised by increased language knowledge and ability to get around in the new cultural environment; and
(4) a final stage in which adjustment is about as complete as possible, anxiety is largely gone, and new customs are accepted and enjoyed.

These and similar adjustment stages have been often described in 'curves', indicating the patterns of change over time in satisfaction in living in the host society or in positive attitude toward it. Some empirical support was found for what has been described as a U-curve of adjustment — depicting the initial optimism and elation in the host culture, the subsequent dip or 'trough' in the level of adjustment, followed by a gradual recovery to higher adjustment levels (cf. Church, 1982; Coelho, 1958; Deutsch &

Won, 1963; Gullahorn & Gullahorn, 1963; Klineberg & Hull, 1979; Lysgaard, 1955; Selltiz & Cook, 1962). This much-popularised observation and prediction of the sojourner adaptation process has been further extended to the 'W-Curve' of adjustment (Gullahorn & Gullahorn, 1963; Trifonovitch, 1977) by adding the re-entry (or return-home) phase during which the sojourner's feelings and attitudes initially dip and subsequently regain strength.

The U-curve and W-curve patterns of change, however, have not always been consistently observed in empirical research. As Church (1982) noted in his review of literature, support for the U-curve hypothesis is weak, inconclusive, and overgeneralised. Not all studies, for instance, have reported that sojourners begin their cross-cultural experiences with a period of elation and optimism (Klineberg & Hull, 1979). Even those supporting the hypothesis have shown marked differences in the time parameters of the curve, making the U-curve description too variable to be sufficiently useful.

Another group of studies focused on the 'effectiveness' of sojourners while they are in foreign cultural environments. These studies have attempted to identify factors that promote or deter sojourners' overseas effectiveness (cf. Kealey & Ruben, 1983). In doing so, researchers have focused on different factors as promoting effectiveness, ranging from personality characteristics (such as patience and honesty) and technical skills, to communication behavior characteristics (such as interaction management and listening skills). For the most part, selection of overseas effectiveness factors in these studies tend to be based on specific practical interests pertinent to specific situations of cross-cultural adaptation, not on rigorous theoretical reasoning.

Nor has a consistent conceptual and operational definition of 'effectiveness' been developed. Hawes & Kealey (1980), for example, studied Canadian technical assistance personnel working in developing countries by defining overseas effectiveness as personal/family adjustment, intercultural interaction, and task accomplishment. Based on this definition, Hawes & Kealey observed that interpersonal skills, identity, and realistic predeparture effectiveness were the best predictors of overseas effectiveness. Gudykunst, Hammer & Wiseman (1977), on the other hand, assessed sojourners' subjective ratings of comfort and satisfaction with life in the other culture as indicators of overseas effectiveness. Collett (1971) relied on ratings by host culture members of the acceptability or competence of the visitors. In Peace Corps studies, field supervisor ratings of an individual's job effectiveness have often been used (cf. Argyle, 1982).

The approaches to cross-cultural adaptation reviewed thus far (particularly those of culture shock, psychological adjustment phases and curves, and effectiveness) have tended to view cross-cultural adaptation experiences as problematic and negative. Countering this view, an alternative approach was proposed by Adler (1972/1987). Adler viewed culture shock and adjustment in a broader context of intercultural learning and growth, in which culture shock is regarded as a profound learning experience that leads to a high degree of self-awareness and personal growth. Thus, culture shock is viewed not as a 'disease for which adaptation is the cure, but is at the very heart of the cross-cultural learning experience, self-understanding, and change' (p. 29).

Similarly, Ruben (1983) questioned the problem-oriented conventional perspectives on cross-cultural adaptation in his discussion of a study of Canadian technical advisors and their spouses on two-year assignments in Kenya (Ruben & Kealey, 1979). In this study, the intensity and directionality of culture shock was found to be unrelated to patterns of psychological adjustment at the end of the first year in the alien culture. Of greater interest was the finding that, in some instances, the magnitude of culture shock was positively related to social and professional effectiveness within the new environment. These findings suggested implications that directly contradicted the problem-oriented perspective on the nature of cross-cultural adaptation.

For Adler and Ruben, then, culture shock experiences are the core or essence, though not necessarily the totality, of the cross-cultural learning experience. Culture shock is regarded as a fundamental experience in that the individual must somehow confront the physiological, psychological, social, and philosophical discrepancies between his or her own internalised cultural disposition and that of the host culture. The cross-cultural learning experience, accordingly, is viewed largely as a transitional experience reflecting a 'movement from a state of low self- and cultural awareness to a state of high self- and cultural awareness' (Adler, 1972/1987:15). This emphasis on cultural learning and growth has broadened the traditional, problem-oriented perspective on the culture-shock phenomenon.

Need for integration: a critique

Studies in cross-cultural adaptation, as represented by the above review, have provided considerable information and insights. Overall, the field has benefited from the vastness and diversity of the anthropological, sociological, and social psychological approaches. Yet it has also suffered from complexity and lack of coherence in definitions, viewpoints, and conceptualisations of cross-cultural adaptation. There are intellectual, ideological, and applied 'problem' orientations peculiar to different disciplines and individual scholars. The field's growth has often been stunted by provincial traditions, and extensive cross-fertilisation and integration has not occurred. As such, the early characterisation of the fragmentation of science by Ludwig von Bertalanffy (1956) still applies to the conditions that face serious scholars of cross-cultural adaptation today. Bertalanffy stated,

> Modern science is characterised by its ever-increasing specialisation, necessitated by the enormous amount of data, the complexity of techniques and of theoretical structures within every field. This, however, has led to a breakdown of science as an integrated realm: The physicist, the biologist, the psychologist and the social scientist are, so to speak, encapsulated in a private universe, and it is difficult to get word from one cocoon to the other. (pp. 1–2)

Indeed, the complexity of the field of cross-cultural adaptation makes it difficult to synthesize all the existing approaches and to interpret the results meaningfully. Yet a synthesis must be attempted. Without an integrated understanding of the various academic endeavors, efforts to describe and explain the cross-cultural adaptation process are likely to lack accuracy, clarity, coherence, and comprehensiveness. The existing information and various insights need to be synthesized, the areas of convergence and divergence among them need to be identified, and their limitations and problems must be delineated. Specifically, four main areas of concern in the existing approaches point to the critical need for developing an integrative theory:

(1) inconsistent use of concepts,
(2) lack of coordination between group- and individual-level approaches,
(3) lack of integration between the studies of immigrants and of sojourners, and
(4) the narrowness of perspectives that view cross-cultural adaptation as either a positive (desirable) or a negative (undesirable) phenomenon.

Inconsistent use of concepts

In reviewing literature in the field of cross-cultural adaptation, one is most likely to be left with a sense of disarray. Different terms are used by different investigators to refer to essentially the same process, and the same terms are defined by different investigators in different ways. For example, a variety of terms have been used to refer to the process immigrants and sojourners go through in a new and unfamiliar culture including 'acculturation', 'adaptation', 'adjustment', 'assimilation', 'integration', 'resocialisation' and 'transculturation', to name a few. Each of these terms, in turn, has been defined conceptually and operationally from many divergent viewpoints and approaches.

This general failure to share the common definitions is a fundamental impediment to systematic understanding of the cross-cultural adaptation process. Although anthropological, communication, sociological, sociolinguistic, and social psychological investigators share a common interest and a common topic of inquiry, each pursues the process in their own way, often looking at different aspects of the same phenomenon. A lack of common terminologies across disciplinary boundaries is symptomatic of, and at least partially responsible for, the lack of coherence and cross-fertilisation among conceptual and research activities that characterise the present state-of-the-art in the field of cross-cultural adaptation.

Lack of integration: group-level and individual-level approaches

As pointed out previously, the anthropological and sociological studies have traditionally analysed cross-cultural adaptation on a group basis. The group approach emphasises the definition of ethnic boundaries, and examines the cultural or sociocultural and institutional factors that affect relationships between or among ethnic groups, without reference to the functions of individuals.

On the other hand, social psychological studies have focused primarily on immigrants or sojourners and analysed their individual adaptation patterns. This approach has been pursued without seriously considering the influence of the group-level institutional factors on the individual adaptation process. This exclusive emphasis on the individual is not unique to studies of cross-cultural adaptation. Traditional approaches to adaptation and stress in general have developed from psychodynamic studies of ego psychology. In these approaches, adaptation is almost exclusively equated with intrapsychic mechanisms that allow individuals to control the environmental stimuli impinging on them and to maintain a state of personal well-being. Almost all adaptation and stress literature has neglected consideration of the relationship between societal–cultural structure and psychological adaptation (cf. Mechanic, 1974:32).

Yet, a fuller understanding of adaptation — either of cultural strangers or of the general population — can be achieved when the societal and cultural conditions of the environment are compared with the individuals' personal characteristics. Still, concepts and empirical findings in the group-level inquiries must be considered for their potential usefulness to the individual-level inquiries. Such an integration can be best realised in an approach that views cross-cultural adaptation as a multidimensional process. In this perspective, the individual stranger and the host environment are viewed as co-influencing the adaptation process. The interethnic dynamics of the host society and the position of the individual's ethnic community must be considered in accounting for the individual's reactions to their changed life conditions. Neither the group-level approaches in anthropology and sociology nor the individual-level approaches in psychology, social psychology, and sociolinguistics are by themselves sufficient to build a comprehensive understanding of cross-cultural adaptation. What is needed is a unifying perspective by which both group- and individual-level approaches can be integrated into a comprehensive framework.

Lack of integration: studies of immigrants and of sojourners

As reviewed earlier, studies of immigrants and of sojourners have evolved as two separate areas of inquiry with distinct academic traditions. The lack of cross-fertilisation and integration is an outcome of the overly specialised approaches of individual researchers and of their distinct academic disciplines rather than a reflection of the reality of cross-cultural adaptation itself. This is not to say that the two groups' adaptation experiences are identical. The immigrants (or refugees) who reside in a new culture for a long, indefinite period are likely to go through a greater amount of adaptive change. Sojourners, on the other hand, are likely to experience less adaptive changes in their relatively short stay of, say, one to several years. As Brislin (1981) noted:

> During the short-term sojourns, hosts frequently do not expect culturally appropriate behavior in all situations; mistakes are forgiven as long as the sojourner seems sincerely interested in learning about the culture. Over a long period of time, on the other hand, hosts expect greater sophistication and may react negatively if sojourners have not learned appropriate behaviors. (p. 271)

In either short-term or long-term situations, however, individuals must adapt to at least those aspects of the host culture critical to their survival and adequate social performance. Long-term and short-term approaches can be integrated by relating the adaptive changes of the long-term and short-term residents to the different levels of adaptation, and by uncovering the patterns commonly observed in both groups. To date, few studies have made such an attempt (cf. Taft, 1977). Brein & David's (1971) review, for example, deals only with the adaptation of sojourners and makes no mention of the literature on immigrants. These studies could potentially inform each other and thereby facilitate the discovery of the principles that describe and explain the phenomena of cross-cultural adaptation.

Implicit biases

The line between theory and ideology must be more clearly drawn so that scientists may approach the reality of cross-cultural adaptation with maximum clarity and objectivity. The ideologies of the assimilationists and of the pluralists appear to have clouded attempts to understand cross-cultural adaptation. Even though scholars in the field have seldom made their ideological position explicit, there has been an implicit dispute between the assimilationists and the pluralists. The assimilationists have tended to equate cross-cultural adaptation with disappearance of ethnicity, while the pluralists have tended to emphasize the persistence of ethnicity.

At the root of these conflicting perspectives is a tendency to view opposites as divorced from each other and irreconcilable. Even the simplest of opposites, such as buying and selling, are viewed as two different and separate events despite their being also completely *inseparable* as two sides of *one* event, namely, the single business transaction itself. In the same manner, the cultural assimilationist view and the cultural pluralist view represent two sides of the same cross-cultural adaptation phenomenon. Adaptive change can never be complete, and, at any given moment in any given individual, both the aspect that indicates adaptation and the other aspect that indicates lack of adaptation can be observed. Whether one is an assimilationist or a pluralist, the fact remains that no immigrant or sojourner can completely escape adaptation as long as they remain in, and are functionally dependent on, the host society.

In addition to ideologically-based biases, efforts to build a broad-based theory have been also neglected by the 'variable-analytic' nature of research. Empirically-minded quantitative researchers in effect have generated numerous narrow conceptualisations of cross-cultural adaptation by 'plugging' variables into a regression equation without careful theoretical considerations. Indeed, many studies appear to have been aimed primarily at developing measurement devices, and there is a paucity of research aimed at constructing or testing theoretical explanations of the adaptation process.

As a result, the many existing 'models', 'indexes' and 'scales' are varied and inconsistent. Proponents of a variety of perspectives often disregard or 'argue past one another' (Bentley, 1981:xvi), with little mention of the relations that may exist between separate measures of concepts such as 'acculturation'. Nor is there mention of the association between alternative measures of the same concept. The propositions of one scientific theory or model do not necessarily add up, or bear a coherent relationship, to the propositions of any other model.

The problems discussed above point to the serious need for a theoretical framework that provides a greater cohesiveness and completeness in describing and explaining the process by which individuals adapt to a new cultural environment. The field is ready for such a theory, as has been emphasised in recent reports (cf. Berry, 1980; Fabrega, 1969; Ross, 1978). A theory that does integrate this diversity of concepts and approaches is explicated in Part II.

PART II
THE THEORY

3 ORGANISING PRINCIPLES AND ASSUMPTIONS

If all of human knowledge, everything that's known, is believed
to be an enormous hierarchic structure, then the high country
of the mind is found at the uppermost reaches of this structure
in the most general, the most abstract considerations of all.
Robert M. Pirsig

A key challenge for the field of cross-cultural adaptation as a whole, and for this investigator in particular, is to consolidate the diverse perspectives and approaches that exist today into a coherent theoretical system. Such a theoretical system must adequately accommodate all the crucial elements, and their interrelationships, that operate in the process by which individuals come to grips with a new and unfamiliar cultural environment. With this basic consideration, this book presents an integrated theory of cross-cultural adaptation.

This investigator approaches the cross-cultural adaptation process with several organising principles. The domain of the present theory will be identified by listing a number of boundary conditions and by specifying the term, cross-cultural adaptation. This theoretical domain will help define the phenomena beyond which the proposed theory is, and is not, intended to describe and explain. The goals and structure of the theory will also be explained. Aiming to increase our understanding of, and our ability to make predictions about, the cross-cultural adaptation phenomenon, the theory is organised into a structure of assumptions–axioms–theorems. The perspective of General Systems Theory on individuals vis-a-vis environment will be presented as the metatheoretical grounding of the present undertaking.

Theoretical domain

A theory deals with a specific domain that constitutes its 'stuff'. A number of boundary conditions are specified below to clarify the present theoretical domain. These conditions help clarify the aspects of cross-cultural adaptation to which the present theory is generalisable.

Boundary conditions

The present theory includes in its domain all individuals who have been born and raised in one culture and have moved to another culture for varied periods of time. Here, the cross-cultural move refers to physical relocation of individuals into a societal/national/linguistic environment that is different from the culture of their childhood. The cross-cultural adaptation process is viewed as common to both long-term 'settlers' (e.g., immigrants and refugees) and short-term sojourners (e.g., exchange students, Peace Corps volunteers). All are considered to go through at least some adaptive experiences even though the degree of intensity and extensiveness may differ between the two groups. Instead of limiting the present theory to any one group of international migrants based on the circumstances of migration or length of residence in the host society, these conditions are accounted for in the theory as factors that influence an individual's adaptation.

This boundary condition, however, limits the present theory to those individuals who move to another culture *after* their socialisation in the original culture has been more or less completed. Children who move to another culture at a young age or who are born after their parents have moved to a new culture are not included in the present theoretical domain. Unlike their parents, they have not yet completed their primary socialisation process in the original culture, and are more susceptible to new cultural influences. The younger they are, the more likely they are to be receptive to host cultural influences. Teenagers whose first-culture socialisation has been substantial, although not quite completed, can be considered by the present theory with special attention to their premigration maturity levels.

Excluded from this theoretical domain are those who move from one region or subculture to another region or subculture within a societal/national boundary (e.g., rural–urban migrants, regional migrants). The present theory also does not include the experiences of those individuals who have returned to their original culture after a long-term residence in another culture. Although the regional/subcultural migration and the 're-entry' process of returnees into their original culture are likely to share great similarity to the adaptation process, returnees typically do not encounter linguistic and cultural differences as substantial as the international migrants do.

For the population identified above, the present analysis is focused on the individual rather than on the group. By focusing on the individual, the process and the consequences of cross-cultural adaptation is examined from its 'bottom-line' reality. Whatever change occurs in a group through contact with another culture, it cannot be understood without understanding the changes among its individual members. Also, because individuals operating in a given environment are influenced by the sociological and cultural factors (studied in the anthropological and sociological approaches), these factors must be taken into consideration as well as environmental and predispositional characteristics.

In addition, the theory limits its focus to the adaptation of individuals without specifically dealing with possible changes that occur in the host environment. Although both the individual and the host society undergo adaptive changes as a result of prolonged intercultural contact, the influence of the individual on the host society is incomparably smaller than the substantial influence of the host culture on the individual. The dominant culture of the host society controls the life activities of individual immigrants and sojourners, which necessitates adaptation of the individuals, not *vice versa*. The adaptive change of an Australian immigrant in the United States, for example, will be far more rapid and extensive than any influence that the immigrant can bring about in the United States culture at large (cf. Amersfoort, 1974/1982; Berry, 1980; Torbiorn, 1982).

This focus on adaptation of individual immigrants and sojourners, and not on the adaptation of the host environment, in no way makes light of the significant role that the environment plays. Instead, it reflects the angle from which cross-cultural adaptation occurs. This angle helps delimit the theoretical domain to the experiences of individual immigrants and sojourners, not the host environment. As the theory unfolds in the following chapters, it will become apparent that, even though we begin our theoretical thinking from the position where each individual resides, we will ultimately include the larger environment of the host society into our theoretical considerations — as an integral part of the present scheme.

Specification of terms

Based on the above boundary conditions, *the present use of the term, cross-cultural adaptation, refers to the process of change over time that takes place within individuals who have completed their primary socialisation process in one culture and then come into continuous, prolonged first-hand contact with a new and unfamiliar culture*. In this new cultural context, the individuals are, at least to some extent, *dependent* on the host society and experience some uncertainty and unfamiliarity in carrying out their daily activities. Cross-cultural adaptation takes place regardless of the circumstances or the specific time and space in which individuals move from one society to another. In all cases, they are strangers who willingly or unwillingly undergo some degree of change in their original cultural patterns.

As discussed in Chapter 2, a multitude of terms are used to refer to the process of cross-cultural adaptation with some differences in their respective emphasis. For example, 'assimilation' and 'amalgamation' have been often used to emphasise the acceptance of cultural elements of the host society by the individual. The term, 'acculturation', has been defined by some as the process in which individuals acquire some (but not all) aspects of the host cultural elements. In a more limited sense, 'adjustment', has been sometimes used to refer to the mental-emotional state of comfort, satisfaction, and positive attitude. 'Integration', on the other hand, has been used in some studies that focus on the development of social relationships in the host environment.

The complexity of terminological usage in the field increases further when we consider the variations in operational definitions (or indicators) of each of these terms. In assessing acculturation levels of immigrants, for example, many psychological studies have focused on the respondents' own 'subjective' accounts. Others have observed more 'objective' indicators such as the individuals' interpersonal relationships with native members of the host society, language skills (assessed by observers), and other demographic information (such as occupational status, income, and housing). In more extensive studies, both of these categories have been utilised in operationalising the level of acculturation. (For a review of various uses of these terms, see Alba, 1976; Amersfoort, 1974/1982; Bochner, 1973; Brislin, 1981; Dyal & Dyal, 1981; Y. Kim, 1976; Nagata, 1969; Olsen, 1968; Pettigrew, 1978; Shibutani & Kwan, 1965, among others.)

As such, different terms have been used to refer to different aspects of individual experiences in new cultural environments. Finding a precise consensual meaning attributed to these terms, therefore, is difficult and may even bring an unnecessary semantic confusion. *Because the present theory includes all of these aspects, the term adaptation is used as a broad concept that accommodates the above and other existing meanings — subjective, objective, assimilative, acculturative, and adjustive.*

Along with the term, adaptation, the term, 'stranger', is employed to accommodate every cross-cultural migrant. Strangers are conceived here as individuals who are initially different and unknown to the new and unfamiliar cultural environment (Gudykunst & Kim, 1984). The present theory is intended to describe and explain the nature of the cross-cultural adaptation process regardless of the specific circumstances of migration, the cultural/national setting in which it occurs, or the specific cultural/national background of the individual.

Theoretical goals

When theorising, scientists generally have two distinct goals: *understanding* and *prediction*. Understanding as a scientific goal refers to presenting a thorough and accurate system of information as to how a certain reality being investigated operates. Further, the essential meaning of the term is knowledge about the interaction of units in a system, and the degree to which such understanding is provided by a given theory is assessed in terms of its 'explanatory power'. On the other hand, prediction means that we can foretell the value of one or more units making up a system, or that we can anticipate the condition or state of a system as a whole (cf. Dubin, 1969:9–10). In both instances the focus is on the outcome, and the degree to which a prediction is provided by a given theory is judged in terms of its 'predictive precision' (cf. Blalock, 1984, Dance & Larson, 1976).

Although these two goals are neither inconsistent nor incompatible, they seldom have been achieved together in theory building in human sciences. For example, Homan's (1961) theory of 'social exchange' proposed that two individuals' liking for each other is positively related to the frequency of their interaction because frequent interaction allows understanding of each other's idiosyncrasies, enabling them to adapt to them. This proposition can be viewed to have not only face validity but also to have great power in permitting broad understanding of a wide range of social phenomena. When applied to specific interpersonal dyads, however, this theory lacks predictive precision.

This gives rise to what Dubin (1969) referred to as two paradoxes. The first is the 'precision paradox': We can achieve precision in prediction without any knowledge of how the predicted outcome was produced. This means that a theory can achieve high precision in predicting when changes in system states will occur and what states will succeed each other without possessing knowledge of how the system operates as a whole. Furthermore, we can predict individual values of variables without knowing the connection between the forecasting indices and the outcome predicted. The second is the 'power paradox': We can achieve powerful understanding of social behavior without being able to predict its character in specific situations, as was exemplified in Homan's theory.

Few existing conceptualisations of cross-cultural adaptation and related phenomena serve both functions of understanding and prediction. They have tended, instead, to focus either on understanding or prediction. Sociological theories, such as Gordon's (1964) theory of interethnic dynamics, and a few social psychological theories, such as the acculturation paradigms developed by Taft (1957) and Berry (1984), present conceptual schemes designed to help *understand* the general acculturation process. These and other similar models focus on broad relationships among the variables composing the adaptation process. They are by themselves not sufficient, however, to make predictions with a great deal of specificity.

The opposite trend has been observed in the majority of the social psychological conceptions of the short-term cross-cultural adaptation of sojourners. These conceptions have been often motivated by practical needs to *predict* 'success' or 'failure' of sojourners living in a foreign culture. The conceptual focus has been typically on a particular 'dependent' variable, or on an interrelated set of dependent variables (such as 'level of satisfaction' and 'attitude toward the host society'). Therefore, the initial result of collecting testable predictive statements is likely to be a simple inventory of supposed causes of the dependent variable(s) under consideration — with little concern for a comprehensive understanding of the adaptation process as a whole.

The present theory attempts to strike a balance between the two theoretical goals, i.e., to provide a comprehensive understanding and to make specific predictions. The theory first presents a new conceptualisation of the *process* of cross-cultural adaptation as a communication process based on the General Systems perspective. In this conceptualisation, the theory describes how individuals undergo adaptive changes through their continuous communication with the cultural environment.

Theoretical structure

This theoretical description of the adaptation process presents a number of metatheoretical *assumptions*, from which *axioms*, or laws of interaction, will be explicated defining the cross-cultural adaptation process. Axioms are employed in the present theory as propositions that are assumed to be true. As Dubin (1969) stated, an axiom states the relationship between two or more units of a model for the entire range of values over which the units are related by the law (p. 177). For example, an axiom is stated, 'A is positively related with B'. Strictly speaking, an axiom will be untestable because it will never be possible to control for all 'relevant' theoretical units.

This theorising scheme needs to be differentiated from the one proposed by Blalock (1969), who argues for the use of axioms to delineate causal relationships between concepts. Blalock's system is principally based on the deductive process of establishing a series of causal axioms (e.g., 'A causes B' and 'B causes C'), based on which propositions (e.g., 'A causes C') are logically derived. In the present scheme of theory development, axioms are exchangeably used with principles that describe, rather than predict, the nature of cross-cultural adaptation.

These axioms (or principles) will serve as the basis on which theoretical predictions, or *theorems*, will be derived. For example, if one axiom relates constructs A and B, a second C and D, and a third E and F, then there must be additional propositions enabling us to make deductive statements connecting these three axioms. These deduced theoretical statements are predictive generalisations stated in terms of covariations or temporal sequences. A theorem is often stated, 'The more ... , the more ... ', or 'If ... then', setting forth the value of one construct that is associated with a corresponding value of another construct. Theorems are linked to assumptions and axioms as shown in Figure 1. Because theorems are derived from assumptions and axioms, their empirical validation will indirectly validate the axioms and, ultimately, the assumptions.

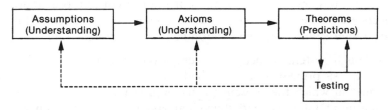

FIGURE 1   *Structure and goals of the present theory*

Finally, the theory emphasises the importance of utilising existing empirical data in the process of theory development. It endorses the position of Blalock (1969) and Dubin (1969) that theory must be grounded in empirical data. Although the theory is not restricted by available empirical data, appropriate research evidence can strengthen the validity and the practical relevance of the propositional statements. Thus, in developing the present theory, we will be continually shuffling back and forth between deductive–theoretical reasoning and inductive–empirical proofs.

General systems perspective: assumptions

In developing the present theory, a number of assumptions are made to establish a set of foundational notions about the cross-cultural adaptation process. Strangers' adaptive experiences in a new cultural environment are all-encompassing involving virtually all aspects of life. Strangers face the host environment in its totality, just as new-born babies learn to discover its many elements and their interrelatedness. The all-inclusive nature of the adaptation process necessitates a theoretical perspective comprehensive enough to accommodate its complexity. At the same time, the multifaceted nature of the adaptation process calls for an interdisciplinary emphasis, based on which the cultural, sociological, sociolinguistic, psychological, and anthropological perspectives may be integrated into a coherent system of knowledge.

The General Systems Theory naturally renders itself to serve these theoretical purposes — that is, to be comprehensive and multidimensional. It is a conceptual network, or a perspective, on a 'higher' (or more general) level than a theory about a specific phenomenon. This abstract nature of the systems perspective enables this investigator to use some of its concepts and principles as a set of fundamental assumptions underlying the present content-specific theory. The basic building block of General Systems Theory, of course, is the *system*, which refers to any entity or whole that consists of interdependent elements. For the present purpose, individual strangers are viewed as systems and are understood to function through on-going interactions with the environment and its inhabitants.

Although systems concepts are employed throughout this book, a number of basic principles are described here to help clarify the fundamental manner in which the present theory approaches the individual-social communication interface and individual adaptation in a given cultural environment. (For detailed discussions of the systems perspective in relation to human communication activities, see Boulding, 1956/1977; Ruben & J. Kim, 1975; Ruesch & Bateson, 1951/1968; among others.)

Evolution of individuals as open systems

No one lives an environment-free life. Individuals always live in a given environment, with which they exchange information along with materials and energies. Each of us operates much like a radar set — continually sending out messages, which then come back to help us define the social world. The environment that we take into account is an infinite array of ongoing event data, on which our senses and minds impose structure, meaning, and utility. This continual give-and-take with the environment is characteristic of *open systems* such as humans. Individuals exchange materials, energies, and information with the environment. A human system is 'closed' when there is no longer any import or export of energies in any of its forms, and therefore no change of components.

This openness, or interaction with the environment, is not only a characteristic of humans but also of all other living systems including animals and plants. What typifies human systems, however, is the elaborate and complex symbolic interchange of information with the sociocultural environment. This process of interaction and information exchange between an individual human system and the environment is called *communication*. As described in Figure 2, communication is an interactive process of sending messages, or *encoding* activities, and of receiving and processing messages, or *decoding* activities. We continually engage in generating 'information output' to the environment as well as in generating meaning for the 'information input' by transforming it internally.

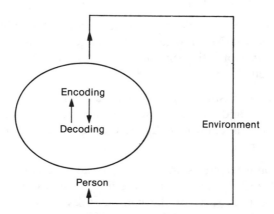

FIGURE 2   *Communication as a person–environment interaction process*

Communication messages are not limited to linguistic or other explicitly coded symbols such as traffic signs, mathematical symbols, and computer languages. They also include spontaneous expressive non-verbal messages that are often non-intentional and implicit. This means that all actions and events (as well as non-actions and non-events) have communicative aspects as soon as they are recognised by a person. A person, as an open communication system, is continually engaged with his or her environment symbolically. As Watzlawick, Beavin & Jackson (1967) prominently stated, one of the axioms of human communication is: 'One cannot not communicate'. Communication, in this sense, can be seen as one of the two basic life processes of all human systems (Ruben, 1975; Thayer, 1968).

Like all other living systems, humans are characteristically *homeostatic*, attempting to hold constant a variety of variables in our internal meaning structure to achieve an ordered whole. When individuals receive messages that disrupt their internal order, they experience *disequilibrium*. In this state, *stress* confronts the individual, who in turn struggles to regain internal equilibrium. Stress, then, is a manifestation of a generic process that occurs whenever the capabilities of an open system are not adequate to the demands of the environment. In stressful situations, the so-called 'defensive mechanism' (or protective, insulating response) is activated in individuals to hold the internal structure constant by some psychological maneuvering. Individuals attempt to avoid or minimise the anticipated or actual 'pain' of disequilibrium commonly referred to as 'stress' by selective attention, self-deception, denial, avoidance, and withdrawal (Lazarus, 1966:262).

When environmental challenges threaten internal equilibrium, individuals by necessity strive to 'meet' and manage the challenge through their *adaptive activities* of acting on, and responding to, the environment. According to Ruben (1983),

> Living systems act instinctively to meet the challenge or threat and to restore harmony and balance. Once regained, equilibrium continues until the system is controlled by new environmental demands, or *stressors* . . . . (p. 137)

The tension between stress and adaptation and the resultant internal transformation essentially characterises the life processes of humans. It is this tension that is necessary for the continued existence of individuals facing environmental challenges. Adaptive transformation, thus, means the resolution of internal stress that promises the qualitative transformation of a person toward growth — a greater internal capacity to cope with varied environmental conditions. Adaptation to the environment is the main causative agent of a human system's evolution. As Dobzhansky (1962) stated, 'evolutionary change *comes from* the environment' (p. 17). Although the environment does not 'impose' changes on the system, individuals as living systems do not cease to evolve as they are continuously in communication with it.

This *stress–adaptation–growth dynamic* is cyclic and continual. Once an environmental threat propels the system into disequilibrium, the person acts to restore harmony by restructuring his or her internal communication system in order to accommodate the challenge. Internal equilibrium is regained until the system is confronted by new environmental challenges. Here, stress and growth are integrated in the adaptation process because neither occurs without the other. This on-going adaptive relationship with the environment constitutes our life activities in which each of us strive to adjust and readjust to changes, challenges, and irritants in an environment. Through the encoding–decoding of information, individuals manifest a *natural* tendency to survive, function, and develop in any given environment. This communication process between our internal system and the external world leads to an adaptive change in our thought and attitude, and a greater understanding of appropriate actions to take in a specific social encounter.

Culture, enculturation and cultural identity

All of us are born into this world knowing literally nothing of what we need to function acceptably in human society. Nor are we born prepared to engage in various activities out of which our sense of reality and self is constructed. It is through *communication* that we *learn* to relate to our environment, just as we 'survive' physically by eating when hungry and building shelters against the cold. Through continuous interaction with the various aspects of the environment, individuals undergo a progression of stages, integrating numerous culturally acceptable concepts, attitudes, and actions into themselves. In this growth process, most individuals simultaneously go through qualitative changes and yet maintain their overall integrity.

This continuous evolution of individuals in relation to their environment occurs in and through *communication*. Because we cannot interact with and adapt to our environment without the activities of information encoding and decoding of information, communication is the central pillar of all human learning. We learn to speak, listen, read, interpret, and understand verbal and non-verbal messages in such a fashion that the messages will be recognised, accepted, and responded to by the individuals with whom we interact. Once acquired, our communication activities function as an instrumental, interpretive, and expressive means of coming to terms with our environment.

A crucial feature of this communication–adaptation process is the bonding process between individuals or the forming of groups (cf. Dance & Larson, 1976; Ruben, 1975). In the communication–adaptation process, individuals acquire membership in the social groups on which they depend and 'find a place' in society. As Ruesch and Bateson (1951/1968) commented,

> When persons convene, things happen. People have their feelings and their thoughts, and both while they are together and afterwards, they act and react to one another. They themselves perceive their own actions, and other people who are present can likewise observe what takes place . . . as a result of such experiences people's views of themselves and of each other may be confirmed, altered, or modified. (pp. 5–6)

From the viewpoint of the individual, then, *culture* is the data field from which to learn and understand. Culture, 'the mass of life patterns' (Adler, 1976:366), serves as a universe of information to the individuals in a given society. Throughout the years of socialisation, children acquire an understanding of, and the culturally-patterned modes of responses to, their world. The familiar culture is the 'home world', which is associated closely with the family or 'significant others'. An unfamiliar culture, on the other hand, is one that is out of harmony with one's basic understanding of self and reality.

Cultures vary in world view, beliefs, values, norms and other assumptions, as well as in their communication patterns. In each culture, individuals are connected to each other through a common system of encoding and decoding. Specifically, cultures vary in language and verbal behavior, manner of movement, sitting, standing, gesturing, postures, tones of voice, facial expressions, and the way of handling time, space, and material (cf. Gudykunst & Kim, 1984; Hall, 1976, 1983). It is culture that programs us to interpret verbal and non-verbal messages by defining what is real, what is true, what is right, what is beautiful, and what is good.

As such, culture conditions individuals to certain patterns of thinking, feeling, and behaving in varied social transactions. Frank (1975) observed the inseparable relationship between culture and communication by viewing the cultural field 'as arising from the patterned transactional relations' (p. 128) of all individuals, each of whom carries on continual interaction with other members of the group. Further, all the varied patterns, rituals, institutional practices, and symbols of group life appear as so many different modes of communication in and through which each person can approach, negotiate, and seek consummation. We may thus view the economic, political, legal, and social patterns and transactions as defined and prescribed cultural modes of symbols and behavior.

Culture, thus, can be viewed as the sum of the consensuses of the individual communication patterns manifest by the members of a society, giving coherence, continuity, and distinctive form to their way of life. As Sapir (1931) noted, 'every cultural pattern and every single act of social behavior involves communication in either an explicit or implicit sense' (p. 78). The intertwined dynamics of culture and communication was further recognised by Peterson, Jensen & Rivers (1965), who pointed out that

> communication . . . is the carrier of the social process. It is the means man [woman] has for organising, stabilising, and modifying his [her] social life . . . . The social process depends upon the accumulation and transmission of knowledge. Knowledge in time depends upon communication. (p. 16)

The unwritten task of every culture is to organise, integrate, and maintain the psychological patterns of the individual, primarily in the formative years of childhood (Berger & Luckmann, 1967). Throughout the socialisation process, children learn and acquire most of the factors and processes that make them fit to live in the company of others. This internalised learning enables individuals to interact easily with other members of their culture who share a similar image of reality and self. The process in which individuals adapt to the surrounding cultural forces throughout the years of socialisation is commonly called *enculturation*.

Adaptation to the pervasive cultural forces is at the core of the enculturation process. Throughout the socialisation process, children become adapted to the fellow members of their cultural group, which, in turn, gives them their status and assigns to them their role in the life of the community. By the time they reach adulthood, these cultural patterns are 'programmed' into their nervous system and become part of their 'character' or 'personality', determining in part the manner in which they will manage future events. The impressions received from the surroundings, from others, and from the self, as well as the retention of these impressions for future reference, become integral parts of our internal meaning systems (cf. Cronen, Chen & Pearce, 1988).

Implied in the communication–enculturation process is the fundamental pliability of individual human systems. The enculturation of human beings is so pervasive that most behavior rarely rises to the level of consciousness. Culture is imprinted in each individual as a pattern of perceptions, attitudes, and behaviors that is accepted and expected by others in a given society below the level of conscious thought. Because we are programmed by culture from the very day we are born, we are rarely conscious of the hidden cultural programming that influences the way we think, move, and express ourselves verbally and non-verbally. We hardly realise that these invisible cultural influences determine how we solve problems and how economic and governmental systems are put together and function.

Such inseparable relationships between cultural patterns and individuals' internalised conditions are incorporated into an individual's *cultural identity*. The cultural forms for expressing and understanding communication behavior are internalised from the teachings of early significant others and become *the* world, with a strong emotional and protective overtone. As individuals incorporate into their world view the essential experience of value systems, attitudes, and beliefs, as well as the concerted communication patterns of their culture, they also develop a cultural identity.

From the present systems perspective, cultural identity is not a thing or a 'fixed' personality structure, but a complex process of continuing *interpretive activity* internal to individuals as a result of their enculturation experiences. As individuals mature in a given cultural milieu, their internal conditions incorporate the various cultural attributes. Such internalised cultural attributes, in turn, provide an invisible bond with other members who also have internalised the same cultural attributes. In this sense, shared cultural identity 'breeds' the sense of 'fellowship' and in-group loyalty. It is this 'we-feeling' and self-conception and self-designation of oneself as a member of a certain cultural group that has been emphasised most frequently in social psychological explications of cultural identity (cf. Giles, 1977; Giles & Johnson, 1981; Tajfel, 1978b; Tajfel & Turner, 1979; Turner, 1987).

In forming cultural identity, individuals also acquire a general 'efficacy', a sense of an agency in their lives. Utilising the cultural modes of communication, they are able to conform with greater or lesser fidelity to these sanctioned patterns. Successful adaptation of individuals, then, depends directly on their ability to communicate in a given cultural environment. Successful adaptation is possible only where their internal communication patterns sufficiently overlap with those of others in the same cultural group.

This internal capacity based on the acquired communication patterns is called *communication competence*, that is, the mental capabilities by which individuals organise themselves in and with their sociocultural milieu, developing ways of seeing, hearing, understanding, and responding to the environment. Through communication competence, they integrate themselves to the reality and the reality to themselves. In Ruben's (1975) words, it can be thought of as

> sensing, making-sense-of, and acting toward the objects and people in one's milieu. It is the process by which the individual informationally fits himself [herself] into (adapts to and adapts) his [her] environment. (pp. 168–169)

The general criteria for communication competence can be viewed as two interrelated elements: *appropriateness* and *effectiveness*. According to Spitzberg & Cupach (1984), appropriateness refers to the interactants' perception that they understand the content of the encounter and have not had their norms or rules violated too extensively. Effectiveness, on the other hand, refers to their fidelity in relating to some specific environmental expectation or task in a given sociocultural context. (See, also, Wiemann & Backlund, 1980, for a review of literature on communication competence.)

Here, communication *competence* should be distinguished from actual communication *performance*. Competence is the capability of an individual, while that individual's performance is the 'actual behavior in actual cases' (Hymes, 1972:18), which will depend on the specific situation. Competence, therefore, is the foundation for mediating environmental conditions with the adaptation of an individual, and thereby enabling the individual to manage given situations with fidelity.

As individuals become capable of adhering to the modal cultural patterns and the prescribed use of group-sanctioned symbols, they are better able to manage themselves and their environment. Through the use of these and other culturally sanctioned communication patterns, they perceive themselves, and are perceived by others, as 'well-adapted' and socially 'competent'. As Ruesch (1951/1968) stated, 'the ability to communicate successfully becomes synonymous with being mentally healthy' (p. 87). We are well aware that such a definition is a relativistic one; but it is obvious that people are mentally healthy only when their means of communication permit them to manage their surroundings successfully.

When the means of communication are not available and breakdown occurs, or when people are transplanted to surroundings that use a different communication system, they become at least temporarily maladapted.

The foregoing systems concepts and principles can be summarised into the following assumptions:

Assumptions

Assumption 1: A person is an open communication system that interacts with the environment through input and output of information.

Assumption 2: A person has an inherent drive to maintain his or her internal equilibrium in the face of changes in environmental conditions.

Assumption 3: A person's internal equilibrium is disturbed when the person–environment symmetry is broken.

Assumption 4: To regain internal equilibrium and reduce stress, a person adapts by altering his/her internal conditions.

Assumption 5: Stress and growth are inseparable as aspects of adaptation. Both are necessary to define the nature of a person's internal growth.

Assumption 6: The stress–adaptation–growth dynamic lies at the heart of the human system's response to environmental challenge.

Assumption 7: Each culture sanctions a system of communication for its members.

Assumption 8: Through communication, an individual adapts to a given cultural environment.

Assumption 9: As a person adapts to a cultural environment, he/she forms a cultural identity.

Assumption 10: A person's communication competence facilitates, as well as is facilitated by, his/her level of cultural adaptation.

In this chapter, a number of organising principles have been presented to lay a foundation for the present theory of cross-cultural adaptation. The theory is about the cross-cultural adaptation experiences of grown-up individuals who were born and raised in one culture and have moved to another culture. It aims to achieve an optimal balance between the two theoretical goals of understanding and prediction, and to maximally utilise available empirical data. In this weaving of deductive and inductive processes, the theory attempts to provide a linkage between its conceptual reasoning and the corresponding empirical reality. The present theoretical perspective is derived from some of the basic concepts and principles of General Systems Theory that emphasises the holistic, interactive and dynamic nature of individuals as open communications systems, their enculturation process, and their acquisition of cultural identity and communication competence.

4 CROSS-CULTURAL ADAPTATION: AXIOMS

The problem of human adaptation could be presented
as a dialectic between permanency and change.
Rene Dubos

Individuals enter an unfamiliar culture with the cultural communication competence that they have internalised in their home country. The internalised cultural imprinting that governs individuals' identity and behavior remains largely unrecognised, unquestioned, and unchallenged until they encounter people with different cultural attributes. As Boulding (1956/1977) stated, the human nervous system is structured in such a way that 'the patterns that govern behavior and perception come into consciousness only when there is a deviation from the familiar'. (p. 13)

Strangers adapting

Intercultural encounters provide such situations of deviation from the familiar, assumed, and taken-for-granted, as individuals are faced with things that do not follow their unconscious cultural program. They now need to learn and acquire a new system of communication patterns acceptable in the host society. As strangers in the new land, they are subject to a greater or lesser necessity to conform to the communication patterns of the host society. Permanent immigrants or long-term settlers generally have a greater need to conform than temporary sojourners, yet no one is completely free from having to understand, and manage, the various communication patterns sanctioned and operating in the host culture.

Acculturation and deculturation

This process of learning and acquiring the elements of the host culture is called *acculturation* (cf. Shibutani & Kwan, 1965:470). Specifically, acculturation of strangers involves the cultural patterns established in the host society at large and regarded by the majority of people as the 'standard' for that society. In many ethnically diverse societies, the standard cultural patterns refer mainly to those of the dominant culture. In the United States, for example, the standard cultural patterns refer mainly to those of the anglo-white Americans. Although acquiring minority cultural patterns is a part of the overall adaptation process of newcomers, the most compelling pressure to conform comes from the dominant elements of the host society.

In this process, strangers are re-enculturated, only this time into the host society. This second-time enculturation does not occur so smoothly as their childhood enculturation, because of the distinct cultural identity and communication patterns internalised in their childhood. As acculturation occurs in the strangers, *unlearning* (or undoing) of at least some of the old cultural patterns occurs (at least in the sense that new responses are adopted in situations that previously would have evoked old ones). The cost of acquiring something new is inevitably the 'losing' of something old in much the same way as 'being someone requires the forfeiture of being someone else' (Thayer, 1975:240).

This cultural discontinuity in strangers' internal cultural identity and attributes has been recognised by a number of investigators as *desocialisation* or *deculturation* (Bar-Yosef, 1968; Eisenstadt, 1954). These two phenomena are not necessarily observable in a direct one-on-one basis. Acquiring knowledge and skill in the host language may not necessarily result in the unlearning of the corresponding amount of knowledge and skill in the original language, as has been indicated in studies of bilingual children (e.g., Arnberg, 1987; Beardsmore, 1986; Phinney & Rotheram, 1987). As we consider the make-up of strangers after a given time in the host milieu, however, we will note that their internal attributes are no longer the same as they once were before being exposed to the host culture.

In this dynamic interplay of acculturation and deculturation, strangers gradually undergo an adaptive transformation in their communication system. Ultimately the new cultural patterns replace many of the old patterns and the overall transformation of strangers becomes noticeable, particularly to others. (See Figure 3.)

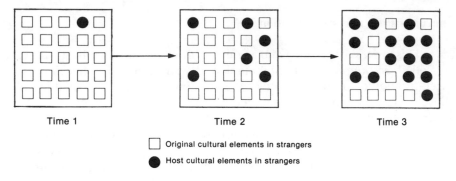

Time 1   Time 2   Time 3

☐ Original cultural elements in strangers

● Host cultural elements in strangers

FIGURE 3   *Deculturation and acculturation in the adaptation process*

Stress–adaptation–growth dynamics

As discussed previously, human systems are characteristically homeostatic attempting to hold constant a variety of variables in our internal structure so as to achieve an ordered whole. When individuals receive messages that disrupt their existing internal order, they experience disequilibrium. In this state of disequilibrium, stress confronts the individual. As such, strangers inevitably experience acute stress as they go through the experiences of acculturation and deculturation. They lack 'intersubjective understanding' (Schuetz, 1944:499) of the social world inhabited by the members of the host society. As Parrillo (1966) observed:

> For the natives, then, every social situation is the coming together not only of roles and identities, but also of shared realities — the intersubjective structure of consciousness. What is taken for granted by the native is problematic for the stranger. In a familiar world, people live through the day by responding to daily routine without questioning or reflection. To strangers, however, every situation is new and is therefore experienced as a crisis. (p. 3)

As long as there are discrepancies between the demands of the host environment and the capacities of the strangers' internal communication to meet those demands, the strangers must adjust and readjust themselves to better function in the host society. Everyone requires on-going validation of his or her 'place' in a given environment, and the inability to meet this basic human need can lead to symptoms of mental, emotional, and physical disturbance (Berger & Kellner, 1970). The shifting of the self-world relationship brings about a heightened level of consciousness through an increased awareness of the split between inner, subjective experiences and external, objective circumstances.

When experiencing internal stress or disequilibrium, strangers 'instinctively' react to maintain or restore their inner balance and stability. Through various psychological maneuvers, they temporarily escape from the necessity of having to deal with stressful conditions. Often the 'problem-solving' approach is not used by strangers when they are under high stress, but, instead, more primitive, rigid, and less adequate attempts are made to protect feelings or master the situation. Consequently, strangers may become more aggressive or hostile toward the new country, attacking its values, customs, food, climate, and so on. As coping mechanisms, they may yearn for home, become dependent on others, be excessively concerned with unimportant details, rationalise their inabilities, or simply avoid problematic situations by ignoring them (cf. Lazarus, 1966).

Unfortunately, these defensive reactions do not facilitate learning about a new environment. Although defensive reactions to stressful situations may temporarily reduce inner tension and anxiety, strangers cannot avoid the necessity to 'face' and cope with the host environment if they are to perform satisfactorily in it. Although internal protective reactions are frequently necessary for strangers, such reactions are generally temporary. Sooner or later, the strangers must stop protective reactions that merely postpone dealing with the impending problems of adaptation. As long as they remain in the host society, and as long as the quality of their performance in the host society depends on how well they can communicate with host nationals, they eventually must acquire the information that will improve their functional relationship with the host environment.

To acquire the necessary communication competence of the host society means going through many stressful emotional 'lows'. Strangers must weather internal conflicts — conflicts between their original cultural patterns and the host cultural patterns — through active communication participation in the host society. In this process, *stress* is inevitably present: it is 'part-and-parcel of the stress-adaptation cycle' (Ruben, 1983:143). The psychological movements of individuals' internal systems into new dimensions of perception and experience often produce forms of temporary personality disintegration, or even 'breakdown' in some extreme cases. *Stress, in the present context, can be viewed as the internal resistance of the human organism against its own cultural evolution.*

As strangers face the demands of the host environment and cope with the accompanying stress, parts of their internal organisation undergo small changes. The interior organisation of strangers is in flux as they continue to communicate with and adapt to the host environment. The periods of 'crisis' will be temporary as the strangers work out new ways of handling problems through sources of strength in themselves and in their social environment. A crisis, once managed by the strangers, presents an opportunity to strengthen their coping abilities and potential for adaptive changes. Stress, then, is responsible not only for suffering, frustration, and anxiety, but also for providing the impetus for adaptive personal trans-formation and growth — the learning and creative responses to manage new cultural circumstances.

Stress, adaptation, and growth, together, define the internal dynamics of strangers' cross-cultural experiences in a 'draw-back-to-leap' pattern similar to the movement of a wheel. (See Figure 4.) Each stressful experience is responded to by strangers with a 'draw back', which then activates their adaptive energy to help them reorganise themselves and 'leap forward'. This stress–adaptation–growth cycle involves communication activities that shift between out-looking, information-seeking behavior and tension-reducing, defensive retreat, and the resultant capacity to see a situation 'with new eyes'. The break-up of the old internal conditions usually results not in chaos or breakdown, but in the creation of a whole new internal structure that is better adapted to the host environment.

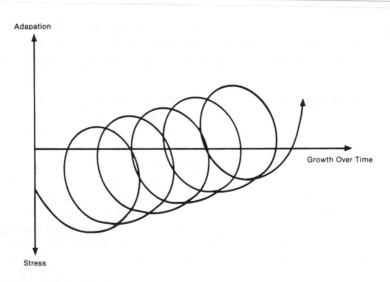

FIGURE 4　*Stress–adaptation–growth dynamics of adaptive transformation*

The adaptation process, thus, is not a smooth, linear process, but a transformation of individuals through the successive interplay of *degeneration* and *regeneration*. The stress, adaptation, and resultant internal growth essentially characterise the strangers' conscious and unconscious movement forward and upward in the direction of greater success in meeting the demands of the host environment. The resolution of stressful difficulties promises the qualitative transformation of strangers toward a greater internal capacity to cope with varied environmental conditions. The increased internal capacity, in turn, facilitates the subsequent handling of stress and adaptation, learning and unlearning, acculturation and deculturation, crisis and resolution.

At this point, recall from Chapter 2 that many studies of the 'culture shock' phenomenon have focused on these initial-phase stress reactions of strangers. These studies have typically viewed culture shock as a negative, problematic, and undesirable phenomenon to be avoided. Viewed in the present systems terms, however, *culture shock is a manifestation of a generic process that occurs whenever the capabilities of a living system are not sufficiently adequate to the demands of an unfamiliar cultural environment.* It is a necessary precondition to adaptive change, as individuals strive to regain their inner balance by adapting to the demands and opportunities of their new life circumstance (See, also, Adler, 1972/1987; J. Bennett, 1976; Kim & Ruben, 1988; Ruben, 1983, for similar arguments.)

In this view, the present theory conceptualises cross-cultural adaptation as a process of dynamic stress–adaptation–growth interplay. This conceptualisation shows the unity of stress and change in the adaptation process: neither occurs without the other and each occurs because of the other. To the extent that stress is said to be responsible for suffering, frustration, and anxiety, it also must be credited as an impetus for learning, growth and creativity for the individual. Temporary disintegration is thus viewed as the very basis for a subsequent increase in the awareness of life conditions and ways to deal with them.

Empirical research has provided some supportive indication, although indirect and rudimentary, that the stress of meeting with new cultural elements lays the groundwork for subsequent adaptation. For example, Eaton & Lasry (1978) reported that the stress level of more upwardly mobile immigrants was greater than those who were less upwardly mobile. Among Japanese-Americans (Marmot & Syme, 1976) and Mexican-American women (Miranda & Castro, 1977), the better adapted immigrants had a somewhat greater frequency of stress-related symptoms (such as anxiety and need for psychotherapy) than the less adapted group. Additionally,

Ruben & Kealey (1979) suggested that the Canadians in Kenya who would ultimately be the most effective in adapting to the new culture underwent the most intense culture shock during the transition period. Other acculturation studies of immigrants and foreign students in the United States have shown that, once the initial phase has been successfully managed, individuals demonstrate an increased cognitive complexity, a positive orientation toward the host environment and toward themselves, and behavioral capacities to communicate with the natives (cf. Coelho, 1958; Y. Kim, 1976, 1978a,b, 1980). (See, also, Gullahorn & Gullahorn, 1963; Torbiorn, 1982; for further discussions on the stress and adaptation phenomena.)

The stress–adaptation–growth dynamics of strangers' cross-cultural experiences speak of profound human pliability, resilience and potential for growth. Except for a small portion of strangers who are unable, or unwilling, to cope with the stress of cross-cultural adaptation, most strangers in foreign cultures have demonstrated an impressive capacity to manage their cross-cultural encounters successfully and without damaging their overall psychological health. This observation can be extended to individuals under even more extreme life conditions, such as those in concentration camps and prisons who have shown repeatedly that humans are capable of coping with severely stressful situations by adaptively transforming themselves.

It must be pointed out that not all individuals are equally successful in making transitions toward adaptation. Certain individuals, although in the minority, may strongly resist such change, thereby increasing the stress level and making the stress–adaptation–growth cycle intensely difficult. Some may not be able to cope with intense stress experiences due to lack of psychological resilience. Others may find themselves in situations that present too severe a challenge to manage. *Most individuals in most circumstances*, however, undergo the stress–adaptation–change cycle and achieve at least a minimum functional effectiveness in the host environment.

Strangers communicating

As strangers accumulate adaptive experiences, they cultivate the capability to code and decode verbal and non-verbal messages so that the messages will be recognised, accepted, and responded to. Through prolonged and varied communication experiences, strangers gradually acquire the coping mechanisms that help discern and deal with the dynamics of the host environment. Once acquired, communication capabilities function as an instrumental, interpretive, and expressive means of coming to terms with the host environment, and of feeling more at ease and less stressed.

Indeed, communication is at the heart of cross-cultural adaptation — as it is in the enculturation process of native-born children. The cross-cultural adaptation process is essentially a process of achieving the communication capacities necessary for strangers to be functional in the host society. In the continuous process of message encoding and decoding, up-to-date information about the self, the host environment, and the relationship of the self to the host environment leads to the acquisition of appropriate techniques, and eventually increases the individual's mastery of life. Through effective communication, strangers are able to gradually increase their control over the environment and over life itself — just as the capacity of a balloon expands with the increased amount of incoming air.

Conversely, the development of adaptive communication capacity occurs through countless acts of communication. Communication activities of strangers serve to develop their internal communication capacities: one learns to communicate by communicating. Furthermore, the acquired host communication competence has a direct bearing on the overall cross-cultural adaptation of strangers, serving as their primary means of utilising the resources of the host environment. It also functions as a set of adaptive tools assisting strangers to further participate in the communication processes of the host society, and to attempt to meet their personal and social needs. Through communication, they adapt to and relate to the new environment, and acquire membership and a sense of belonging in the various social groups of the host society on which they depend.

Dimensions of communication

In understanding the complex process of communication between strangers and the host cultural environment, Ruben's (1975) parameter of human communication provides a useful and comprehensive framework. In this parameter, each person's communication activity is conceptualised in two closely interrelated, inseparable communication processes —*personal* (or intrapersonal) and *social*.

Personal communication refers to the 'private symbolisation' (Ruben, 1975) activities of individuals — all the internal mental activities that occur in individuals that dispose and prepare them to act and react in certain ways in actual social situations. Geyer (1980) refers to this process as 'off-line functions', that is, 'internal information exchange within the system' of individuals when

(1) no inputs are received from the environment,
(2) no outputs are given to the environment, or
(3) there are 'outputs' but the system directs these back into itself as 'inputs' — as when a conclusion of a thinking process is not transmitted to anybody else but is used as an element in a further line of thought (p. 32).

Personal communication is linked to social communication when two or more individuals interact with one another, knowingly or not. Social communication is the process underlying 'intersubjectivisation', a phenomenon that occurs as a consequence of 'public symbolisation' (Ruben, 1975). According to Geyer (1980), these externalized communication processes of individuals are referred to as 'on-line functions' of human systems. The actual interface of individuals with their environment occurs through their on-line input–output transactions of messages.

Social communication activities occur in many different contexts — from communication in the macro-level society via newspapers, television and movies, to communication within the micro-level environment such as family, neighborhood, museum, workplace, bank, classroom, and friends. Social communication occurs when strangers make simple, passing observations of people on the street, when they listen to a newly released record album, or when they engage in serious dialogue with close friends. These and numerous other aspects of social communication activities can be grouped into two dimensions: (1) interpersonal communication and (2) mass communication.

Interpersonal communication of strangers refers to their social engagements through people in their immediate micro-level environment. Much of their adaptive learning takes place in the context of interpersonal communication. *Mass communication*, on the other hand, includes all other social processes that occur within larger, societal contexts. Through mass media communication experiences (such as radio, television, magazines, newspaper, movies, museums) and other forms of indirect communication (such as lectures, posters, and computerised networks), individuals participate in 'para-social' activities substituting for, or in conjunction with, direct person-to-person encounters. Mass communication, thus, is a more generalised, public form of communication by which individuals interact with their larger societal environment without involvement in any relationships with specific persons.

Along this line of systems thinking, the present theory focuses on host communication competence in examining personal (or 'off-line') communication processes of strangers. To understand social (or 'on-line') communication processes, we will examine the strangers' participation in the host society in general (host social communication) and in their ethnic community (ethnic social communication). Each of these two communication processes is explained below in relation to cross-cultural adaptation.

Personal communication: host communication competence

The successful adaptation of strangers is realised only when their internal communication systems sufficiently overlap with those of the natives. This internal capacity enables strangers to organise themselves in and with their sociocultural milieu, developing ways of seeing, hearing, understanding, and responding to the environment appropriately. As they become more competent in the host communication system, they are better able to discern the similarities and differences between their original home culture and the host culture and are able to act accordingly.

For the natives, such internal communication capacity has been acquired from so early in life and has been so completely internalised into their personal communication system that, by and large, it operates automatically and unconsciously. For immigrants or sojourners, however, the interpretive frames need to be learned and internalised (acculturation) and, at the same time, some of their original cultural communication patterns must be unlearned (deculturation). Through trial and error, with frequently accompanying stress and despair, they are able to gradually transform their personal communication patterns and achieve an increasing level of host communication competence. Until the strangers have acquired a sufficient level of host communication competence, they are handicapped in their ability to appropriately and effectively receive and transmit messages and retain information, and to perform operations in such a way that they may contribute to furthering their physical, psychological and social fulfilment in the host society.

In a way, strangers become more 'mature' members of the host society through acquiring host communication competence. They become less reliant on others for protection and correction of their behaviors in managing their daily activities, and feel a greater sense of belonging to the host society. Strangers' host communication competence, thus, facilitates the process of achieving the ultimate goal and outcome of cross-cultural adaptation — increased functional fitness and decreased cross-cultural stress. As Ruesch & Bateson (1951/1968) stated, 'the ability to communicate successfully becomes synonymous with being mentally healthy'. (p. 87)

Host communication competence as presently conceptualised, then, is a *continuum*, on which different strangers can be plotted and analysed. At the lowest end of this continuum is a hypothetical 'zero competence', that is, a complete inability to communicate in a new cultural environment. At the highest end, we can theoretically place those individuals whose capability to communicate is at the highest possible attainment.

Host social communication

Strangers actually *participate* in the reality of the host environment through social communication. Through such participation, they become actively 'engaged' in the host society and develop a functional relationship with it, and are given the opportunity to learn and enhance their host communication competence (cf. Cooley, 1909; Dewey, 1916; Duncan, 1967).

The critical importance of host social communication as a cross-cultural adaptation medium has been shown in numerous empirical studies, although findings are still scattered across several human science disciplines. Typically, the group-level anthropological studies of cultural contacts and change have taken communication as a 'given' condition that facilitates the adaptation flow between two or more contacting cultures (cf. Herskovits, 1958), and thus, little scientific attention has been placed on the communication process itself. In sociological studies, strangers' communication behaviors have been included as part of the indexes of 'social integration' or as a factor that is positively associated with the 'majority–minority' relations among ethnic groups within societies (cf. Gordon, 1964; Marden & Meyer, 1968; Pool, 1965).

Like interpersonal communication activities, mass communication activities (particularly the use of mass media) have been observed to promote adaptation of strangers. Gordon (1964) stated, for example, that the mass media (along with public schools) exert 'overwhelming acculturation powers' over immigrants' children (pp. 244–245). Shibutani &

Kwan (1965) also supported this view indicating that

> the extent to which members of a minority group become acculturated to the way of life of the dominant group depends upon the extent of their participation in the communication channels of their rulers. (p. 573)

The underlying assumption is that access to, exposure to, and use of the mass media of the dominant group influences ethnics and migrants in their processes of learning about and taking part in the dominant society (Subervi-Velez, 1986).

Recently, a few communication researchers have begun to pay closer attention to the communication patterns of immigrants. Nagata (1969), for example, made a first conceptualisation of the immigrant adaptation process based on various communication variables (such as interpersonal communication relations, mass media behavior, and perceptual and attitudinal orientations). In his study of Chicago area Japanese-Americans, Nagata observed a progressive increase in such communication variables. (See also Chang, 1972, for a similar study.) Ryu's study (1976) suggested the positive role of mass media in the adaptation of Korean immigrants in the United States. Other studies of sojourners and immigrants have repeatedly shown that individuals who are more active in interpersonal communication with members of the host society are better adjusted psychologically as well as financially (cf. Y. Kim, 1976, 1978a, 1980; Selltiz et al., 1963).

Strangers themselves are also keenly aware of the vital role that communication plays in their overall functioning in the host society. The majority of the Indochinese refugees in the United States, for example, expressed a strong need for communication training and general cultural orientation. A similar view was expressed by the social and educational service agencies and organisations serving refugee resettlement and adaptation. The agencies considered cultural and communication barriers one of the most serious problems impairing their service delivery to refugee clients (Y. Kim, 1980).

Indeed, the critical importance of the host communication activities of strangers cannot be over-emphasised. Adaptive transformation occurs in and through such communication activities, which, in turn, facilitate learning of all other aspects of the host culture including its economic, social, political and aesthetic dimensions.

Ethnic social communication

Along with host interpersonal and mass communication activities, strangers in many societies today have access to individuals of the same national or ethnic origin. Whether we speak of British compounds in India, American military posts in West Germany, Puerto Rican barrios in New York city, Chinatown in Tokyo, or a Japanese student association in a Canadian university, there are ethnic communities that provide strangers with opportunities to interact with fellow countrymen [women]. In large cities in countries like Australia, Canada, England, Germany, and the United States, where there has been a large influx of immigrants, many immigrant groups have organised some form of 'mutual aid' or 'self-help' ethnic community group. Such ethnic organisations render assistance to those who need material, informational, emotional, and other forms of social support (De Cocq, 1976). In many larger immigrant groups, ethnic media (including newspapers, radio stations, and television programs) perform various informational, educational, and entertainment services for their members.

These ethnic support systems serve adaptation-facilitating functions for new immigrants and sojourners during the initial phase of their adaptation process. Because many strangers initially lack host communication competence and other resources to be self-reliant in the new environment, they tend to rely on ethnic sources of support, compensating for the lack of support from host nationals. In the long run, however, heavy reliance on ethnic sources for their social activities would contribute to the sustenance of ethnic identity (Burgess, 1978), and deter the development of strangers' host communication competence. Because of the relatively 'easy' communication experiences in dealing with ethnic individuals and media, strangers are likely to delay or avoid confronting the stressful experiences of host social communication that are essential for adaptation. The relatively stress-free ethnic communication activities offer temporary relief and refuge, but in doing so discourage the long-term development of host communication competence and participation in the host social processes.

Strangers, therefore, cannot remain rigidly ethnic and also become highly adapted to the host culture. The longer strangers avoid or only minimally interact with the host communication environment, the longer it will take for them to acquire host communication competence. To the extent that strangers participate in ethnic communication channels, they are likely to maintain perspectives different from the normative patterns of the host culture and will experience difficulty in understanding and relating to the host environment.

In sum, the personal and social communication processes are functionally interrelated by a reciprocal causal relationship. (See Figure 5.) Strangers' host communication competence promotes their social engagements with the host environment. Their participation in host social communication processes, in turn, facilitates their host communication competence. This reciprocal and mutually defining relationship between host communication competence and social communication activities is analogous to computer operations in which the former is comparable to the capabilities of a software program and the latter to the actual application of the software for a specific purpose. Added to this interaction of host communication competence and participation in host social communication activities are ethnic social communication activities. Initially, ethnic social communication serves the adaptive process by compensating for the lack of host communication competence and host social communication activities. In time, ethnic social communication is likely to inhibit strangers' development of host communication competence and social participation.

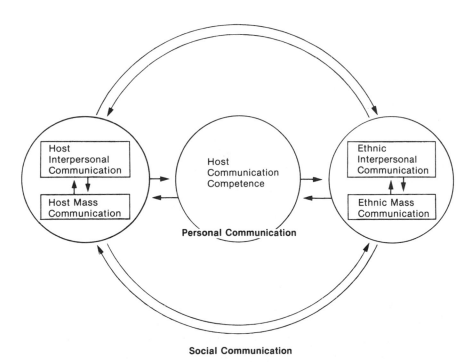

FIGURE 5 *Interrelated processes of host communication competence, ethnic social communication, and host social communication*

Host environment and predisposition

The personal and social (interpersonal, mass) communication processes of strangers cannot be fully understood in isolation from the host environment or without understanding their individualised backgrounds. By adding these dimensions to the present discussion of communication and adaptation, we can address issues concerning the observed differences among individual strangers in their adaptation patterns.

Host environment: receptivity and conformity pressure

Host environment refers to the social milieu that strangers encounter through interpersonal and mass communication activities. Through interpersonal communication activities, strangers interact with a small part of the host society such as their work place, neighborhood, and community. Strangers share a direct functional relationship with this micro-environment. Through mass communication activities, strangers are exposed to the 'macro'-environment of the host society, its political, social, religious, economic, and other events and activities.

To understand and explain the cross-cultural adaptation process, both the micro-and macro-environment need to be examined. Specifically, the present theory is concerned with the extent to which the environment is receptive toward strangers and the extent to which it exerts pressure on strangers to conform to the host cultural patterns. Environmental receptivity refers to the opportunities offered to strangers to participate in on-going social activities. Other terms such as 'interaction potential' (Y. Kim, 1979a) or 'acquaintance potential' (Cook, 1962) have been used for environmental receptivity in relation to strangers' interpersonal communication activities. For instance, United States military personnel who live in a remote military camp have limited access to local people in their daily activities. On the other hand, Peace Corps volunteers who live primarily with natives in local residences have greater access to the host social processes.

The 'conformity pressure' (Zajonc, 1952) of the host environment refers to the extent to which the environment challenges strangers to adopt the normative patterns of the host culture and its communication system. Although very few systematic studies have examined the role of environmental pressure in cross-cultural adaptation, societies and sub-societies clearly show different levels of tolerance (or rigidity) for strangers and their different cultural attributes. Generally, heterogeneous and 'free' societies such as the United States tend to exert less conformity pressure on strangers than homogeneous and 'rigid' societies such as the Soviet Union.

The above two environmental factors — receptivity and conformity pressure — help define the relative level of encouragement and challenge that a given environment offers to strangers. A society offering an optimal influence on strangers' adaptation would be one in which receptivity and conformity pressure are in an optimal balance.

Predisposition: adaptive potential

An additional dimension in explaining strangers' communication–adaptation is the nature of their experiential backgrounds prior to migrating to the host society. Strangers' predispositional factors precede the actual adaptation process, and set the tone for subsequent stranger–host communication encounters. The present analysis focuses on three predispositional factors that have direct bearing on strangers' communication–adaptation processes:

(1) cultural and racial background,
(2) personality attributes, and
(3) preparedness for change.

These predispositional factors collectively characterise the strangers' overall *adaptive potential*.

Clearly, strangers from a culture similar to the host culture would begin their adaptation process with a greater advantage, compared to those who must bridge a more substantial cultural gap. A similar advantage is found among strangers whose racial/physical make-up closely resembles that of the natives. These cultural and racial similarities equip strangers with a greater potential for successful adaptation in the host environment. Strangers' themselves also contribute to their own adaptive potential with differential personality attributes. Those who are more open-minded and receptive toward the host culture and who are stronger and more resilient under stressful circumstances are likely to be better able to manage the uncertainties and challenges of the host environment. In addition, strangers' adaptive potential is influenced by the degree of their preparedness for change. Those who are better educated and better informed about the host culture (through training and other forms of learning) begin their adaptation process with a greater adaptive potential.

Cross-cultural adaptation outcomes

In time, changes take place within strangers as a cumulative result of prolonged communication and adaptation experiences with the host environment. Such adaptive changes in strangers have been examined in numerous aspects — from tastes for different foods, dress habits, and leisure activities, to religious practices, social values, and attitudes toward host culture and home culture. In the present theory, three interrelated aspects — functional fitness, psychological health, and intercultural identity — are examined as the most direct and critical changes that are likely to be observed in strangers.

Functional fitness

Strangers conduct continuous 'experiments' in the host society. They try and fail, they try and fail less disastrously, they try another alternative and partially succeed. Learning some of the host culture and unlearning some of the original culture gradually brings about an internal transformation in strangers. In time, we see them deviate from the accepted patterns of their original culture and acquire the new patterns of the host culture. A natural outcome of this stress–adaptation–growth process is an increased functional fitness, that is, a greater congruence and compatibility between the strangers' internal conditions and the conditions of the host environment. This notion of person–environment fit implies an interactive systems perspective that, unlike assessments based solely in terms of individual traits, regards human behavior as a function of both the person and the environment (cf. Caplan, 1979; French, Rodger & Cobb, 1974; Murray, 1938; Pervin, 1968). Functional fitness, further, requires some 'compromise' in the internal structure of a person in the face of pressure from the host environment.

As such, the increased functional fitness of strangers promotes their life chances in the host society. Successfully adapted strangers have the desired level of appropriate and effective ways of communicating with the host environment. As they achieve an increasing level of fitness in the host culture, they are better able to meet their basic survival needs and social necessities (e.g., friendship, occupation, and status), as well as philosophical drives (e.g., creativity, actualisation and fulfilment). The increased functional fitness further enhances the potential effectiveness of the strangers' performance and control in the host environment.

Psychological health

An increase in functional fitness will, in turn, reduce the stranger's overall cross-cultural stress, as well as defensive reactions to stress such as withdrawal, denial and hostility. As strangers achieve a greater functional fitness in the host environment with increased communication competence, their experience of internal stress due to cross-cultural challenges will decrease.

Issues of mental health (or illness) have been a subject of great interest among researchers, as well as practitioners. Culture shock studies have been mainly concerned with this psychological-health aspect of sojourn experiences, as was reviewed previously. Immigrant studies have also been conducted in psychology and psychiatry examining the issues of mental illnesses (e.g., Williams & Westermeyer, 1986). In the present theoretical framework, the psychological health (or illness) of strangers is viewed as a direct outcome of their communication–adaptation experiences and as directly related to the level of functional fitness achieved in the host environment.

Intercultural identity

Another related aspect of the cross-cultural adaptation outcome is the development of an intercultural identity. Strangers are capable of adapting to the host environment and of growing and developing through the process. The psychological movements of strangers into new dimensions of perception and experience produce 'boundary-ambiguity syndromes' (Hall, 1976:227), in which the original cultural identity begins to lose its definiteness and rigidity and the emergent identity shows an increasing 'interculturalness'.

From the present systems perspective, intercultural identity, like cultural identity (cf. Chapter 3), refers to the complex *process* of interpretive activity inside a stranger *and* the resultant *self-conception* in relation to a cultural group. As strangers undergo adaptive transformation, their internal attributes and self-identification change from being cultural to being increasingly intercultural, and their emotional adherence to the culture of their childhood weakens, while accommodating the host culture into their self-conception. In other words, a stranger's cultural identity becomes increasingly flexible — no longer rigidly bound by membership to the original culture, or to the host culture — and begins to take on a more fluid intercultural identity (Adler, 1982; Gudykunst & Kim, 1984; Kim & Ruben, 1988).

Such an intercultural identity is likely to have the cognitive, affective, and behavioral flexibility to adapt to the situation and to creatively manage or avoid conflicts that could result from inappropriate switching between cultures. As pointed out earlier, the cross-cultural adaptation experiences of strangers contribute to the expansion of their internal capacity beyond the cultural parameters of the original culture. Through the dynamic and continuous process of stress–adaptation–transformation, strangers' internal conditions gradually transform toward becoming increasingly intercultural.

So far in this chapter, the process and outcomes of cross-cultural adaptation has been theoretically based on the General Systems perspective, focusing on strangers' communication experiences. The adaptation process has been described as a communication process in which strangers learn and acquire dominant communication patterns of the host society. Just as native-born individuals acquire their cultural communication patterns through interaction with their significant others, strangers acquire the cultural communication patterns of the host society and develop relationships with the new social environment through communication. Influencing this communication–adaptation process are the adaptive predisposition of strangers and the characteristics of the host environment. Three aspects of strangers' adaptive change — increased functional fitness, psychological health, and intercultural identity — have been identified as direct consequences of prolonged communication–adaptation experiences in the host society. These theoretical principles of the process and outcome of cross-cultural adaptation can be summarised into the axioms shown opposite.

Axioms

Axiom 1: Cross-cultural adaptation occurs in and through communication.

Axiom 2: Cross-cultural adaptation necessitates at least a minimum level of acculturation of the host culture and a minimum level of deculturation of the childhood culture.

Axiom 3: Individuals continually undergo the internal dynamics of stress–adaptation–growth *vis-à-vis* the host environment, maintaining their overall integrity.

Axiom 4: Host communication competence and host social (interpersonal, mass) communication interactively and collectively facilitate cross-cultural adaptation.

Axiom 5: Ethnic social (interpersonal, mass) communication indirectly facilitates the initial short-term cross-cultural adaptation, compensating for the lack of host communication competence and host social (interpersonal, mass) communication.

Axiom 6: Ethnic (interpersonal, mass) communication indirectly deters the subsequent cross-cultural adaptation by discouraging the long-term development of host communication competence and host social (interpersonal, mass) communication.

Axiom 7: Receptivity and conformity pressure of the host environment facilitates the development of host communication competence and host social (interpersonal, mass) communication.

Axiom 8: Adaptive predisposition facilitates the development of host communication competence and host social (interpersonal, mass) communication.

Axiom 9: Achieved outcomes of cross-cultural adaptation experiences at a given time include increased functional fitness, psychological health, and intercultural identity.

Axiom 10: The increased functional fitness, psychological health, and intercultural identity, in turn, facilitate subsequent development of host communication competence and host social (interpersonal, mass) communication.

5 THEOREMS AND THE MODEL

*The arbitrary structural and dimensional categories are
not independent of each other . . . . Each is one facet on a
multifaceted, complexly organized, and, let us say, living
crystal. Each is intrinsic to the unity of the crystal.
Alternation in one facet affects the structural relations
of the entire crystal.*
Douglas Heath

In the preceding two chapters, the nature of the process and outcomes of
cross-cultural adaptation has been described and explained from a
communication-systems perspective. We examined the fundamental communication process through which human systems interact with and adapt
to a given environment. The process in which individuals enculturate to
become a cultural being was explained as a communication process. We also
noted that, once enculturated into a given culture, individuals acquire and
internalise communication competence in that culture, which serves as the
means for becoming functional in a given society. In this process, a distinct
cultural identity is formed linking an individual to his or her cultural group,
reflecting the deeply internalised cultural attributes.

This sketch of the systems view of human–environmental interfaces
and the cross-cultural adaptation process have been captured in the basic
metatheoretical assumptions (presented in Chapter 3) and reviewed here.

Based on these assumptions, we have examined the process in which
an individual born and raised in one culture adapts to a new culture as a
sojourner or an immigrant. Once enculturated, encountering and adapting
to a new culture necessitates the acculturation of the host cultural
communication patterns as well as the deculturation of the original cultural
communication patterns. In this interplay of acculturation–deculturation,
strangers experience stress caused by the discrepancy between their internal
conditions and the conditions of the host environment. Stress, thus, is a

Assumptions

Assumption 1: A person is an open communication system that interacts with the environment through input and output of information.

Assumption 2: A person has an inherent drive to maintain his or her internal equilibrium in the face of changes in environmental conditions.

Assumption 3: A person's internal equilibrium is disturbed when the person–environment symmetry is broken.

Assumption 4: To regain internal equilibrium and reduce stress, a person adapts by altering his/her internal conditions.

Assumption 5: Stress and growth are inseparable as aspects of adaptation. Both are necessary to define the nature of a person's internal growth.

Assumption 6: The stress–adaptation–growth dynamic lies at the heart of the human system's response to environmental challenges.

Assumption 7: Each culture sanctions a system of communication for its members.

Assumption 8: Through communication, an individual adapts to a given cultural environment.

Assumption 9: As a person adapts to a cultural environment, he/she forms a cultural identity.

Assumption 10: A person's communication competence facilitates, as well as is facilitated by, his/her level of cultural adaptation.

necessary condition for subsequent adaptation as it stimulates adaptive changes in strangers. Without experiencing stress, no adaptation is believed to occur. Adaptation, in this sense, is a developmental process in which the human organism attempts to reduce internal disequilibrium and the accompanying stress through continuous development of host communication competence and participation in interpersonal and mass communication activities of the host environment.

The focal concept in the present theory is the stress–adaptation–growth dynamic of intercultural communication experiences of strangers. Except for a few, most strangers follow the process of adaptation as articulated in the present theory, demonstrating an impressive capacity to manage cross-cultural challenges successfully without damaging their overall psychological health and integrity. As has been demonstrated amply by numerous immigrants and sojourners who have successfully overcome severely stressful situations and transformed themselves adaptively, the process of cross-cultural adaptation is clearly an empirical phenomenon.

Axioms

Axiom 1: Cross-cultural adaptation occurs in and through communication.

Axiom 2: Cross-cultural adaptation necessitates at least a minimum level of acculturation of the host culture and a minimum level of deculturation of the childhood culture.

Axiom 3: Individuals continually undergo the internal dynamics of stress–adaptation–growth *vis-à-vis* the host environment, maintaining their overall integrity.

Axiom 4: Host communication competence and host social (interpersonal, mass) communication interactively and collectively facilitate cross-cultural adaptation.

Axiom 5: Ethnic social (interpersonal, mass) communication indirectly facilitates the initial short-term cross-cultural adaptation, compensating for the initial lack of host communication competence and host social (interpersonal, mass) communication.

Axiom 6: Ethnic social (interpersonal, mass) communication indirectly deters the subsequent cross-cultural adaptation by discouraging the long-term development of host communication competence and host social (interpersonal, mass) communication.

Axiom 7: Receptivity and conformity pressure of the host environment facilitates the development of host communication competence and host social (interpersonal, mass) communication.

Axiom 8: Adaptive predisposition facilitates the development of host communication competence and host social (interpersonal, mass) communication.

Axiom 9: Achieved outcomes of cross-cultural adaptation experiences at a given time include increased functional fitness, psychological health, and intercultural identity.

Axiom 10: The increased functional fitness, psychological health, and intercultural identity, in turn, facilitate subsequent development of host communication competence and host social (interpersonal, mass) communication.

To understand the cross-cultural adaptation process and outcome, therefore, the present theory emphasises an understanding of the communication patterns and activities in and through which strangers experience the host environment. In addition, the theory incorporates the strangers' adaptive potential prior to migration and of the receptivity and conformity pressure of the host environment as factors that influence their communication processes. Finally, the theory identifies three crucial areas of the outcomes of this communication–adaptation process as: becoming increasingly functional, psychologically healthier, and intercultural in identity.

These theoretical principles about how strangers communicate, adapt, and undergo changes have been summarised into the 10 axioms (shown opposite) as universal, trans-cultural, trans-societal principles that individual strangers follow in their process of adapting to a given host environment.

Theorems

Collectively, the above assumptions and axioms provide the content and structure of the present theory, describing and explaining:

(1) how and why strangers adapt and go through a process of transformation in an alien cultural environment;
(2) what happens to the strangers' internal systems as a result of cumulative adaptive communication experiences; and
(3) how their adaptive potential and the host environment influence the communication–adaptation process and outcome.

From the axioms, specific constructs of each dimension are identified as follows:

Theoretical dimensions and constructs

Dimension 1: Personal Communication

Host communication competence

Dimension 2: Host Social Communication

Host interpersonal communication
Host mass communication

Dimension 3: Ethnic Social Communication

Ethnic interpersonal communication
Ethnic mass communication

Dimension 4: Host Environment

Receptivity
Conformity pressure

Dimension 5: Adaptive Predisposition

Cultural/racial background
Personality attributes
Preparedness for change

Dimension 6: Adaptation Outcomes

Functional fitness
Psychological health
Intercultural identity

These constructs are then linked with one another by the nature of their relationships indicated by the axiomatic principles to generate a series of predictive theorems listed below.

Theorems

Theorem 1: The greater the development of host communication competence, the greater the participation in host interpersonal communication.

Theorem 2: The greater the development of host communication competence, the greater the participation in host mass communication.

Theorem 3: The greater the participation in host interpersonal communication, the greater the participation in host mass communication.

Theorem 4: The greater the development of host communication competence, the greater the functional fitness.

Theorem 5: The greater the development of host communication competence, the greater the psychological health.

Theorem 6: The greater the development of host communication competence, the greater the intercultural identity.

Theorem 7: The greater the participation in host interpersonal communication, the greater the functional fitness.

Theorem 8: The greater the participation in host interpersonal communication, the greater the psychological health.

Theorem 9: The greater the participation in host interpersonal communication, the greater the intercultural identity.

Theorem 10: The greater the participation in host mass communication, the greater the functional fitness.

Theorem 11: The greater the participation in host mass communication, the greater the psychological health.

Theorem 12: The greater the participation in host mass communication, the greater the intercultural identity.

Theorem 13: The greater the participation in ethnic interpersonal communication, the greater the initial short-term development of host communication competence.

Theorem 14: The greater the participation in ethnic mass communication, the greater the initial short-term development of host communication competence.

Theorem 15: The greater the participation in ethnic interpersonal communication, the lesser the subsequent long-term development of host communication competence.

Theorem 16: The greater the participation in ethnic interpersonal communication, the lesser the subsequent long-term development of host interpersonal communication.

Theorem 17: The greater the participation in ethnic mass communication, the lesser the subsequent long-term development of host communication competence.

Theorem 18: The greater the participation in ethnic mass communication, the lesser the subsequent long-term participation in host interpersonal communication.

Theorem 19: The greater the participation in ethnic mass communication, the lesser the subsequent long-term participation in host mass communication.

Theorem 20: The greater the adaptive potential in predisposition, the greater the development of host communication competence.

Theorem 21: The greater the adaptive potential in predisposition, the greater the participation in host interpersonal communication.

Theorem 22: The greater the adaptive potential in predisposition, the greater the participation in host mass communication.

Theorem 23: The greater the receptivity of the host environment, the greater the development of host communication competence.

Theorem 24: The greater the receptivity of the host environment, the greater the participation in host interpersonal communication.

Theorem 25: The greater the receptivity of the host environment, the greater the participation in host mass communication.

Theorem 26: The greater the conformity pressure of the host environment, the greater the development of host communication competence.

Theorem 27: The greater the conformity pressure of the host environment, the greater the participation in host interpersonal communication.

Theorem 28: The greater the conformity pressure of the host environment, the greater the participation in host mass communication.

The model

The above theorems together offer a 'from-the-ground-up' explanation of the process and outcomes of cross-cultural adaptation, with a central focus on the communication experiences of individual strangers. Based on the causal linkages provided in these theorems, we are now able to draw a diagram that represents the overall structure of the present theory, as shown in Figure 6. The single arrows indicate unidirectional causality while the two arrows side-by-side indicate bidirectional causality.

Given the overall theoretical structure described in Figure 6, the present theory re-emphasises the argument made earlier in Chapter 3 that cross-cultural adaptation is not solely a psychological, sociological, or anthropological issue but that the diverse academic interests must be integrated into a single, comprehensive framework. Such a framework must consist of a set of unifying principles for the diversity observed in existing approaches, and of constructs that are sufficiently abstract and general to help consolidate and simplify the many different elements and processes in the complex adaptation process.

The present multidimensional model, based on its systems perspective and communication focus, realises at least some of the necessary inter-disciplinary integration. It clarifies the interrelatedness among:

(1) personal and social communication processes of strangers,
(2) adaptive predispositional factors,
(3) host environmental conditions, and
(4) the resultant internal transformation of strangers.

These dimensions are dynamically interrelated in the present framework as they are in the reality of the adaptation experiences of individual strangers. As such, the present theory echoes Ruesch & Bateson (1951/1968), who viewed the systems-based communication approach as central to unifying diverse perspectives in human sciences.

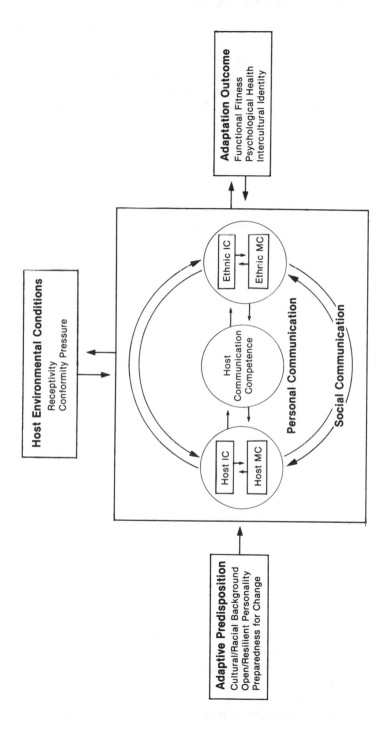

Note: IC-Interpersonal Communication, MC-Mass Communication

FIGURE 6   *A communication model of cross-cultural adaptation*

... communication is the only scientific model which enables us to explain physical, intrapersonal, interpersonal, and cultural aspects of events within one system. By the use of one single system we eliminate the multiplicity of single universes, the multifarious vocabularies, and the controversies which arise because we, the scientists and clinicians, cannot understand each other. (p. 5)

In addition to providing an interdisciplinary integration, the present theory incorporates both the views of those who consider cross-cultural experiences as primarily problematic and the views of those who regard cross-cultural experiences as learning and growth experiences. It does so by recognising that the cross-cultural adaptation process involves both stressful and growth experiences, and that the dynamic tension between these two experiences is essential for subsequent adaptive transformation and growth.

A similar systems reasoning allows a theoretical conciliation of the apparent conflict between assimilationist and pluralist ideological positions. As has been pointed out earlier, the present theory assumes that adaptation of human systems is neither desirable nor undesirable on the theoretical level, but that it takes place naturally and inevitably as long as individuals engage in communication with the environment. Their internal transformation necessarily follows adaptation, regardless of their ideological choice.

Realistically, an average stranger will not become fully competent in the host communication system to the extent that his or her communication modes are identical with the natives. The individual makes a workable adaptation, nonetheless, as a result of both continuous exposure to the natives and the many trials and errors in interacting with them. Gradually the strangers are transformed so that they become increasingly capable of managing their daily activities. In this process, at least some of the original cultural attributes must be unlearned and some of the host cultural attributes must be acquired. At any given moment, both the original and the new cultural attributes are present in a stranger.

At this point, readers are reminded of the boundary conditions of the present theory. As noted in Chapter 2, this theory does not directly attempt to explain the changes that occur in the host culture itself, but only the changes that take place in individual strangers' internal conditions. The theory further recognizes that some strangers, although small in percentage, may not follow the adaptation patterns identified in the theory. Perhaps due to innate temperament or by circumstantial conditions extremely susceptible to ill effects from any change or trauma, these strangers may not be able to, or may be unwilling to, undergo the adaptive changes identified in the present theory. In principle, these limits and individual variables define the parameters of the capabilities of human systems in coping with environmental changes in general, and cross-cultural stress in particular. These issues of human systems limitations and of environmental conditions leading to the extremity of a stranger's failure to adapt, however, lie beyond the present theoretical domain, although it is an important issue to be investigated.

Given these boundary specifications, this theory offers a conceptual framework that is comprehensive and integrative. It is proposed as a culture-general system of description and explanation that clarifies the meaning of cross-cultural adaptation experiences and helps to predict the specific nature of the relationship between its dimensions and constructs. The present assumptions, axioms, and theorems are culture-general and apply to all cross-cultural adaptation contexts. Given this broad generalisability, the theory incorporates differences in the individual backgrounds and in the host environmental conditions to explain the communication patterns and adaptive transformation of strangers. The theory clearly suggests that, *if* strangers are to become successfully adapted, they must above all enhance their host communication competence and actively participate in the interpersonal and mass communication processes of the host society. Yet, according to the theory, strangers must 'face' the experiences of stress, particularly during the early stages, if they are to 're-invent' themselves to become successfully adapted in the host milieu.

The predictive propositions such as the ones reviewed above will need to be validated and refined through empirical studies. In the following three chapters, each of the theoretical constructs will be discussed in detail and a number of the specific indicators will be identified for empirical observation.

PART III
ELABORATION OF
THE THEORY

6 HOST COMMUNICATION COMPETENCE

> *If what we can express in any present moment cannot be comprehended, or if what we can comprehend at that moment is not being expressed, our existence as humans is threatened.*
> Lee Thayer

A central premise of the theoretical system has been that strangers' successful adaptation is possible only when they are able to communicate successfully with the host environment. To do so requires that the strangers' internal communication patterns overlap sufficiently with those of the natives. Just as children acquire and internalise their cultural communication patterns to become well-adapted members of their society, strangers must acquire sufficient host communication competence to be able to manage their daily activities appropriately and effectively and thereby become functionally fit in the new cultural milieu.

The concept — host communication competence — can be examined in detail by analysing its key empirical indicators:

(1) knowledge of the host communication system,
(2) cognitive complexity in responding to the host environment,
(3) affective (emotional, aesthetic) co-orientation with the host culture, and
(4) behavioral capability to perform various interactions in the host environment.

Although these factors overlap functionally, are interdependent, and operate simultaneously within a person, they serve the present purpose of identifying elements that are crucial in the strangers' adaptation experiences.

Briefly, knowledge of the host communication system refers to the capacity of strangers to identify and understand messages in different situations of interaction with the host environment. Affective co-orientation refers to motivational readiness and emotional participation in the cultural values, attitudes, and aesthetic/emotional experiences of the host culture. This factor deepens strangers' understanding of the subtle feelings and attitudes embedded in various messages from the host environment, and thereby, enriches their communicative experiences. Behavioral capability refers to the ability to select behaviors that are effective and appropriate in various social situations. This behavioral competence is distinguished in the present conceptualisation from 'performance'. The latter involves all three dimensions of host communication competence — cognitive, affective, and behavioral, as well as environmental factors and the performance of the other person.

The present analysis of host communication competence corresponds to Kuhn's (1975) conceptualisation of a human communication system, in which the state of an individual communication system is examined by its 'detector', 'selector' and 'effector' processes. According to Kuhn, the 'detector' process refers to the concept-perception function that processes information, the 'selector' process refers to the goal or value function of the individual, and the 'effector' process refers to the ability of the individual to physically carry out the selected behavior.

Also, the present scheme is generally in agreement with the other existing conceptualisations of communication competence and adaptation. For instance, interpersonal communication competence was analysed by Spitzberg & Cupach (1984) in terms of (1) motivation, (2) knowledge, and (3) skill. Taft (1977), in his discussion of cross-cultural adaptation, explained adaptation in terms of three dimensions — 'cognitive', 'dynamic' and 'behavioral'. Also, Brislin, Landis & Brandt (1983) similarly identified the effects of cross-cultural training of sojourners as 'changes in thinking (cognitions), affective reactions (feelings), and behavior' (pp. 7–8). In a survey of factors identified as predictors of overseas success of sojourners, Kealey & Ruben (1983) concluded that such predictors generally fell into cognitive, affective, and behavioral competence. Grove & Torbiorn (1985) also identified 'applicability of behavior', 'clarity of the mental frame of reference' and 'emotional adequacy' as the main indicators of successful cross-cultural adaptation. As such, there has been substantial agreement among researchers on the cognitive–affective–behavioral subprocesses of an individual stranger's capacity to adapt. (See Figure 7.)

Below, a number of cognitive, affective and behavioral elements of

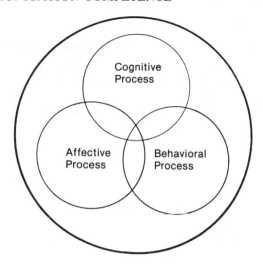

FIGURE 7   *Three interrelated elements of host communication competence*

host communication competence are presented for their direct relevance to the present theoretical concern, cross-cultural adaptation.

Knowledge of host communication system

Differences in the ways in which experiences are organised and interpreted constitute some of the main differences between cultures. As Campbell (1964) pointed out, communication between strangers and host nationals becomes possible only when both sides understand each other's messages by extending the domains of common perception and inter-pretation. Frequently, however, the 'burden' lies heavily, or exclusively, on the strangers to learn to understand the messages of the natives, not *vice versa*. It is usually strangers, not natives, who need to learn the host communication patterns to function in the existing host environment.

Typically, however, strangers are faced with high degrees of un-certainty. They are unfamiliar with various aspects of the new cultural environment, particularly the 'mentality' (thought patterns) of the natives. Their initial perception of the unfamiliar host environment tends to be simple, often dictated by gross stereotypes about the environment rather than accurate insights. Their 'think-as-usual' patterns become unworkable in dealing with the host environment because they do not share the common underlying assumptions of the host population.

In this uncertain situation, securing adequate information about the environment is an obvious necessity for the adaptive process. Actions can be carried out most successfully when the strangers have acquired sufficient information about the host environment. As articulated by Gudykunst (1988) based on uncertainty reduction theory (Berger & Calabrese, 1975), strangers' adaptation is essentially a process of reducing the unpredictable elements of the host society by increasing their knowledge about the environment. Strangers search for patterns, trends, consistencies and inconsistencies in the host environment, gradually increasing their knowledge and understanding of the new milieu. Through varied communication encounters with natives, and through exposure to mass communication processes, the strangers become more conscious of many of their behaviors and attitudes previously taken for granted. They realise that their culturally-bound ways of thinking and behaving are no longer universally accepted. They learn different ways of responding, from very simple behavior such as how to apply for a bank account and how to express gratitude to a friend, to more complex social interactions such as developing and maintaining an intimate relationship with a native of the host culture.

The crucial importance of cognitive competence in the strangers' adaptation was recognised by the Social Science Research Council (1954) when it defined cross-cultural adaptation as primarily 'a matter of range of presentation and of perceptual reality' (p. 993). The relevance of cognition in cross-cultural adaptation has continued to be recognised in many subsequent works on cross-cultural adaptation of immigrants and sojourners (cf. Berry, 1980; Chance, 1965; Taft, 1975; Torbiorn, 1982). For example, empirical data from a study of Korean immigrants in the United States (Y. Kim, 1977b) suggests that strangers' knowledge of the host society becomes increasingly extensive, accurate, and refined over the years and that such increased cultural learning is reflected in the development of more complex cognitive structures for perceiving the host environment. The reverse also appears to be true. Strangers who are cognitively more complex have been observed to have a greater capacity to acquire the information they need than those who are less cognitively complex (Yum, 1982).

Knowledge of the host language

Knowledge of the host language is perhaps the most critical, and certainly the most salient, aspect of host communication competence.

Language is a 'veil' over the reality of the culture in which it is used, involving an *agreement* of its users about what there is to be seen and how it should be seen. To learn the host language, therefore, is to learn not only the linguistic codes *per se* but also to gain access to the accumulated records of the host cultural experiences. To be proficient in the host language requires an understanding of not only its phonemic, syntactic, and semantic rules but also its pragmatic rules.

It is the pragmatic rules that profoundly involve cultural and sub-cultural connotations of verbal expressions, particularly of slang, idiom, humor, and metaphors that are highly contextual and so require an intimate knowledge of the relevant experiences of users. For strangers, acquiring sufficient host language knowledge often accompanies an extensive and continuous experience of frustration. Even those who are well equipped with the host language through textbook learning often find themselves unfamiliar with its pragmatic usage. Many phrases used in daily conversation can be learned only through personal exposure to situations in which the phrases are actually used.

The critical importance of host language knowledge in cross-cultural adaptation can be explained in terms of its central role to all communication activities that involve spoken or written messages. First, language is as much a means of organising and structuring the world as it is a means of representing experiences. It serves as the primary 'conduit' for information between communicators, and, as such, strangers must learn the host language if they wish to function and participate in the host environment. In a sense, strangers are subject to 'coercion' by the host environment in much the same way as they are pressured by the economic, political, legal, and social patterns. They cannot communicate with the natives effectively unless they utilise the group-accepted language in a way that can be recognised, understood and responded to by the natives. Without the host language knowledge, they are unable to participate in direct encounters with natives as well as in host mass communication processes. To an extent, this inability can be compared to the lack of social opportunities among the host nationals who are illiterate (although they do speak the language).

Second, host language competence is not limited to simply acquiring the ability to express and understand verbal messages. It also enables the cultural stranger to *think* in the way the native speakers think, as language patterns and thought patterns are closely interrelated. As articulated in the Sapir–Whorf hypothesis, each linguistic system is

> not merely a reproducing instrument for voicing ideas but rather is itself the shaper of ideas, the program and guide for the individual's mental

activity, for his [her] analysis of impressions, for his [her] synthesis of his [her] mental stock in trade. (Whorf, 1952, in Hoijer, 1982:211).

Third, the host language is an instrument of status and power for strangers. As Bourdieu (1979) pointed out,

> a person speaks not only to be understood but also to be believed, obeyed, respected, distinguished. Hence the full definition of competence as the right to speech, i.e., to the legitimate language, the authorised language which is also the language of authority. (p. 19)

This language-based reality of social 'empowerment' often serves as subtle, hidden discrimination against strangers whose host language knowledge is limited. Conversely, acquiring host language knowledge means gaining access to the 'mainstream' and enhancing social standing in the host society.

Considerable research attention has been devoted to the general effectiveness of language orientation in promoting cross-cultural adaptation. Almost all studies on cross-cultural adaptation have included language competence, and have presented empirical evidence for the paramount importance of host language competence in various 'indicators' of adaptation. For example, Nishida (1985) found that English competence of Japanese students in the United States stood out most clearly as significantly related with interactional effectiveness. Also, Indochinese refugees in the United States reported that those refugees who were fluent in English had a labor force participation rate similar to, or higher than, that of the U. S. population; refugees who spoke 'a little' English had an unemployment rate twice the national average; and refugees who spoke no English had an even higher unemployment rate (Office of Refugee Resettlement, 1982; see also Jaeger & Sandhu, 1985 for similar findings). Often, the language used by strangers and the proficiency of such usage has been a measure of the extent of adaptation. DeFleur & Cho (1957) included 'language behavior' as one of the crucial areas in their 'index of acculturation'. (See also Breton, 1964; Chance, 1965; Graves, 1967; Y. Kim, 1976, 1977a; Price, 1968; Richmond, 1967.)

Knowledge of host non-verbal behavior

Equally as critical as host language knowledge is knowledge of host non-verbal behavior. The adequacy and effectiveness of communication is governed not only by words but also by the use of more or less standardised behaviors, ceremonies, rituals and norms. Implicit, non-verbal messages such as facial expressions and body movements, vocal patterns and spatial–temporal behaviors establish the emotional/attitudinal under-currents of interactions, and help define the nature of the relationship between interactants.

Like language, much of non-verbal behavior is shaped by cultural conditioning from early childhood, which acts to encourage, inhibit, or otherwise alter the direct expression of motivational/emotional ex-periences. Ekman & Friesen (1971) termed these factors *display rules*, which may be defined as cultural rules or expectations about the manage-ment of emotional expressions. Further, cultural conditioning also regulates the 'rhythm' of interaction, or 'action chain' (Hall, 1976), which is carried out in various non-verbal forms of behavior such as gesturing or other body movements signifying turn-taking and turn-yielding, or initiating and terminating interactions.

Clearly, strangers need to learn these non-verbal behavior patterns of the host culture just as they need to learn the host language if they are to become communicatively competent. Many embarrassing and awkward moments are bound to occur as long as they seriously lack such non-verbal knowledge. To the extent that strangers are unaccustomed to such interaction patterns, they are likely to be 'out of sync' in communicating with the natives.

Stuttering, foreign accents and other paralinguistic patterns that deviate from host language speech patterns are additional handicaps for strangers. Also critical to the patterned, synchronised non-verbal patterns of the host culture are the time-related behaviors, including the 'pace' of carrying out various formal and informal tasks and the strictness of observing punctuality. For instance, an immigrant from a 'monochronic' time culture such as the United States would find it necessary to adapt his or her time orientation and behavior in adapting to a 'polychronic' time system such as the one in Mexico (Hall, 1976).

Unfortunately, the task of learning a new system of non-verbal behavior is monumental due to its subtleties, implicitness, and com-plexities, and can be acquired only through direct experiences of observing and participating in communication activities with the natives over an extended period. In the meantime, the inadequacy of strangers' less conscious elements of non-verbal behavior creates tension and discomfort in themselves and in the natives, if not outright communication 'breakdown' (cf. Segalowitz & Catbonton, 1977; Taylor & Simard, 1975). Such lack of synchronised non-verbal behaviors further contributes to natives' perception that strangers are less than competent and adequate socially.

Knowledge of host communication rules

Underlying the verbal and non-verbal codes and behaviors of the host culture are its communication rules, that is, a coherent system of expected patterns of behavior that serves to organise interaction between individuals in the host society. Culture provides the 'rules of the game' that enable individuals to make sense out of events, activities, actions, and behaviors. Communication rules function as directives that govern the flow of messages from one person to another, limiting the possibilities of communication actions of the participating persons (Ruesch, in Ruesch & Bateson, 1951/1968:21). The rules partly serve to define the meaning a situation has, and to define the meaning that any given action has within that situation. For the individual, the rules provide a set of recipes that specify how a given end state may be achieved, and, thus, render the behavior of each person more or less predictable and understandable to others.

Communication rules apply to all levels of behavior, both verbal and non-verbal. Some rules are formally coded within the written or spoken language, as in the case of public and organisational rules and regulations. Others are left implicit, mostly dealing with the nature of interpersonal relationships, intimacy levels, status, or dominance levels. These informal, relational rules are not formally coded or immediately visible, but are implicitly embedded with patterns of non-verbal behavior. They are learned during primary socialisation and, among adults, operate semi-automatically (Noesjirwan, 1978).

The operating rules of a culture, however, have specifiable consequences, and these consequences are visible and measurable. Cultural differences exist, for instance, in the expected consequences for action due to different rules (Applegate & Sypher, 1988; Cronen, Chen & Pearce, 1988). The objectively same situation will elicit different behavioral choices, while the objectively same sequence of behaviors may elicit different interpretations. Pearce & Stamm (1973), in presenting the theory of 'coordinated management of meaning', conceptualised such behavioral choices and interpretations thereof within individual communicators as providing emergent communication rules.

For strangers to learn the communication rules of the host culture, therefore, requires a deepened cultural understanding. They must go beyond simply knowing the verbal and non-verbal patterns, and be able to 'see' how and why the natives communicate in the way they do. It is only when strangers have acquired a general cultural understanding that they are able to share the 'experiential equivalence' or 'shared memory' to interpret the hidden, unspoken communication rules operating in the natives (cf. Parrillo, 1966; Sechrest, Fay, & Zaidi 1982).

Such a deeper-level understanding of the host cultural communication rules involves the knowledge of historical, political, economic, religious and educational practices of the host society. If, for example, strangers are to adapt to a predominantly Moslem culture, they must have some under-standing of the Moslem heritage underlying various social dynamics of that cultural milieu. Without such background knowledge, they are likely to make 'cultural projections' (Hall, 1976:164) in attempting to make sense of many of the communication rules and behaviors of the natives. Background knowledge about the host culture further includes the group's institutions and subgroups, arts, sciences and technology, attitudes, beliefs, values, reciprocal role requirements, and all other dominant thought patterns of the host environment. Since the cultural knowledge of any structurally complex group can never be complete, even for a life-long member of the group, the newcomers' knowledge of host communication rules can be understood only in relative terms.

Without sufficient knowledge about the host culture and its history, the strangers sometimes may be the comical butt of jokes, ridicule, or serious prejudice. A Monterey Bay, California conflict reported by Orbach & Beckwith (1982:137–139) between Vietnamese refugee fishermen and the traditional local fishing community (predominantly Italian-Americans) is a case in point. The Vietnamese entered the industry with independent operations before they were aware of the formal and informal rules of the industry. In Seadrift, for example, pot-fishing for crabs was an important local fishery business. Pot fishermen had their own territories: loose geographical areas where it was understood that one fisherman or group had preferential rights to set their gear. These territories were informal and unwritten without legal boundaries of any kind, but were nonetheless commonly understood and accepted in the operation of the fishery. For the Vietnamese entrants into the industry — especially those who were not knowledgeable in English — to learn about this informal rule was beyond their reach. This conflict, then, extended to arguments with buyers over fish prices, incidents of 'citizen's arrests' of Vietnamese, the vandalising of Vietnamese equipment, and boat sinking.

Such communication rules operating in the host environment need to be understood in order for strangers to be competent enough to deal with challenges of the host culture. In the case of the Vietnamese fishermen, they learned the fishery-related rules the hard way. In time, and after repeated contacts, the strangers' cultural understanding will increase so that they may not only understand the natives' communication rules, but may even participate in the implementation of the rules. As the strangers' ability to 'fill-in' (Ruesch, 1968/1951:47) the unspoken assumptions behind the host communication behaviors increases, they are better able to manage their life activities in the host society.

Cognitive complexity

Along with the knowledge of host language, verbal behavior, non-verbal behavior, and communication rules, strangers acquire necessary cognitive complexity as they adapt to the host environment. During the initial phases of adaptation, strangers' perceptions of the new environment tend to be overly simplistic, inaccurate, and unrealistic. They tend to categorise events and people into certain stereotypical molds. Thus, cultural stereotypes become salient as screening devices when strangers need to maintain the easiest and most economical structure in their perception of an unfamiliar milieu.

As strangers learn more about the host culture, however, their perceptions become more refined and complex, enabling them to detect numerous variations and nuances in the host environment. As they increase their knowledge about the host environment, they also increase their internal information-processing capacity in such a way that it becomes more compatible with that of the host nationals. To the extent that culture is a learned phenomenon, strangers are capable of acquiring the cognitive patterns of the host culture. Cultural learning further enables them to recognise their cognitive patterns as distinct from those of the host culture and to gradually increase their capacity for 'perspective taking' (Fogel, 1979:25) and 'co-orientation relation' with members of the host society (Pearce & Stamm, 1973).

The cognitive complexity of cultural strangers, therefore, can be defined as the *structure* of their knowledge/thoughts/ideas, that is, *how* they know what they know with regard to the host cultural milieu. We may consider the content aspect of strangers' cognitive competence as the substance of their ideas and knowledge that constitute the requisite information necessary to perform various social transactions (cf. Spitzberg & Cupach, 1984:119). The structural aspect of strangers' cognition, therefore, refers to the cognitive ability and manner in which strangers acquire, interpret, and respond to the information necessary to perform satisfactorily in the host society. This structural attribute of strangers' personal communication system is, in the description of Koestler (1967), like

> a series of 'filters' or 'scanners' through which the vital input traffic must pass on its ascent from sense-organ to cerebral cortex. Their function is to analyse, de-code, classify and abstract the information that the stream carries, until the chaotic multitude of sensations, which constantly bombard the senses, is transformed into meaningful messages. (p. 77)

Cognitive differentiation and integration

The two aspects of cognitive complexity that have been most widely recognised in cognitive psychology are 'differentiation' and 'integration'. According to Schroder, Driver & Streufert (1967, 1975), individuals who possessed a complex cognitive structure tended to better differentiate the number of dimensions in their personal constructs, to better articulate and abstract the dimensions, and to better integrate them into a meaningful whole. In the context of cross-cultural adaptation, strangers' cognitive complexity can be examined as part of their host communication competence based on the degree of detailed and comprehensive understanding of the host environment. For instance, a new immigrant in the United States may perceive that American people are all friendly. With accumulated communication experiences with the natives, however, the immigrant's cognitive structure is likely to become more realistic than the initial stereotypical perception, recognising that there are numerous subgroup and individual variations among Americans in friendliness. Similarly, an Australian international student in Italy may not be able to distinguish subtle differences in the regional dialects until having been exposed to such differences over a period of time.

A number of studies have shown the increasingly differentiated perceptual organisation of immigrants and sojourners over time. For instance, Coelho (1958) found that Indian students in the United States showed increasingly differentiated perspectives on the American culture, by being able to articulate the host culture with increasing detail, variety and scope over a period of 36 months. Similarly, Y. Kim (1976) observed among Korean immigrants in the United States an increasing trend in their ability to identify and elaborate on the similarities and differences between the Korean and the American cultural differences in interpersonal relationships.

The importance of cognitive structure was recognised by Brewer & Miller (1984) when they conceptualised interethnic relations as the process of change in individuals from 'categorisation' to 'decategorisation', or from impersonalised or undifferentiated perceptions to a more personalised and differentiated (individualised) perception of the host environment. According to Brewer & Miller, differentiation meant the 'distinctiveness of individual category members within that category' that occurs when one learns information unique to individual outgroup members. Personalisation, on the other hand, was viewed as responding to other individuals in terms of their relationship to the self, which necessarily involves making direct self–other interpersonal comparisons that cross category boundaries (p. 287). From this conceptual scheme of Brewer & Miller, strangers' perceptions of the host environment are likely to become increasingly decategorised over time.

The above categorisation–decategorisation distinction by Brewer & Miller corresponds closely to the concept 'category width'. Strangers' interaction in the host society can be seen as progressing from 'narrow' categorisation to 'broad' categorisation. In the initial stage of adaptation, strangers perceive others' behavior using narrow categories, which often results in inaccurate or inappropriate perceptions. This is based on the assumption that narrow categorisers would categorise behavior narrowly using their own cultural meaning system, and that they should have more adaptation problems occurring from their categorising strategy (cf. Detweiler, 1980; Stening, 1979).

In this developmental process, strangers become increasingly capable of discerning the differences between various cultural patterns of the environment. The gross 'stereotypical' perception of communication messages is changed into a more refined and discriminating perception. At the same time, the exaggerated differences or similarities between the two cultural patterns appear to become diminished as the strangers begin to see underlying commonalities in human experiences and to differentiate behavioral tendencies of the cultures in various specific social contexts. They become increasingly capable of recognising and identifying the contextual and individual variations of the cultural patterns, and find it increasingly difficult to make gross stereotypes of the host society.

Cognitive flexibility

Closely related to the strangers' cognitive complexity is a capacity to be mentally flexible in dealing with ambiguity and unfamiliarity. An individual's cognitive flexibility is dependent on the number of descriptive and explanatory ideas at his or her disposal for the ability to make sense of and to integrate new information into a pre-existing cognitive structure. The cognitive style opposite to cognitive flexibility is, of course, cognitive rigidity. As Ruben & Kealey (1979) reviewed, this cognitive flexibility, often called communication empathy, has been considered by many researchers as an essential communication component for sojourners in promoting their cross-cultural adaptation. As much as cognitive flexibility of strangers is likely to facilitate their adaptation, cognitive rigidity is likely to bring about their alienation in the host society.

Cognitive flexibility was referred to by Barnlund & Nomura (1985) as 'decentering', or 'the process of becoming aware of and temporarily suspending the constructs normally used to interpret events so as to consider fresh ways of construing them' (p. 348). As such, the critical importance of cognitive flexibility in cross-cultural adaptation lies in strangers' ability to 'bend' their way of thinking and to be receptive to the host cultural patterns. Cognitive flexibility is also related to the mental ability that imagines, plans, and considers a new world of information. One may say, then, that strangers with a high level of cognitive flexibility 'flex' their outer as well as their inner reality in a way that maximises their functioning in various activities. This flexibility of perception and thought patterns is a key to openness and acceptance of the host culture and, thus, to successful cross-cultural adaptation.

An indirect empirical support for the relationship between cognitive empathy (as well as cognitive complexity) and cross-cultural adaptation was provided by Seelye & Wasilewski (1981). Among immigrant children (aged 6–13), Seelye & Wasilewski found positive associations between/among increased flexibility in interpersonal interaction, a flexible coping style, a repertoire of linguistic and psychomotor behavior patterns peculiar to the host culture, and an understanding of the functionality of behavioral options within each cultural situation.

It must be emphasised that the above approaches to cognitive complexity — differentiation/integration and flexibility — are based on the common assumption that the complexity of a person varies across different content areas and that individuals differ in the degree to which they manifest a given level of complexity within a particular domain of cognition (cf. Crockett, 1965:53). This means that, as strangers develop a greater cognitive complexity in experiencing the host environment, they become more capable of differentiated, integrated, and decategorised understanding of the environment. Instead of narrow categorising of environmental data, they are able to utilise a broader and more comprehensive perspective. Further, the gross stereotypical perception will be changed to a more 'personalised' perception in which individual differences, rather than group differences, play a more significant role in strangers' perceptions.

It follows, then, that strangers with high cognitive complexity are better able to maximise their adaptation or functional fitness in the host society. They will have more ways of reacting to a given condition, will be less blindly or randomly influenced by environmental pressures, and thus will be less prone to experiencing psychological disturbances and social malfunctions. The more complex strangers' cognitive structures become, the greater their autonomy and freedom from the dictates of the environment.

Further, the complexity of an individual's cognitive structure is a developmental and cumulative process. As Schroder and his associates (1967) explained, the level of cognitive complexity in a given content area is not static over time but develops further with new learning experiences. Maturity itself involves development of cognitive complexity, which enables individuals to see a situation in broader, relativistic perspectives. Additionally, a mature person's cognitive image contains not only what is, but what might be. It is full of potentialities as yet unrealised. This developmental progression of cognitive complexity in relating to the host environment is demonstrated in the strangers' adaptation to new cultures. Just as comparative analyses of children, adolescents, and adults reveal an increasing cognitive complexity, research on immigrants and sojourners indicates that, in general, strangers' perception of the new culture becomes more complex and refined with increased host environment interactions (cf. Y. Kim, 1977a).

Through the cumulative experiences of adaptation in the host culture, strangers gradually attain sufficient cognitive capacity to differentiate along more dimensions and categories between the original culture and the host culture and to synthesise the dimensions of these cultures into an integrated perspective. Given the same amount of information, a stranger with higher cognitive complexity can perceive events in the host society in a more advanced, refined, differentiated, elaborated and integrated manner. The change in cognitive complexity enables the person to think more compatibly with host nationals.

Affective co-orientation

Not only must strangers acquire the extensive cognitive repertoire and complexity that facilitates their understanding of messages from the host environment, they must also develop the adaptive affective patterns — the emotional 'drives' or 'reflexes' toward a successful adaptation in the host environment. This affective co-orientation enables the strangers to position themselves in a psychological orientation that is 'favorable' or 'compatible' with that of the host culture. Taft (1977) identifies this affective process as the 'dynamic' aspect of culture:

> There are certain universal human needs and modes of functioning that must be satisfied in all cultures. In broad terms, these needs refer to the maintenance of life processes, the need to maintain a structural society to enhance as well as regulate social relationships, and to provide for the self-expressive needs of individuals. While these needs are universal, each culture prescribes different models for satisfying them. (p. 134)

Affective co-orientation with the host environment is examined here in terms of three main aspects:

(1) adaptive motivation, or the willingness or 'drive' to participate in the host culture;
(2) affirmative attitude toward self and others in the host environment; and
(3) aesthetic/emotional appreciation, or the capacity to share the aesthetic/emotional experiences of the natives.

These affective characteristics of strangers are considered to promote their adaptation in the host culture by facilitating the ability to share congruent and compatible affective experiences with the natives.

Adaptive motivation

Strangers' communication behavior at a given time is influenced by their anticipation of the future, that is, how they envision their relationship with the host environment. Anticipatory desire reflects the internal willingness or commitment to learn about and participate in the host cultural environment. This psychological posture is called here adaptive motivation. This motivation underlies strangers' self-guiding propensity to imagine what does not yet exist, including what they would like to achieve in the host society. In some cases, no external pressures may be as strong in influencing their behaviors as self-motivation. The more intense their adaptive motiva tion, the more they are likely to show enthusiasm and dedication in their effort to become functional in the host society.

Such affirmative orientation has been observed to facilitate immigrants' participation in host communication processes. Selltiz and her associates (1963), for example, found that foreign students in the United States varied considerably in their interest in getting to know Americans and that such variations in interest were associated with their actual social relations with Americans. Taylor & Simard (1975), in their study of intercultural interaction in Canada, concluded that the lack of interaction between ethnolinguistic groups was more a function of motivation than of language capacity. (See, also, Y. Kim, 1976, 1978a, 1980 for similar findings.)

Adaptive motivation is, indeed, one of the key differentiating attributes between sojourners and settlers (immigrants and refugees). Sojourners, or short-term residents, thinking of their short-term visit abroad as transitory (limited to the period of assignment), may generally negate any serious motivational commitment to adaptation. With little motivation, learning the host communication and culture and participating in the host communication processes are likely to be less important in their sojourn experiences (Aitken, 1973). Coelho (1958), in his study of Indian students in the United States, reported a significant difference in adaptive motivation between students who were planning to stay in the United States and those planning to return to India.

Similar observations have been made in comparing the adaptation patterns of Cuban refugees and Puerto Rican immigrants in the United States. Cuban refugees, knowing that they could not go home for a long time, accepted the United States as a permanent home. This acceptance facilitated their adaptive motivation, and thus, their adaptation. On the other hand, Puerto Ricans (Hispanic by language and culture though granted United States citizenship in 1917) have been much less successful than Cubans: more than 40% of them live below the official poverty line for a family of four (Friedrich, 1985:38). One paradoxical reason may be that Puerto Ricans are free to come and go between the mainland United States and Puerto Rico, and therefore are less motivated to adapt to the host culture.

Affirmative self/other attitude

Closely related to the adaptive motivation of strangers is their attitudinal orientation toward themselves and the host environment.

Strangers cannot be highly motivated to adapt to the host environment without accepting and affirming it. As Amir (1969) pointed out, intergroup contact is clearly related to this attitude, which in turn influences the outcome of the cross-cultural interaction. The affirmative attitude often translates into the ability to withhold evaluation, refrain from cultural absolutism, and accept rather than reject. It further leads to the development of the capacity to participate in the host culture. For instance, Punetha, Giles & Young (1987), in their study of Sikh, Hindu and Muslim immigrants in Britain and of the indigenous Britons, reported that the psychological distance the immigrant groups perceived between themselves and the indigenous population was in line with their desire to maintain a quite separate cultural identity.

The positive or negative attitudinal orientation of strangers toward their host environment is considered to be closely associated with the positive or negative attitude toward themselves. The more accepting they are of their life in the host society, the more accepting of the host society they are likely to be. On the other hand, a negative self-image is likely to facilitate the strangers' self-alienation and withdrawal from the host environment, and, thus, deter their adaptation processes.

Empirical data are available in support of the association between positive self-image (or confidence) and communication–adaptation patterns of strangers. Among the findings are studies of sojourner adaptation by Morris (1960), Selltiz and her associates (1963), and Sewell & Davidsen (1961). These researchers observed that the sojourners' confidence in their ability to speak English was an important influence on their actual command of the language and on the development of social relations. Also, as pointed out by Lazarus (1966), individuals who are insecure are likely to seek social support from less threatening ethnic individuals. More recently, studies of Indochinese refugees in the United States have also emphasised the importance of the refugees' positive self-image in their adaptation (Office of Refugee Resettlement, 1984). Discussions with teachers and students in English-as-a-Second-Language (ESL) classes indicated that lack of self-confidence, depression, and trauma impeded the refugees' learning.

Aesthetic/emotional appreciation

Along with the strength of adaptive motivation and affirmative self- and other-attitude, strangers' affective co-orientation is reflected in, and is influenced by, the extent to which they are able to fulfill their aesthetic (and emotional) needs in the host environment. Such aesthetic/emotional fulfilment is achieved when they are capable of understanding and experiencing the subtle and unspoken aesthetic/emotional responses of the natives. Mansell (1981) emphasised the importance of the aesthetic fulfilment of individuals in an alien culture:

> The concept of aesthetic awareness is linked with ineffable, intuitive feelings of appreciation and celebration. This form of awareness creates a consciousness which transforms individuals' perceptions of the world and imports a sense of unity between self and surrounding . . . It is in this transformative mode of experiencing that many people create access to the momentary peaks of fulfilment which makes life meaningful. (p. 99)

Aesthetic/emotional needs are often difficult to gratify within an unfamiliar culture due to their spontaneous, unstructured, and mostly unspoken nature. Because of the difficulties involved in cultivating the aesthetic sensibilities of the host culture, many strangers turn to their ethnic groups to pursue satisfaction in their original culture. In doing so, they tend to withdraw emotionally from the host culture until they have learned to make the necessary adaptation to its affective modes. (See Chapter 7 for a detailed discussion on the role of ethnic communication.)

Through repeated exposure to varied social situations and communication encounters in the host environment, strangers gradually come to appreciate the aesthetic and emotional tendencies of the natives without criticism, and even participate in them actively. This aesthetic and emotional transformation can be compared to the process in which older generations gradually become adapted to younger generations' tastes for music, fashion, and fun. As strangers develop their aesthetic and emotional co-orientation with the natives, they become better able to understand and 'feel' their sentiments and moods. They may even join together in their humor, excitement, and joy, as well as their anger, sarcasm, and disappointment. In such appreciation, their communication experiences with the natives will no longer be 'monophonic' but 'stereophonic'.

Behavioral competence

Along with cognitive and affective capacities, strangers need to develop behavioral competence in the host communication system. Behavioral competence here refers to the 'enactment tendencies' (Buck,

1984:vii), or motor-skill capacity to express the internal cognitive and affective experiences outwardly in communicating with other persons. Through trial and error, strangers are able to expand their behavioral capability to integrate sequences of verbal and non-verbal activities in a relatively smooth and automatic manner. In this process, strangers learn to perform many of the required social roles in the host society without having to formulate a conscious mental plan of action. Like natives, they are equipped with what Schuetz (1964) called 'matter of course recipes for action' (p. 140). Strangers initially learning the host language, for example, often go through a mental 'rehearsal' before speaking, but no longer need to do so as they become proficient in the language. At this level, much of their speaking activity becomes internalised, natural and automatic. Insofar as these internalised action plans are executed successfully, strangers' communication experiences are likely to be less stressful and more rewarding.

Normally, all three processes in individuals are well co-ordinated and balanced. For strangers, however, they do not necessarily match congruently, typically lacking in one or more of the three components. For example, a stranger may be quite knowledgeable about the host culture and yet may find it almost impossible to understand and share many of the aesthetic sensibilities. Another stranger may be adequately skilled in performing specific social roles but may find some of the operant values in their role performance disagreeable. Yet another stranger may be sufficiently knowledgeable and capable of participating in the emotional experiences of the host nationals, but may be incapable of successfully expressing themselves through verbal and non-verbal performances.

When such internal imbalance is severe, strangers experience disequilibrium or stress, as discussed earlier. Because the three components are interdependent in communication, and because each is subject to change, everyone experiences stress from time to time. If, however, the stress is intense or prolonged, strangers may experience a trauma reflecting a functional 'breakdown' of their internal communication system. Naturally, then, the cognitive, affective, and behavioral processes are linked with many of the psychological problems associated with the strangers' maladaptation. Negative self-image, low self-esteem, low morale, a sense of social isolation, dissatisfaction with life in general and a bitter attitude of being helpless victims of circumstance are associated primarily with the inability to relate successfully to the host milieu. This inability stems from a lack of affective competence, which in turn brings about psychological imbalance.

In the long run, these internal subprocesses have a tendency to reinforce each other and achieve a balance (cf. Amersfoort, 1974/1982:36). As stated in Chapter 3, humans have inherent 'homeostatic' tendencies toward a balance among the three subprocesses. It is the integration of the cognitive, affective and behavioral subprocesses that enables strangers to become fully 'engaged' in their encounters with the natives. Their host communication experiences are no longer inadequate, but proficient. In this process, strangers are increasingly capable of achieving a sense of efficacy — of 'completeness' in interfacing with the host environment.

7 SOCIAL COMMUNICATION

Successful communication with self and others implies correction by others as well as self-correction.
Jurgen Ruesch

All the adaptive cultural learning of strangers takes place in the context of social communication. By participating in various interpersonal and mass communication activities, strangers receive input from the new environment that potentially provides them with the basis for adaptive transformation. The information from their immediate interpersonal environment and the larger societal environment transmits images of the host culture and communication patterns and presents them with feedback that helps them understand and correct their own communication patterns. In this process, the strangers' participation in host society interpersonal and mass communication activities facilitates, as well as is facilitated by, host communication competence. The greater their social communication participation, the greater their host communication competence, and the better adapted they are likely to be in the host environment. In addition, it has been theorised that the strangers' participation in ethnic social communication activities initially facilitates, but eventually deters, the development of host communication competence and host social communication activities. This chapter examines in detail strangers' participation in their host and ethnic social processes through interpersonal and mass communication activities.

Host interpersonal communication

The process of migration from society to society can be compared to the up-rooting and re-rooting of transplantation. All migrants are removed from most, if not all, of the long-standing friends, family, relatives and co-workers with whom they participated in interpersonal communication activities. In the new society, they are faced with the task of constructing a new set of relationships that is critical to meeting their personal and social needs: making a living, learning the new language, seeking companionship and emotional security, or finding a new social identity. In carrying on communication activities in a variety of social contexts, strangers gradually rebuild their relational network. At a given time, the relational network in the strangers' immediate social milieu, in turn, presents us with information about their interpersonal communication activities.

Individuals' relational networks (or similar terms such as social networks, communication networks, personal networks, ego networks, egocentric networks and personal community) have been extensively investigated and theorized in anthropology, sociology and other human sciences. By utilising some of the concepts and tools developed in such studies, we can examine the nature and configuration of strangers' relational networks. (Readers interested in communication-centered network theories and methods are referred to Albrecht & Adelman, 1987; McCallister & Fischer, 1978; Rogers & Kincaid, 1981 for detailed discussions.)

In examining a relational network, a clear set of criteria needs to be established. Each relationship in a given network is different from the rest, and there are potentially several ways to examine a relationship, based on where one draws the line in defining the scope/boundary of relational linkages to be included in analysis. As McDermott (1980) pointed out, relational networks can be fruitfully examined at two levels: (1) the overall general social networks in which an individual is embedded, and (2) the smaller, more influential network of relational ties that develop from contacts within the networks. The first general category of interpersonal relations is broad, including those that are formal and informal, casual and intimate, kin and non-kin. Also included are first- and second-order relationships with others who are not directly in contact with the 'Ego' (the person at the center of a network) but are known to the Ego indirectly (Smith, 1976:21). The second approach is limited in its analysis to only that called the 'primary network', which consists of significant others, or those persons who substantially influence the formation, maintenance, or modification of an individual's cognitive, affective and behavioral attributes.

For the present purpose of understanding strangers' interpersonal communication, either approach can be taken. Generally speaking, however, the more restrictively a stranger's relational network is defined, the further away from random will its makeup be and the more closely will it reflect his or her adaptation level. A network of friends is based on the Ego's more deliberate choices, for example, unlike the overall network of acquaintances. If a group of sojourners is observed to be relatively limited in its interaction with host nationals, however, we might have to extend our network boundary to include everyone the sojourners regularly encounter.

Whichever boundary conditions one chooses to employ in examining the strangers' relational networks, the analysis of the network characteristics presents effective ways to understand the strangers' participation in interpersonal communication processes of the host society. Network analyses have the promise of capturing *emergent* patterns of strangers' interpersonal communication activities by focusing on the structure and contents of relational networks at a given time.

Adaptive functions of relational networks

The relational networks of strangers potentially serve many important functions in facilitating their adaptation. Perhaps the most widely recognised adaptive function is the provision of emotional support to strangers who rely on it for their sense of security and well-being. The relational network helps ease the loneliness, stress and difficulty that the strangers may encounter, particularly during the initial phase of the adaptation process. Although relationships can sometimes cause anguish, the overall social support they provide generally outweighs the troubles.

Second, the relational network provides strangers with information and 'feedback' that potentially facilitates their adaptive changes. Through various interpersonal contacts in the network, strangers can learn the communication rules, tacit cultural assumptions, standards of verbal and non-verbal behavior, and aesthetic and emotional sensibilities of the host culture. Consciously and unconsciously, they rely on the other network members for interpreting various attributes and actions of others and of themselves. By conferring with host nationals (or with ethnic friends who are successfully adapted), strangers can confirm or reject presumed meanings and motives in the natives' communication behaviors. They learn not only *what* to do, but also *how* they are doing relative to the natives (and to the ethnics).

Such adaptive information and feedback provide strangers with the basic corpus out of which their cognitive, affective, and behavioral capacities are cultivated. Through interpersonal encounters with host nationals, strangers 'reorganize' the internalised communication systems of their original culture and acquire new cultural parameters. In time, the attributes of the stranger and the natives tend to 'converge' (Rogers & Kincaid, 1981). As Rogers & Kincaid (1981) stated in presenting their 'convergence theory',

> The uniqueness of an individual's personal network is responsible for the uniqueness of his [her] meaning. The codes and concepts available to interpret information are based on each individual's past experiences which may be similar, but never identical, to another individual's. As an individual's patterns of interaction with others become similar (overlapping) to those of another individual's, so do their codes and concepts for interpreting and understanding reality. (p. 45)

The above adaptive functions of the relational networks of strangers are closely associated with at least two network attributes: (1) the proportion of host or outgroup ties (in relation to ethnic or ingroup ties) and (2) the strength of host ties (in relation to ethnic ties). Although other network attributes can be analysed, these two are considered most directly pertinent to understanding the cross-cultural adaptation process.

The size and proportion of host ties

For strangers who have not yet developed a sufficient level of host communication competence, developing relationships with the natives is a challenging or even threatening task. Simard (1981), in her study of relationship formation across ethno-linguistic boundaries among French and English Canadian college students, clearly indicated that it was more difficult to form new acquaintances cross-culturally than intra-culturally. Such difficulty, according to Simard, was not only due to differences in language *per se* but also, and more importantly, to psychological barriers such as ethnic identity. Gudykunst (1983) reported a similar result from his study of intra- and intercultural communication: that respondents perceived initial conversations as developing more easily in intracultural encounters than in intercultural encounters.

Notwithstanding cross-cultural psychological barriers, strangers, in time, develop at least a limited number of interpersonal ties with host nationals. These relationships serve as crucial social contexts from which strangers learn and participate in communication activities, which, in turn, facilitates the development of host communication competence. Thus, the ratio of host interpersonal ties to the number of ethnic interpersonal ties in a stranger's relational network indicates a relative level of host communication competence and adaptation.

An extensive pool of supportive empirical data exists. Selltiz, Christ, Havel & Cook (1963), in their study of international students in the United States, showed that those more actively involved with Americans expressed more satisfaction in their sojourn experiences and more favorable attitudes toward the United States. Studies by Christie (1976) and Dosman (1972) indicated that 'elite' or 'affluent' sectors of the American Indian reserve communities in Canada tended to be 'plugged into' off-reserve networks — usually consisting of both Indians and non-Indians or representatives of the Bureau of Indian Affairs. Such bonds made the transition to urban life a simpler and more stable process. Studies of foreign students and visitors in the United States and elsewhere have found similar results regarding the linkage between the number of host nationals in relational networks and cross-cultural adaptation (e.g., James, 1961; Johnston, 1963; Ossenborg, 1964; Kelman & Ezekiel, 1970; Weinstock, 1964).

Studies of immigrants have revealed further that, although newly-arrived immigrants are likely to be attracted to their own ethnic group for interpersonal communication activities, their relational networks gradually include an increasing number of ties with the natives. The ties with host nationals replaced some of the ethnic ties, making the stranger's relational network increasingly heterogeneous over a period of time (J. Kim, 1980; Y. Kim, 1976, 1977a, 1977b, 1978b, 1980; Mirowsky & Ross, 1983; Yum, 1983). As strangers gradually adapt, their relational ties become increasingly mixed with individuals outside their own group (See Figure 8), suggesting that the original culture initially serves as an important determinant of interpersonal ties but becomes less important over time (Y. Kim, 1986a, 1987).

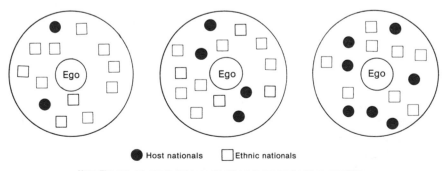

● Host nationals   ☐ Ethnic nationals

Note: The network size is held constant here to emphasize its composition.

FIGURE 8   *Adaptive change in the composition of a relational network*

Accordingly, the role of ethnic ties has been generally viewed as interfering with the cross-cultural adaptation process (Anderson & Christie, 1978:1). Studies such as the ones cited above have assumed ethnic communication activities as dysfunctional to the adaptation process of strangers. Someone whose personal network consists primarily of in-group members, therefore, is considered less competent in communicating with the natives. Supportive evidence for this assumption was provided by J. Kim (1980), whose study of Korean immigrants in Chicago showed that the immigrants' ethnic communication had a negative effect on their acculturation particularly at later stages of the acculturation process.

Given the above roles of host and ethnic relational ties, the heterogeneity of network composition has been investigated extensively. Typically, it has been assessed by simply counting the number of ethnic and non-ethnic ties in an interpersonal network, and then computing the ratio between the two relational categories. But no systematic attempt has been made to determine if non-ethnic ties must necessarily include members of the dominant majority group in the host society (e.g., white Anglo-Saxon Protestants in the case of the United States). Also, as noted by Alba (1976), we do not know whether a stranger's interpersonal network should include others from many different backgrounds, or whether they may all be from one group so long as it is different from the stranger's ethnic group. This issue remains to be explored.

The strength of host ties

Once the overall composition of the stranger's relational network is identified, we can examine the 'strength' of the ties maintained with host nationals (as well as ethnic individuals) in the network. The strength of tie refers to the level of intimacy, solidarity, or 'bondedness' of the relationship (Marsden & Campbell, 1983) — the overall level of interdependency and commitment to the relationship between the involved parties and, thus, the relative degree of difficulty of breaking the tie.

Of the multitude of relationships that a person develops, some are more important to the person than others. Some relationships are by nature public, impersonal, or superficial while others are more private, personal, and intimate. A given relationship that begins as merely superficial may develop into an intimate sharing of information and understanding, as articulated by Altman & Taylor's (1973) 'social penetration theory'. Focusing on the movement of relationships toward intimacy, this theory identifies two key dimensions to the developmental process of intimate relationships as *breadth* and *depth*. The breadth of a relationship refers to the number of personal characteristics that one relational partner makes accessible to the other and the quality of information made available about those characteristics. The depth of a relationship indicates the core personal characteristics about which one has information. In the onion analogy used by Altman & Taylor to explain the social penetration process, the outer layers of personality structure, like the outer skin of an onion, consist of all the demographic and biographical information that could be known about another. The greater the surface area that becomes exposed to a relational partner, the greater the breadth of the relationship. Each of those areas in turn has underlying layers, with the inner core representing a person's basic needs, feelings and values. The more a relational partner is able to penetrate into these inner aspects of personality, the greater the depth of the relationship.

Applying this characterisation of intimacy to a relationship that a stranger has developed with a host national, we can infer that this stranger–host relationship has been transformed from what Tajfel & Turner (1979) called an 'intergroup' relationship, based on a relatively un-differentiated perception of each other's cultural membership, to an 'interpersonal' relationship based on a refined and personalised under-standing of each other. In conceptualising the intergroup–interpersonal communication continuum, Tajfel and Turner (1979) stated:

> At one extreme . . . is the interaction between two or more individuals which is fully determined by their interpersonal relationships and individual characteristics and not at all affected by various social groups or categories to which they respectively belong. The other extreme consists of interactions between two or more individuals (or groups of individuals) which are fully determined by their respective memberships of various social groups or categories, and not at all affected by the interindividual personal relationships between the people involved. (p. 34)

In this framework, the degree of intimacy, or 'interpersonalness', of relational ties with host nationals that strangers have at a given time helps us to understand the level of their host communication competence and adaptation. Strong ties are far from random in makeup; they generally reflect the mutual choices of friendship based on similarity in the psychologi-cal attributes of the parties involved. By the time strangers have incorp-orated into their relational network a number of strong relationships with host nationals, they may be considered no longer 'strangers'.

Research findings have repeatedly shown that strangers become more capable of developing strong relational ties with host nationals as time goes on. (See Figure 9.) Selltiz and her associates (1963) reported that, as time went on, foreign students in the United States met more different kinds of people and visited more American families, and that, by the end of their first year, they had made at least one close American friend. In Y. Kim's studies of Chicago-area Koreans (1976, 1977b, 1978a), Mexicans (1978b), and Indochinese (1980), it was consistently found that the immigrants' intimate ties with host nationals (White Americans in particular) increased over time in terms of numbers as well as in the comparative ratio to their ethnic intimate ties. The immigrant–host tie strength was closely associated with the immigrant's host communication competence (as measured by cognitive complexity, attitudinal/motivational orientation, and linguistic competence). Yum (1983) also reported in a study of social network patterns (network size, frequency of interaction, density) among five ethnic groups in Hawaii that the hypothesised relationships between the social network patterns and the level of information acquisition were statistically significant among immigrant groups (Korean and Samoan immigrants) that were relatively new to the island's immigration history.

A special case of intimate tie is the marital relationship. Although marriages occur mostly between persons of the same ethnic/racial background, intermarriages of strangers to host nationals do occur. Intermarriages (at least successful ones) serve as a social context through which strangers can develop intimate relational ties with host nationals

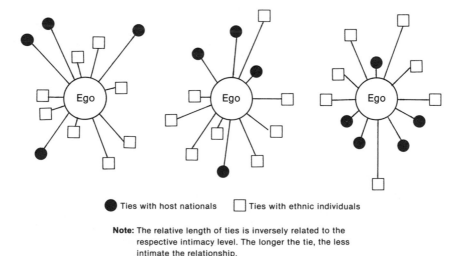

● Ties with host nationals   □ Ties with ethnic individuals

Note: The relative length of ties is inversely related to the respective intimacy level. The longer the tie, the less intimate the relationship.

FIGURE 9   *Adaptive change in the intimacy of host and ethnic relational ties*

through their spouses' relational networks (e.g., spouses' family and friends). Intermarriages occur more frequently across successive generations of immigrants. A number of studies (e.g., Alba, 1976; Friedrich, 1985; Tinker, 1973) have documented increasing rates of intermarriages across generations in various immigrant groups in the United States. (Such intergenerational trends of intermarriages, however, are beyond the scope of the present theory, which is limited to immigrants and sojourners.)

While strong ties, particularly marital relationships, play a vital role in facilitating the stranger's cross-cultural adaptation, 'weak ties' (Granovetter, 1973; Weimann, 1983) should not be considered insignificant in the adaptation process. All relationships with host nationals serve as sources of information based on which strangers learn the host culture and communication patterns. From the societal point of view, weak stranger–host ties serve a vital function of providing linkages between its various ethnic groups. Along with the mass communication processes, relational linkages between strangers and hosts, weak or strong, help spread societal news, information, innovations and regulations. In Weimann's (1983) analysis of relational patterns between members of different social groups (e.g., occupation and age) of a kibbutz community in Israel, weak ties were observed to serve as the most frequent informational 'bridges' between members of different groups.

The 'mapping' of strangers' relational networks, then, provides us with information on their cross-cultural adaptation process, particularly when we examine the two essential attributes presented above — (1) the extent to which host nationals are included in the network and (2) the tie strength of these stranger–host relationships. These basic relational network characteristics provide useful information about the strangers' host communication competence and of their overall adaptation.

Host mass communication

Like relational networks, mass communication processes offer strangers experiences through which they participate in the host environment. As discussed in Chapter 4, mass communication refers to all institutionalised public forms of social communication that disseminate and perpetuate the cultural reality of a society. Mass communication includes the communication activities involved with restaurants, schools, churches, supermarkets, highways, political campaigns, and the fashion industry, as well as with the mass media, theater, museums, art galleries, and libraries (Ruben, 1975:174). Through these and other mass communication processes, the society provides a cultural reality to which strangers (as well as natives) are exposed. By participating in these societal processes, strangers learn about various on-going events, norms, attitudes, beliefs, values and other information about the host culture.

Adaptive functions of host mass communication

Although mass communication scholars have traditionally investigated the cross-cultural adaptation process, they have contributed a number of theories and propositions that bear significant implications for the process. T. Gordon (1974), for example, conceptualised the socialisation function of mass communication:

> the media's major socialisation influence is on (1) the images and stereotypes we possess of our environment, our social systems; (2) the long-term value systems we possess; and (3) what we view as priority concern — by way of the media's agenda-setting function. (p. 13)

Also, Lasswell's (1948/1964) well-known formulation of the mass communication process recognises three major functions: (1) surveillance of the environment, (2) correlation of the components of society in making a response to the environment, and (3) transmission of the social inheritance (p. 51). Both T. Gordon's and Lasswell's views clearly point to the adaptive function of mass communication processes by transmitting not only topical events but also societal values, norms of behavior, and traditional perspectives for interpreting the environment. Just as the mass media contribute to the socialisation of younger generations, they help facilitate the adaptation process of strangers.

Adaptive functions of host mass communication have long been alluded to in studies of immigrant adaptation. Gordon (1964) stated that the mass media (along with public schools) exert 'overwhelming acculturation powers' over immigrants' children (pp. 244–5). Shibutani & Kwan (1965) also supported this view, indicating that

> the extent to which members of a minority group become acculturated to the way of life of the dominant group depends upon the extent of their participation in the communication channels of their rulers. (p. 573)

In a study of Canadian immigrants, Richmond (1967) observed that the newspapers and magazines explicitly and implicitly 'convey a knowledge of Canadian norms of behavior and social institutions, without which the

immigrant will remain incompletely absorbed into the Canadian way of life'
(pp. 138–9).

Because mass media processes are public, they are capable of
extending the scope of strangers' cultural learning beyond their immediate
interpersonal environment. As DeFleur & Cho (1957) pointed out in their
study of first-generation Japanese women:

> [Mass media] to a considerable extent acquaint the individual who
> consume them with American mass culture. Extensive consumption of
> the products of the American mass media would indicate a somewhat
> greater facility with the majority culture patterns than would be the
> case of those who remained isolated from these sources. (p. 248)

Participating in the mass communication processes of the host society,
therefore, enables cultural strangers to learn about the broader ranges of
the host cultural elements — its aspirations, tradition, history, myths, art,
work, play and humor, as well as specific current issues and events. Through
these messages, mass communication experiences offer the strangers an
adaptive function that complements their interpersonal communication
processes: they provide strangers with images of the host culture that are
not readily available in their immediate interpersonal environment.

While complementing the limited scope of cultural messages provided
by interpersonal communication processes, the adaptive function of a
specific mass communication experience is likely to be weaker than that of
a specific interpersonal communication experience. Unlike the public and
impersonal nature of mass communication processes, communication
activities involving interpersonal relationships are high in intensity with
simultaneous feedback. In the primarily unidirectional mass communication processes, the direct control experienced in interpersonal communication situations is seldom present. A study of Korean immigrants in
Chicago (Y. Kim, 1977a) provided supportive evidence for the relatively
weak adaptive function of mass communication. The statistical association
between American mass media consumption and cognitive complexity (in
perceiving American society) was significantly weaker than between
interpersonal communication with Americans and cognitive complexity.

Within these constraints, however, mass communication experiences
have been assumed to be positively associated with various other aspects
of cross-cultural adaptation. Graves (1967) and Nagata (1969), for instance,
included the possession of a TV set as one of the items in their index of
immigrant acculturation. A similar assumption was made for the adaptive
function of radio by DeFleur & Cho (1957), who used the amount of daily

exposure to radio (as well as TV) as one of the adaptation variables in 'recreational behavior' (p. 249). As an extension of 'visual orientation' for knowledge as well as entertainment, movie-going was employed by DeFleur & Cho (1957), in their study of Japanese-Americans, as one of the key considerations in determining the 'acculturation orientation' of Japanese immigrant women (p. 249). Also, Spindler & Goldschmidt (1952) used movie-going (together with radio possession) as a component in their 'index of social acculturation' among Menomini Indians.

Later studies of immigrants in the United States by Y. Kim (1976, 1977a–c, 1978a–b, 1980) provided further empirical support for the adaptive functions of using the host mass media. The immigrants' exposure to American mass media (the amount and frequency of exposure to radio, television, magazines, newspapers and movies), together with their relationships with Americans (White Americans in particular), was found to be significantly related to cultural learning as manifested in the immigrant's refined understanding of American friendship patterns. (See, also, Hong, 1980; Kapoor & Williams, 1979; Kim, Lee & Jeong, 1982; Pedone, 1980; Ryu, 1976, for other empirical data supporting the adaptive function of host mass media use.)

This adaptive function of host mass communication has been postulated by Y. Kim (1979b) to be more significant during the initial phase of the adaptation process. During this phase, the stranger has not yet developed sufficient host communication competence to develop and maintain satisfactory interpersonal relationships with host nationals. The initial communication experiences of direct contact with the natives are often frustrating and stressful to strangers; they feel awkward and out of place in relating to others. The direct negative feedback from the natives, subtle or explicit, can be too overwhelming for the strangers. They would, then, be more likely to avoid or withdraw from direct interpersonal encounters when they can and, instead, resort to less personal, less direct mass communication as alternative, virtually pressure-free, sources of learning about the host environment. This inference is shared by Ryu (1976), who studied foreign students' reliance on mass media as a source of adaptation and found a greater use of host media among the new arrivals.

Host mass media contents

Of the stranger's various mass communication experiences, exposure to the content of information-oriented media such as newspapers, magazines and television news has been observed to be particularly associated with adaptation when compared to other media that are primarily entertainment oriented. In studies of Korean, Japanese, Mexican and Indochinese immigrants in the Chicago area, Y. Kim (1976, 1977a–c, 1978a–b, 1980) repeatedly observed that the immigrants' use of information-oriented media content was far more strongly associated with interpersonal relationship formations with host nationals than their use of overall radio, television, and magazine content. Such media behavior strongly suggests that the adaptive function of mass communication experiences is further limited by the level of the strangers' host communication competence. Unlike many interpersonal communication situations, strangers themselves have the freedom to participate or not to participate in mass communication activities. Particularly, mass communication activities (such as reading news magazines or attending theater performances) require a substantial understanding of the host communication system. The reception and interpretation of the messages are almost completely determined by the strangers themselves. Strangers must be both motivated to receive messages and capable of understanding them before the messages can have any effect on their adaptive learning. Future research needs to investigate in detail the quality of strangers' mass communication experiences in relation to their adaptation.

All in all, strangers' participation in host mass communication processes facilitates, as well as is facilitated by, their adaptation. A few empirical studies have demonstrated the mutually facilitative relationship between host mass communication experiences and adaptation. Nagata (1969), for example, observed that differences in mass media behaviors across first, second, and third generation Japanese-Americans are accompanied by an increasing use of American mass media. Chang (1972) also reported recognisable differences, although not statistically significant, in mass media behaviors among three groups of Korean immigrants ('cultural assimilation group', 'bicultural group' and 'nativistic group') that were distinct in the patterns of change in cultural values. In a cross-sectional analysis of Korean immigrants and their mass media behavior (Y. Kim, 1978a–b), a significant increase of mass media consumption was observed over the years.

In sum, host mass communication experiences serve the end of adaptation, often filling the gap that strangers have in communicating with host nationals interpersonally. Although lacking the intensity of interpersonal communication experiences, mass communication experiences help strangers broaden their perspective of the host culture beyond their immediate interpersonal environment by providing information about the society at large.

Ethnic social communication

Strangers' participation in the host society is not limited to interactions with the natives or with the host mass communication activities. Many immigrants and sojourners today have access to individuals of the same national or ethnic origin. In many cases, ethnic support groups and ethnic neighborhoods have grown into large communities with their own churches, media, business associations, and other social institutions. These communities offer organised programs and activities designed to serve and 'protect' the various political, economic, cultural, and educational needs and interests of the community. Schools for teaching youngsters the homeland culture and language and celebrations of religious and other cultural events provide the means of forming crucial ties between old and new societies.

Within such ethnic communities, earlier arrivals help the newer arrivals find housing, jobs, or other basic necessities, introduce them to friends and churches, and give information and advice about various questions that the newly arrived individuals might have. In larger communities, ethnic newspapers, radios, television stations, and bookstores flourish offering an institutionalised network of communication that reaches larger segments of the communities. At times, the ethnic communities expand their services beyond their own group to cover the needs of other groups of immigrants and sojourners faced with similar problems in the host society.

Strangers' ethnic social communication activities are influenced by the degree of 'institutional completeness' (Breton, 1964) of the community. Strangers whose ethnic community is extensively institutionalised and offers extensive social, religious, educational and political programs, tend to be more involved in ethnic communication activities interpersonally as well as through media (Inglis & Gudykunst, 1982).

The adaptation process of those who have access to a substantial number of fellow ethnic individuals becomes somewhat more complex because of their communication activities in both ethnic and host cultural contexts. Traditionally, strangers' participation in ethnic communication has been viewed to have a deterrent effect on their adaptation. Reflecting the 'assimilationist' ideological stance that predominated the earlier work in cross-cultural adaptation, ethnic communication has been generally viewed to promote 'ethnicity' and discourage integration into the host society. For example, Shibutani & Kwan (1965) stated, 'to the extent that . . . a minority group participated in different sets of communication channels, they develop different perspectives and have difficulty in understanding each other' (p. 982). Broom & Kitsuse (1955) similarly argued: 'A large part of the acculturation experience of the members of an ethnic group may be circumscribed by the ethnic community' (p. 45).

More recently, however, an exactly opposite view has been expressed, arguing for the vital importance of ethnic communities in serving the needs of the ethnic individuals. Based on the ideology of cultural pluralism, this view places its emphasis less on the necessity of adaptation to the larger society and more on the preservation of original cultural attributes. As noted in Chapter 2, this ideology has generated numerous studies of 'ethnicity' in the United States during the past two decades, resulting in enormous amounts of information about ethnic phenomena, structure, and processes (cf. Bentley, 1981; Burgess, 1978).

Ideological perspectives aside, findings from various empirical studies indicate that considering ethnic communication activities as *either* helpful *or* detrimental to strangers' adaptation is somewhat simplistic. Below, some of the crucial aspects of ethnic communication processes are examined within the present theoretical framework. It is argued that strangers' participation in ethnic communication processes can *both* promote *and* impede their adaptation process depending on the extent that it replaces their host communication activities over time.

Short-term, adaptation-promoting functions

Throughout the history of migration — whether from rural to urban or from country to country — migrants have always tended to form a collectivity. On arrival, strangers faced with the uncertainty and insecurity of being in a new situation find ways to affiliate themselves with their own ethnic group. The task of developing host communication competence (including the host language, non-verbal behavior, communication rules, motivational, attitudinal, and aesthetic/emotional orientation and be-havioral capabilities) is a monumental one. Until they become sufficiently competent in communicating with host nationals, strangers inevitably find their interpersonal communication experiences with host nationals stressful and less than satisfying. Liu Zongren (1984), a Chinese journalist who had studied in the United States for two years, reflected on this point when he stated,

> During my stay in the United States I had met many people, some of whom had become very good friends . . . they had helped me in every

way they could to understand American life. But few of them really understood me or knew why I couldn't feel comfortable among Americans. (p. 200)

Under such circumstances, strangers naturally seek refuge, and opportunities to relieve their cross-cultural stress, from ethnic friends and kin who share common cultural backgrounds and the experiences as strangers in the host society. As Albrecht & Adelman (1984) postulated,

> individuals will be most likely to perceive that those who share a stressful context will be more helpful as sources of support than those who do not share the context, provided that the stressful conditions are seen as reversible to some degree. (p. 20)

Strangers, thus, tend to gravitate toward a place in which they have at least some access to an ethnic support system via either family, friends, relatives, or visible community organisations. By locating themselves in or near an ethnic community, strangers are able to have some psychological and social 'security' in an alien land. Through the emotional support strangers find from ethnic communication activities, they are able to avoid possible serious psychological 'breakdown'.

In fact, many immigrants and sojourners seek such ethnic support systems even before entering the host society. International students' choices of a university are often influenced by the availability of some ethnic ties on, or near to, the campus. Snyder (1976) found, for example, that a sizable personal network existed at arrival for most immigrants in five ethnic neighborhoods (Blacks, Chicanos, Whites, Arabs and American Indians) in Los Angeles. Krause (1978), in a study of Italian, Jewish, and Slavic immigrant women in Pittsburgh between 1900 and 1945, observed that ethnic friends, relatives, neighbors and their own children played a vital role in the settlement of the immigrant women. A particularly visible ethnic clustering comes from the case of Hmong refugees who fled their home country, Laos, and came to the United States after the Vietnam War. Following the patterns of 'group settlement' (Coombs, 1977) or 'chain migration' (Price, 1968), Hmong refugees have clearly demonstrated the critical importance of an ethnic support network in the initial transition period. Also, numerous survey studies have repeatedly demonstrated almost exclusively ethnic friendship networks for first-year immigrants in the United States who have sizable local ethnic communities available (cf. Deusen, 1982; Y. Kim, 1976, 1978a–b, 1980; Silverman, 1979).

In addition to providing strangers with emotional and social support, ethnic ties serve as 'gatekeepers' (Kurtz, 1970), 'patronage' (Mortland &

Ledgerwood, 1987), or 'culture brokers' (Snyder, 1976), providing links between strangers and the host society. Kurtz (1970) observed in his study of the Spanish-American community in Denver that newcomers looked at their ethnic friends and acquaintances as 'leaders' because they have relatively 'greater access to the Anglo system, holding linkage positions which enable them to further the acculturation of minority group members to the urban culture' (p. 41). Similarly, Mortland & Ledgerwood (1987), in a study of an Indochinese refugee community in Boston, identified a patronage system mostly invisible to American service providers. The refugee patrons were observed to be an integral part of the refugee communication network, controlling the flow of information and resources between Americans (including service agencies) and the refugee population.

Adding to the supportive functions of ethnic interpersonal communication is the information provided by ethnic mass communication activities, particularly ethnic media. Media have always been a vital part of communication processes in various ethnic communities. In the United States, ethnic media have existed ever since the first newspaper, the Philadelphia *Zeitung*, began in 1732, aimed at the city's burgeoning German population. Many of the papers catering to Europeans have withered away, while the influx of Hispanics and Asians has given rise to dozens of new publications. In some large cities in the United States (such as Chicago, Los Angeles, and New York), ethnic communities offer radio or television programs for a varying number of hours or days per week as well, although newspapers are still the predominant ethnic media (cf. Kelly, 1985; Subervi-Velez, 1986).

Like ethnic interpersonal communication experiences, ethnic media have been observed to perform the gatekeeping function, serving as vehicles for strangers to learn about and adapt to the host culture (cf. Fishman *et al.*, 1966; Hunter, 1960, Hur, 1981; Marzolf, 1979; Zubrzycki, 1958). Such services are carried out by the media through reports on immigration law changes, tax laws, etiquette, and other information that help strangers adapt to the local area and host society. In addition, ethnic media, especially the broadcast media, provide entertainment and relaxation for community members that helps relieve pressures of dealing with the host environment (Warshauer, 1966).

The above functions of ethnic interpersonal and mass communication activities indirectly facilitate strangers' adaptation, particularly during the initial period of settlement. By providing vital 'helping hands' to newly arrived strangers, ethnic social communication substitutes for host social communication, assisting them to cope with uncertainties and the sense of uprootedness.

Long-term, ethnicity-maintenance functions

Yet the more intrinsic and lasting function of ethnic social communication lies in maintaining strangers' linkage to the 'mother country' and 'mother tongue'. Participating in ethnic activities means participating in ethnic culture. Knowingly or unknowingly, ethnic communication processes reinforce the original cultural patterns in strangers as they continue to practice the use of verbal and non-verbal symbols of the original culture and all its implicit communication rules.

The use of ethnic language, in particular, has received extensive attention in social psychology and sociolinguistics for its significant role in expressing ethnicity in intergroup encounters (Ferguson & Heath, 1981; Giles, 1977; Giles, Bourhis & Taylor, 1977; Giles & Johnson, 1981, 1986; Giles, Robinson & Smith, 1980). Along with ancestry, religion, physiognomy and other ethnic attributes, language characteristics are a central feature of ethnic behavior. Ethnic media also have been viewed as playing a significant role in propagating ethnicity in strangers, striving for preservation of the group's original culture and language and promoting ethnic pride and solidarity among its members (Burgess, 1978; Lazerwitz, 1954). Even a casual analysis of ethnic media reveals that most of their contents promote ethnicity explicitly or implicitly.

A body of direct and indirect empirical evidence is available from several different societies to support the long-term negative effect of ethnic communication on cross-cultural adaptation. For instance, Gal (1978) concluded from a community study of the town of Oberwart (a German/Hungarian bilingual community in Australia) that a long-established ethnic network was associated with a non-standard language. More recently, Milroy (1982) observed that a close-knit ethnic network structure was an important mechanism of language maintenance, in that speakers were able to form a cohesive group capable of resisting pressure, linguistic and social, from outside the group. Milroy further suggested that a change in the ethnic group's non-standard language maintenance would be associated with the breakup of such a structure (p. 185).

Further, the use of the ethnic language has been observed to interfere with the acquisition of the host language. The first-language users are likely to 'fall back' on old knowledge when they have not yet acquired enough of the second language (Krashen, 1981). As suggested by the 'speech accommodation theory' of Giles and his associates (Giles & Smith, 1979; Street & Giles, 1982), individuals within a network removed from host nationals are likely to have very few opportunities to use the standard language of the host society, and so have less desire to 'converge' their language behavior toward that of the host society or to achieve the social approval of the host nationals. As Selltiz and her associates (1963) commented in their study of foreign students in the United States, ethnic relations may increase the sense of security by providing a setting in which strangers feel at home, where they need not worry about possible misunderstanding of their actions, or fear possible rebuffs because of prejudice against people of their color or nationality. On the other hand, it is likely to impede adaptation by reducing the pressure to come to terms, in some way, with the new situation, and by additionally providing a forum in which defensive reactions of criticism and hostility toward the host country are reinforced by similar reactions on the part of fellow ethnic individuals.

Such ethnic ties are likely to become a liability to cross-cultural adaptation particularly if strangers are heavily dependent on them without active involvement with host nationals (Anderson & Christie, 1978:1). Even though ethnic interpersonal relationships are helpful to new arrivals by giving them access to information, emotional support, and other tangible material assistance, they may discourage strangers' direct participation in the host communication processes, and, accordingly, slow down the process of adaptation to the host society.

Ethnic relational networks are likely to slow the strangers' cross-cultural process even further if it consists of individuals who are themselves poorly adapted to the host environment. Maladaptive communication of one immigrant may breed maladaptive communication in another, through subtle or explicit forms of social pressure on the stranger to conform to ethnic culture. Because the network reinforces ethnic communication patterns in the strangers, their learning about the host culture and communication patterns would be minimal. Zongren (1984) expressed his own experience of dilemma when he sensed conformity pressure from his fellow countrymen:

> I had been so absorbed in my studies of American life and language that I never took the time to go out with my Chinese roommates to a movie or to a park . . . I had made more and more American friends and was involved with them in social events, visits, and short trips. When my Chinese friends made plans for a weekend, they stopped counting me in their group. Some, both the Chinese visiting scholars

and a few Chinese from Taiwan that I knew casually, had begun saying that I was a busy man in American society — I sensed their sarcasm. They were probably thinking that I considered it beneath my 'dignity' to go out with them. I felt somewhat guilty about this. (p. 168)

The more prolonged participation in ethnic communication processes, then, the more it is likely to help strangers maintain their ethnicity. The original cultural and communication patterns, ethnic group allegiance and loyalty, and ethnic consciousness and identification may not be substantially revised in spite of the exposure to the host sociocultural environment. The ethnicity-maintenance function of ethnic communication would, therefore, deter strangers' adaptive activities beyond the phase of initial settlement and cultural learning. The relatively stress-free ethnic communication activities offer temporary relief, but no longer facilitate adaptation itself.

There comes a point in the adaptation process when strangers' ethnic communication activities may no longer serve the purpose of adapting to the host society or may even become liabilities to their adaptive endeavor, competing with their host communication activities. To acquire the host culture means to lose at least some of the original cultural patterns. Each stranger has only so much time and energy to engage in communication activities, and, therefore, his or her ethnic communication activities must be reduced in order to make 'room' for host communication activities. As Broom & Kitsuse (1955) aptly put it, 'A large part of the acculturation experience of the members of an ethnic group may be circumscribed by the ethnic community' (p. 45).

Indeed, strangers cannot remain rigidly ethnic and also become highly adapted to the host culture. 'No learning without unlearning', and 'No acculturation without deculturation'. Involvement in ethnic communication processes inevitably reduces their involvement in host communication processes, and the reduced host communication activities in turn decreases their chances for learning and acquiring host communication competence. To the extent that strangers participate in different sets of communication channels with different sets of communication patterns, they are likely to have perspectives different from the salient patterns of the host society and will, therefore, experience difficulty in understanding and relating to the host nationals. If the shift in allocation of time and energy between ethnic and host communication activities is not sufficient to enable participation in various activities in the host society, then the stranger will maintain ethnic communication patterns that are inadequate and 'unfit' in the host society.

The tension between ethnic communication and ethnicity, on the one hand, and host communication and adaptation, on the other hand, can be seen in the life of elderly immigrants whose everyday activities occur almost exclusively within their family and ethnic community. They have little knowledge of the host language and culture, and thus are mostly dependent on interpreters if they are to communicate with host nationals. Even after many years, these immigrants have remained almost the same as they were when they first followed their children and moved to the host country. Contrast this lack of cross-cultural adaptation with the extraordinary level of host communication competence and adaptation achieved by many Peace Corps volunteers or missionaries whose relational network in the host society consists primarily of local people.

The extensive and prolonged reliance of immigrants for support on other immigrants in the ethnic community has been frequently reported. Valdez (1979), in a study of relational patterns of Puerto Ricans in an industrialised city, reported the immigrants' high integration into ethnically homogeneous networks of family, friends, and coworkers. Le (1979, in Deusen, 1982:238) also reported that the personal networks of Vietnamese refugees in Los Angeles consisted predominantly of other Vietnamese and that most refugees preferred to use family or friends as a primary source of help for mental health problems. (See, also, Y. Kim, 1977b, 1978a, 1978b, 1980; King, 1984; Krause, 1978; Silverman, 1979; Yum, 1983, for similar findings.)

Research findings generally support the overall inverse relationship between the degree of ethnic communication and the degree of communication with host nationals (cf. J. Kim, 1980; Y. Kim, 1976, 1977b, 1978a, 1980). Further supportive evidence has been provided in research findings that the marital status of immigrants significantly increases their ethnic communication activities. Alba & Chamlin (1983), for example, argued that those who are 'in-married', that is, married to the same ethnic individual, are likely to be more involved with other ethnic individuals for social support. Similarly, J. Kim (1980), in his study of Korean immigrants in the Chicago area, reported that those who were married to a Korean demonstrated lower adaptation rates. Almost twice the variance in the immigrants' acculturation level was explained in this study by participation in relationships with natives as was explained by ethnic communication. Also, Matsumoto *et al.* (1973) reported that Japanese-Americans in Honolulu and Seattle showed an increasing attenuation of ethnic identity scores across generations.

The eventual negative influence of ethnic communication on cross-cultural adaptation has been further supported by findings from studies of international students. Among these findings is the negative relationship between a strong attachment of students to their home culture and their adaptation to the host society. For instance, it has been observed that those students who were highly identified with their home country were scored low in satisfaction with their stay in the United States and were less successful academically (Selltiz *et al.*, 1963; Sewell & Davidsen, 1961).

Strangers' participation in ethnic interpersonal communication activities has been observed to be closely associated with other aspects of ethnic communication including the use of ethnic media. Like ethnic relational ties, ethnic media can serve an adaptation-facilitating role during the initial phase of settlement. In the long run, however, a heavy reliance on ethnic media is likely to slow the process of adaptation by sustaining ethnicity and traditional ties. Extensive data are available to support this reasoning. A comprehensive work from Canada by Goldlust & Richmond (1974) showed evidence to support their hypothesis that immigrants who relied on ethnic media to the exclusion of Canadian newspapers were likely to be less thoroughly acculturated even after both education level and length of residence were held constant. (See, also, Goldlust & Richmond, 1974; Hur, 1981; J. Kim, 1980; Ryu, 1980 among others, for findings that link ethnic media behavior, ethnicity, and participation in host social processes.)

Other studies have shown that the level of interest in, and the perceived utility of, ethnic media among strangers decreases clearly and consistently as they become more familiar with the host language and culture. This trend, however, did not occur during the initial years of residence in some immigrant groups, demonstrating the adaptive function of ethnic communication during the initial phases of adaptation (cf. Hong, 1980; Kim, Lee & Jeong, 1982; Y. Kim, 1977b, 1980).

In addition, a number of studies in ethnic communities observed demographic and socioeconomic status in relation to communication behavior. Findings from these studies have consistently shown that lower age, higher education and higher socioeconomic status are associated with (1) increased participation in the interpersonal and mass communication processes of the host society and (2) decreased participation in the interpersonal and mass communication processes within the ethnic community. Milroy (1980), for example, presented many examples of ethnic individuals in Belgium who actively sought upward mobility and deliberately avoided close ties within the ethnic community. These individuals, according to Milroy, saw extensive involvements with close ethnic ties as detrimental to their own or their children's opportunities for social advancement. Similarly, Hur (1981) reported that ethnic individuals in Cleveland with lower socioeconomic status tended to rely more on ethnic media, while ethnics with higher socioeconomic status turned more to the metro-area media and magazines.

Research has further shown that, over the years, immigrants and sojourners alike show increased participation in the interpersonal and mass communication activities of the host society and decreased participation in the interpersonal and mass communication activities within the ethnic community. In a study of Southeast Asian refugees in Los Angeles, for example, Le (1979, in Deusen, 1982:238) observed that the refugees using American formal services decreased in accord with the length of time spent in the United States. (For similar findings, see Chang, 1972, 1974; Jeffres & Hur, 1981; Y. Kim, 1976, 1977a-b, 1978b, 1980; Nagata, 1969; Richmond, 1967; Yum, 1982.)

The theoretical reasoning and empirical evidence thus far clearly points out that one must communicate with host nationals and participate in the host mass communication processes if increased adaptation is to be achieved. The informational, emotional, social and material support that the ethnic communication activities provide for strangers is invaluable initially as they struggle to cope with the experiences of dealing with uncertainty and uprootedness. Yet such supportive ethnic communication experiences by themselves cannot make strangers acquire the necessary host communication competence. In the long run, ethnic communication reinforces strangers' ethnicity, not adaptation, particularly if it is not substantially supplemented or replaced by host social communication activities.

Postulating the 'duality' of the short-term adaptation-facilitating function and the long-term adaptation-deterrent function of ethnic communication neither endorses the assimilationist position nor denies the pluralist position. It simply points to the cumulative influences of ethnic involvements in reinforcing ethnicity — following exactly the same theoretical principle that underlies the adaptation-facilitating function of host social communication activities. The maintenance of original cultural attributes of communication may serve many useful purposes desired by individuals and groups that value cultural preservation. For the purpose of cross-cultural adaptation, however, it delays or interferes with the acquisition of host communication competence and active participation in host communication channels.

Strangers, therefore, face an inherent dilemma of choices — whether, and to what extent, they choose to remain ethnic or to adapt to the host environment. The choice remains ultimately one that individual strangers must make taking into consideration the challenges and demands of the host society itself and the nature of their roles and aspirations in that society.

8 HOST ENVIRONMENT AND PREDISPOSITION

> *I am a part of all that I have met;*
> *Yet all experience is an arch wherethro'*
> *Gleams that untravell'd world, whose margin fades*
> *For ever and for ever when I move.*
> Alfred Tennyson

At any given time, the state of strangers' personal and social communication is influenced by the forces of their environment and by the conditions that they had individually brought with them to the host society. It is the host environment that serves as the 'foreground' or social context in which strangers mobilise their resources and to which they strive to adapt. At the same time, it is strangers' own predisposition that serves as the 'background' from which their adaptive responses are mobilised. Together, the environmental and predispositional conditions help set the parameters within which strangers find their uniquely personalised passages of cross-cultural adaptation.

Host environment

Two host environmental conditions that are directly pertinent to the present purpose are receptivity toward strangers and conformity pressure. The first condition, receptivity, refers to the degree to which a given host environment shows openness and acceptance toward strangers. The second condition, conformity pressure, refers to the degree to which the environment overtly or covertly expects or demands that strangers follow its normative cultural and communication patterns. These two host environmental conditions have been theorised as interactively linked with the strangers' personal and social communication processes.

Receptivity

Societies and groups differ in the degree to which they are receptive to strangers and allow (or deny) them the opportunities to become an integral part of the host social processes. Because environmental receptivity offers openness and acceptance, it has also been labeled as 'interaction potential' (Y. Kim, 1979a) or 'acquaintance potential' (Cook, 1962) emphasising the interpersonal context in the immediate host environment. Receptivity of a given host environment can also be examined in the *attitude* of acceptance or denial of strangers expressed in interpersonal and mass communication processes. Such expressions can be explicit, but, for the most part, they are subtle and unconscious, embedded in non-verbal behaviors of the natives. Acceptance may be shown in a simple smile, while non-acceptance may be conveyed in an aloof tone of voice (cf. Giffin, 1970:352).

The attitude of the host society toward a specific out-group may be due to long-standing friendship or power relationship (as exemplified in the relationship between White and Black South Africans). Development of new events in international affairs may also change a longstanding friendly attitude between groups, as was recently observed between the United States and Iran. The attitude of the host society toward an out-group can be also influenced by its own domestic economic or political situation, such as a high unemployment rate or racial turmoil (Lieberson, 1961).

Once a positive or negative climate is formed among host nationals toward a specific out-group, that climate is likely to influence their receptivity toward strangers from that group. Such practices as segregation or integration in housing, selective or open provision of employment opportunities and exclusion or inclusion from meaningful interpersonal contacts are often influenced by the overall social climate. These practices in the host society make strangers' cross-cultural adaptation more trying or easier. Under trying circumstances, strangers are likely to feel insecure and unwelcome in the host culture and to feel discouraged from any attempt to initiate interpersonal communication with natives. The psychological barriers thus developed in strangers (as well as in the native population) limit their opportunities to develop host communication competence. Under more receptive circumstances, strangers would enjoy more opportunities to participate in the host communication processes.

Conformity pressure

Societies also vary in permissiveness, 'plasticity', or tolerance, in allowing strangers to deviate from its normative cultural patterns. Societies that are relatively free, pluralistic and heterogeneous tend to manifest a substantially high tolerance level toward cultural diversity. In contrast, societies that are relatively controlled, totalitarian and homogeneous tend to exert greater conformity pressure on strangers to follow their ideology, beliefs, values, language and behavioral norms.

Conformity pressure is visible in the official or unofficial *language practices* of the host society. In most countries, strangers who need to benefit from what the state has to offer are expected to learn the dominant language according to their needs. Pressure to conform linguistically is particularly acute for immigrants whose livelihood is dependent on jobs in the host society. Similarly, proficiency in the host language is vital to the performance of international students seeking an academic degree. On the other hand, short-term sojourners whose activities are not vitally dependent on the host social system (such as diplomats and military personnel) would be subject to the least amount of conformity pressure.

Conformity pressure varies further in different *regions or groups* within a society. Strangers are likely to find that, in general, large urban centers with a heterogeneous and cosmopolitan milieu offer noticeably more permissiveness than small rural towns. While the social structures of metropolitan areas exhibit greater freedom for new and different elements, the presence of strangers can be a matter of great interest and close scrutiny in villages, as has been discussed in sociological literature (cf. Laumann, 1973; Wellman, 1982).

It must be noted that conformity pressure in a given environment can be too severe for strangers to manage, intensifying their already acute cross-cultural stress and, thus, impairing their adaptive communication activities. Such excessive conformity pressure may be felt by exchange students, for instance, who realise that their academic competence is ignored by their fellow classmates due to the language barrier. In most cross-cultural adaptation situations, however, strangers manage to continue their adaptive communication activities. As they become increasingly proficient in host communication competence and in managing their social communication activities, the environmental conformity pressure is likely to be attenuated.

As such, the relationship between host environmental conditions and the adaptation of strangers is interactive and mutually causal. Individual strangers can, and do, make a difference in a given environmental condition based on their level of host communication competence and social participation. Strangers' adaptive communication processes and host environmental conditions have a 'grip' on each other in a 'push-and-pull' process of interaction between the host environment and the strangers themselves.

Predisposition

Not all strangers migrate for the same reasons, or come from the same backgrounds. Nor are their subsequent adaptation experiences uniform — even if they are all in the exactly same host environment. While adaptation occurs in the basic structures of all strangers, there are countless specific individual strategies to the changed circumstances. Cross-cultural adaptation, thus, consists of infinitely varied responses of individual strangers to the environment: no two strangers share exactly the same adaptation experiences.

Among the multitude of background characteristics that can be examined, the present analysis focuses on three factors that have direct bearing on the adaptive communication processes: (1) cultural and racial background, (2) personality attributes, and (3) preparedness for change. These background conditions collectively characterise strangers' adaptive potential in the host environment.

Cultural/racial background

One source of adaptive predisposition is the degree of *similarity* (or compatibility) between the strangers and the host culture in political, linguistic, economic, religious, technological, and other experiential backgrounds. Strangers whose cultural background (particularly language) is similar to the host culture would begin their adaptation process with greater ease. To the extent that the original cultural patterns coincide with the host cultural patterns, less new learning is necessary to become functionally fit in the host environment. The greater the disparity between the two, on the other hand, the larger the cultural gap to be bridged.

Cultural similarity or disparity can be examined in all the elements of host communication competence discussed in Chapter 6 (including language, non-verbal behavior, communication rules, emotional and aesthetic sensibilities, and behavior patterns). (See Berry & Annis, 1974; Church, 1982; Dyal & Dyal, 1981, Fabrega, 1969; Furnham, 1984; Taft, 1977; Weinberg, 1973, for discussions of the cultural gap and its influence on the adaptation process.) Thus, an immigrant moving from England or an English-speaking part of Canada to the United States, or a French-speaking Vietnamese moving to Montreal would be equipped with a linguistic/cultural background that is considerably similar. Also, a French migrant from the large cosmopolitan center of Paris would likely have greater difficulty in a small rural town in Mexico than in Mexico City.

Almost all studies conducted in the United States examining inter-personal relationship patterns of foreign students have reported that European students interacted with Americans more extensively than did students from Asia (cf. Selltiz *et al.*, 1963:246). Lysgaard (1955) and Sewell & Davidsen (1961), for example, described Scandinavian students as having little difficulty in adjusting to life in the United States, while Lambert & Bressler (1956) and Bennett, Passin & McKnight (1958) reported con-siderable difficulty on the part of students from India and Japan, respec-tively. Similar results have been reported by Furnham & Bochner (1982) for foreign students in England. Many culture-shock studies further agreed that an effective indicator of the intensity of stress reactions of sojourners is the degree of difference between the sojourners' home culture and the host culture (cf. David, 1971).

In addition, the cultural backgrounds of strangers are often translated into different levels of *status* or *prestige*, which influences their com-munication experiences with host nationals. Many societies hold certain esteem (or lack thereof) toward different groups of the world. When negative out-group perceptions are directed toward a particular cultural or racial group, such perceptions are likely to discourage the participation of strangers from that group in the host communication processes. On the other hand, strangers from a group favorably perceived by the natives are likely to enjoy a higher 'standing' and greater receptiveness.

Closely related to cultural similarity/discrepancy and prestige is the degree of *salience* of racially-based physical distinctiveness (Weinberg, 1973). Outstanding physical characteristics such as skin color, facial features, and physique often add to the overall 'foreignness' of strangers, playing a favorable or unfavorable role in the strangers' subsequent communication-adaptation process depending on how it is perceived by host nationals.

Personality attributes

In addition to strangers' cultural and racial background characteristics, their individual personality also influences their adaptive communication activities. Despite the arguments of some researchers negating the relevance and validity of personality factors in cross-cultural adaptation, some supportive empirical evidence is available for postulating a relationship between cross-cultural adaptation and certain personality traits (cf. Kealey & Ruben, 1983). An assumption here is that individuals possess certain basic mental or behavioral 'traits' that are more or less enduring in nature, and that such traits serve as tendencies of individualised ways to respond to environmental stimuli.

Among the personal attributes observed in empirical research are tolerance for ambiguity or risk-taking (Fiske & Maddi, 1961), gregarious-ness (Bradburn, 1969), and hardiness or resilience (Quisumbing, 1982). In addition, Yum (1987) reported a tentative finding that shows a positive correlation between immigrants' 'internal locus of control' (the tendency to place the responsibility for events within themselves) and the extent to which they develop host national acquaintances. Also, behavioral characteristics that reflect extrovertedness, positive orientation, respect for people in general, empathy, open-mindedness, tolerance for ambiguity, and self-control have been identified as contributing to effective adaptation in the new culture.

The personality and behavioral indicators employed in previous studies share considerable semantic redundancy, and can be consolidated into two system-theoretic concepts: (1) openness and (2) resilience. Openness, as a theoretical construct, provides a common base for more specific concepts such as 'open-mindedness', 'tolerance for ambiguity', 'gregariousness' and 'extrovertedness'. Resilience consolidates such concepts as 'internal locus of control', 'tolerance of ambiguity', 'persistence', 'hardiness' (or 'vulnerability'), 'self-control', 'resourcefulness', 'inner security', and 'self–confidence'.

Openness. One of the most fundamental conditions of individuals as open systems is, of course, their degree of openness. Openness here refers to receptivity to external information as well as the internal flow of information within the the individual (Gendlin, 1962, 1978). In this systems perspective, the quality of the individual's communication activities is considered to be directly affected by the person's openness. Openness, like a child's innocence, should enable strangers to minimise their resistance to change and to maximise their inner capacity to 'receive' changes as they occur. As Jantsch (1980) stated, an open person would have a tendency to live 'without any reserve in the structure of the present, and yet to let go and flow into a new structure when the right time has come' (p. 255).

Effective cross-cultural adaptation involves this quality of openness in strangers because it facilitates their interaction with the host environment, enabling them to make as accurate and realistic an assessment of themselves and of the environment as possible. It helps strangers to examine themselves and the environment with 'honesty' and a willingness to be transformed as they encounter new experiences in the host environment. On the other hand, strangers with a 'closed' personality would tend to distort their understanding of the host culture, the original culture, and their own internal conditions. Some individuals may, for instance, 'glorify' the host culture while others may 'romanticise' the original cultural attributes internalised in their personality. A specific indication of closedness was observed by Coelho (1958) in his study of Indian students in the United States, in terms of their rigidity and 'defensiveness' in adhering to their home reference groups.

Age is closely associated with openness for change. Unlike children, older strangers by and large have a personality structure into which their original cultural identity and communication patterns are solidified. Even when they are strongly motivated to learn and adapt to the host culture, many will find it difficult to do so because of their 'old' cultural habits. Many studies have reported that age at the time of migration significantly influences the subsequent rate of adaptation, particularly on second-language acquisition. Findings indicate, for instance, that younger adults tend to acquire English more quickly and attain a higher proficiency than do older adults (cf. Baldassini & Flaherty, 1982; Furnham, 1984; Y. Kim, 1976, 1980). Gal (1978) found a strong rank correlation between an immigrant's age and his or her preference of speaking in the original language. This inverse relationship between age and adaptation was observed even among American tourists in Africa during a six-week tour (Cort & King, 1979), in which the older tourists experienced greater culture shock and were observed to be less tolerant of host environmental ambiguities.

Resilience. Along with openness, the resilience of strangers' personality facilitates their adaptive capacity in the host environment. Individual strangers react to a given stressful situation differently. Some strangers would react to difficult situations with composure and clear thinking, while others in similar situations would 'fall apart' being unable to collect their resources to manage the impending 'crisis'. Resilience, thus, refers to the attribute similar to what is called 'ego strength', or inner 'coping capacity', to withstand internal disturbances (or perceived difficulties) under environmental stress and to persist in the efforts to make things work (Lazarus, 1966:225). It is the opposite of fragile self-control that can be 'blown away' in the face of a slight challenge to the self-image by others.

Resilience, however, must not be confused with stubbornness and tenseness. On the contrary, a resilient personality reflects the qualities of *flexibility* (the ability to 'bend' and empathise with others while believing in oneself) and of relaxedness (the ability to 'let-go' of anxiousness and remain integrated) (cf. MacKinnon, 1978). While stubbornness and tenseness discourage adaptation, flexibility and relaxedness facilitate creative and effective responses to impending problems. For strangers coping with the difficulties of adapting to the host culture, their resilient personality would help them to find what is 'best' in each potentially problematic situation they encounter.

Armed with an open and resilient personality, then, strangers are better able to 'give' when challenged and find a way to 'pull' themselves into a position of good will and respect. Without openness and resilience, they are less capable of absorbing culture shocks and withstanding challenges of the adaptation process, just as a building without give in its structure will easily collapse in a storm. The open and resilient mind of strangers has the strength of the 'triumphant personality' that remains resourceful, creative, and in good spirits for the future.

Preparedness for change

Strangers' adaptive potential is further promoted by their preparedness for change, or psychological 'readiness' and informational familiarity with the host culture prior to, or during, the initial period of adaptation in the new environment. Knowledge about the host communication systems, particularly language, and about relevant norms, rules, customs, history and art as well as economic, social, and political institutions, adds to strangers' preparedness for change.

Among many possible indicators of such preparedness is *formal education experiences* (cf. Furnham, 1984; Y. Kim, 1977a, 1980; Yum, 1982). Schooling, regardless of specific cultural context, is viewed as expanding learners' cognitive capacity for new learning and mental resourcefulness. At times, strangers' formal schooling in their home country may have provided them with some exposure to the language, culture, geography and history of the host society. Such pre-migration familiarity would provide added adaptive leverage for building host communication competence and participating in social processes of the host society.

Along with educational background, gender has been observed to influence strangers' adaptive potential. A number of immigrant studies reported that male immigrants were significantly more skilled in the host language than female immigrants, given the same length of residence in the host society (cf. Baldassini & Flaherty, 1982; Furnham, 1984; Y. Kim, 1976; Office of Refugee Resettlement, 1984). Gender, however, does not qualify as a theoretically sound explanatory factor for the observed differences in adaptation because it is confounded by other background characteristics, particularly education. In many cultures, women tend to possess a lower educational background than men and married women tend not to work outside their home, placing them at a less advantageous position in a cross-cultural adaptation situation (Y. Kim, 1976).

In addition to formal schooling, experiences of *pre-entry training* on the host language and culture have been widely regarded as promoting strangers' adaptation to the host society. An increasing number of cross-cultural training programs have been offered to familiarise trainees with their host culture. Peace Corps volunteers, for example, go through an extensive language and cultural training program before being sent to their assigned location. Training programs are also offered to students in missionary preparation programs, business men and women in multinational corporations, military personnel, diplomats and employees of intergovernmental agencies, and international technical advisors, among others. Recently, training programs have been offered to Southeast Asian refugee camps while the refugees are waiting for permission to enter the United States. (See Brislin & Pedersen, 1976; Landis & Brislin, 1983, for an extensive review of training programs and of studies evaluating training effectiveness.)

Generally, these training programs are geared to providing trainees with some degree of psychological preparedness and familiarity with the host culture before they embark to an unfamiliar culture. Ample data have been made available to demonstrate the contribution of prior familiarity through training and education to the smoother adaptation of sojourners in the host society. Sewell & Davidsen (1961), for example, found that the more guidance international students received prior to coming to the United States, the greater was their academic adjustment and satisfaction with the sojourn. Also, a study of the effects of pre-entry training on Southeast Asian refugees found that subsequent English acquisition was accelerated by the training. The gap in English language abilities between trained and untrained refugees after six months in the United States was particularly great for pre-literate individuals (Office of Refugee Resettlement, 1984).

An additional consideration for preparedness for change must be given to the *circumstances* in which individuals migrate to the host society. Unlike refugees who escape a life-threatening crisis at home (such as war), many immigrants plan ahead for their move and prepare themselves extensively for their new life through reading, studying, communication via personal contacts with the host society, and perhaps even through prior visits. Because of such preparedness, their initial adaptation in the host society is likely to be less abrupt and less stressful (Taft, 1977:124). Also, individuals who have previous sojourn experiences outside their own countries are likely to be better prepared for subsequent cross-cultural transition. Selltiz *et al.* (1963) reported that foreign students in the United States who had previously been outside their own countries, no matter for how short a time, interacted more with Americans during their stay than those who had never before been abroad. (See, also, Church, 1982; Furnham, 1984; Sewell & Davidsen, 1961.)

All in all, we have examined in this chapter a number of crucial factors pertaining to both the host environment and the individual stranger's own background and personality traits that are likely to impede or facilitate the cross-cultural adaptation process. While the personal and social communication processes of strangers provide the central dynamics of cross-cultural adaptation in all situations, the environmental and predispositional conditions present strangers with different amounts of 'push and pull' making their communication experiences unique and individualised. To the extent that strangers' cultural and racial backgrounds are similar to, or render status in, the host society, to the extent that their personality is open and resilient, and to the extent that they are well educated, trained, and otherwise prepared for their move, they are in a more 'advantageous' position to begin their journey of adaptation.

9 ADAPTATION OUTCOMES

At the end of this gradual evolution my inner universe
reaches homogeneity in which no forms but the opposition of forms
is abolished. Everything is equalised.
Hubert Benoit

Once strangers enter a new culture, their cross-cultural adaptation process is set in motion. Gradually, strangers' habitual patterns of cognitive, affective, and behavioral responses undergo adaptive transformations. Through the processes of deculturation and acculturation, some of the 'old' cultural habits are replaced by new cultural habits. Gradually, strangers acquire increasing proficiency in the host communication system, becoming better able to express themselves and more effectively engage in spontaneous social transactions. Such improved personal and social communication enable them to fulfill their various human needs, such as maintaining and enhancing social relationships and providing for channels of self-expression and fulfilment (cf. Maslow, 1970).

In many cases, strangers can attempt to satisfy their needs also by participating in the communication processes of their ethnic communities where they are allowed to communicate in the familiar manner of their original culture. Newcomers in particular tend to rely on their ethnic communication activities heavily for social support, although this will vary according to the extent that their ethnic communities are readily available and institutionally complete. As strangers' personal and social communication patterns converge into the communication characteristics of the host culture, their dependence on ethnic communication activities for satisfying their needs are likely to decrease.

Adaptation occurs naturally as long as strangers continue participating in the interpersonal and mass communication processes of the host society.

As Taft (1977) argued, even those strangers who interact with the natives with the intention of confining themselves to only superficial relationships are likely to become at least minimally adapted to the host culture in time 'in spite of themselves' (p. 150). As such, adaptive changes are not necessarily *planned* or *preferred* by strangers. Nor do adaptive changes necessarily serve to pursue or achieve clear goals concerning tasks to be accomplished. Instead, adaptive changes are a cumulative result of all conceivable communication activities — conscious, unconscious, instrumental, non-instrumental, personal and interpersonal. Although strangers' motivational strength will potentially influence the extensiveness of their adaptive transformation, some change will inevitably occur over time.

Large and sudden modifications are likely to occur during the initial phase of adaptation, producing intense stress in strangers' internal systems. Indeed, such large changes are themselves indicative of adaptive difficulties and disruptions, as has been demonstrated amply in culture shock studies. Over a prolonged period, however, strangers will go through a progression of stages, where each stage in the developmental sequence is a necessary result of the preceding condition of adaptation. Adler (1975) has described, for instance, that the short-term sojourners are likely to move from a stage of low to high self- and cultural awareness. A further elaboration of such incremental perceptual development was provided in Y. Kim's (1976) study of Korean immigrants.

Adaptive changes that take place in individual strangers, then, are to be viewed as falling along a continuum in which individual strangers show *differential rates* or *levels* of adaptation from minimal to maximal (cf. Nagata, 1969; Padilla, 1980). These changes in strangers are further viewed in the present theory as the cumulative consequence of all the prior communication experiences in the host society, which, in turn, is influenced by their pre-migration characteristics (i.e., cultural/racial background, preparedness for change, and open and resilient personality attributes) and host environmental conditions (i.e., receptivity and conformity pressure).

The individual rate of adaptation outcome has been assessed in research by a variety of measures including strangers' feelings of comfort, satisfaction, and happiness, and their attitude toward the host society (cf. Berry *et al.*, 1987). In the present theory, three interrelated adaptation outcomes — (1) increased functional fitness, (2) increased psychological health, and (3) increased intercultural identity — have been identified as the most crucial aspects of adaptive change.

Increased functional fitness

Strangers in an unfamiliar environment instinctively strive to 'know their way around', so that they may effectively control their own behavior in relation to the behavior of others — as they would react adaptively to the changing seasons of spring to winter. Through such adaptive activities, strangers achieve an increasing functional fitness, or 'congruence', between the characteristics of their 'subjective' world and the external realities of the host environment (cf. Brody, 1969; French, Rodger & Cobb, 1974; Taft, 1957). Implicit in this view of adaptation is a compromise in the internal structure of a person and the external pressure of the environment.

Strangers' functional fitness has been theorised to be influenced by and influence their personal and social communication processes. Through an increased cognitive, affective and behavioral capacity to communicate competently in the host communication system, and through increased participation in the interpersonal and mass communication processes of the host society, the strangers are transformed so that their encoding and decoding patterns become increasingly proficient. Such increased communicative proficiency, in turn, promotes their functional fitness in the host environment. Ruesch (1957/1972) described this interactive relationship between communication and functional fitness when he stated:

> one of the criteria for successful communication is the mutual fit of over-all patterns and constituent parts, integration, synchrony, smoothness so that no particular person is overburdened with or completely relieved of work, and thus the exchange of messages become efficient, clear, economical, and well timed. (p. 34)

The present conceptualisation of functional fitness as a crucial adaptation outcome is consistent with the layman's common understanding of the phenomenon. For many people, to be well-adapted simply means to be able to function effectively and to feel that one 'belongs' in a particular environment. It is this ideal that the family, the school, and other social institutions have in mind when they concern themselves with children and citizens — to make them 'well-adapted' to their community.

The increased functional fitness (and communication success) has been indirectly observed in previous studies. Szalay & Inn (1987), for example, examined the 'subjective meaning systems' of Mexican-Americans and Puerto Ricans from New York, and compared them to the meaning systems of Anglo Americans in New York and Puerto Ricans in San Juan. Findings from this study demonstrated a general progression of the meaning systems of Mexican-Americans and Puerto Ricans in New York toward the Anglo

American meaning system. An additional indication for a progressive increase in functional fitness was shown in the finding that the meaning systems of Puerto Ricans in New York were located between their San Juan Puerto Rican and Anglo-American counterparts.

Other indirect methods of assessing functional fitness have been employed in survey studies of immigrants. Y. Kim (1978b, 1980), for example, obtained information about strangers' subjective *sense of belonging* in the host environment and confidence in their future as members of the host society. The assumption here is that strangers' subjective assessments of their present and future in the host environment are indicative of the functional fitness they have achieved. Also, the relative psychological distances between strangers' images of self, of ethnic culture, and of the host culture can be an indirect indication of their functional fitness in the host society (Y. Kim, 1978b, 1980).

These indirect, subjective assessments of functional fitness need to be validated by more objective methods. Since the communication-adaptation process occurs in an interactive relationship between strangers and the host environment, evidence that strangers perceive themselves to be functionally fit (or unfit) gains significance if their perceptions are shared by host nationals. One objective method to assess strangers' functional fitness is to observe strangers interacting with host nationals, assess the smoothness of interaction patterns between them, and obtain the opinions of both strangers and their native interaction partners to test the 'mutuality of interpersonal perceptions' (Y. Kim, 1979a). Data thus obtained will allow a more complete understanding of functional fitness.

Psychological health

As strangers achieve an increased level of functional fitness, they also are likely to experience an increased internal integration, or sense of cohesiveness. Psychological health, as an adaptation outcome, refers to such internal integration — a balance in cognitive, affective and behavioral processes operating in harmony with respect to the challenges of the host milieu. In contrast, maladaptation, or psychological disturbance, occurs when strangers lack an adequately balanced internal capacity that is, at the same time, capable of dealing with environmental challenges. What is commonly understood as culture shock (or even mental illness) can be viewed as a phenomenon reflecting a 'breakdown' in communication between a stranger and the environment and a serious 'disequilibrium' within the stranger's internal system (cf. Taft, 1977:146).

Research of personality organisation based on systems conceptions has emphasised the role of communication competence and intrapersonal integration as keys to human effectiveness and psychological well-being. Seeman (1983), in his review of work in this area, concluded:

> the most frequently mentioned aspect of personal effectiveness centered on a conceptual framework which emphasised synthesis and integration. There was wide agreement that special qualities of organisation and function of the individual as a whole characterised the phenomenon of personal effectiveness. The individual's capacity to regulate the total personal system, the harmonious interplay of part processes, and the existence of adequate communication channels were all required as conditions of effective functioning and optimal utilisation of personal resources. (p. 231)

Psychological health is a phenomenon difficult to observe concretely because it reflects a 'normal' state of individuals that is often taken for granted. On the other hand, symptoms of psychological illness are more easily identifiable because they deviate from normalcy. A number of the most commonly identifiable and widely discussed manifestations of psychological illnesses are the so-called *culture-shock symptoms* that include negative self-image, low self-esteem, low morale, social isolation, dissatisfaction with life in general, a bitter attitude of being helpless victims of circumstance and related psychological distresses (cf. Furnham & Bochner, 1986; Torbiorn, 1982).

In addition, the cross-cultural stress and internal disintegration experiences are frequently manifested in the form of *hostility and aggression toward the host society* as well. As suggested by Zajonc (1952) in his 'frustration–aggression hypothesis', the stranger who experiences a need to conform and cannot, due to lack of host communication competence, is subject to frustration leading to aggression and hostility, which in turn serves to reduce the need to adapt by devaluating the need for it.

Extreme stress reactions of strangers may take the form of escapism or mental illness symptoms. Psychiatry, which in recent years has concerned itself with the clinical description of emergent mental illnesses among immigrants, observed that patients manifested such symptoms as alcoholism and 'paranoid syndrome' (cf. Meznaric, 1984). There has also been growing recognition that the development of mental and behavior disorders in immigrants is not so much due to innate characteristics, but is the result of a severe misfit between individuals and the receiving community. Stress seems particularly acute among those whose native culture differs radically from that of the host community. Also, stress can be intensified even further when there is strong pressure for rapid assimilation and the stranger is unable, or unwilling, to join a familiar group that might offer tension reduction and flexibility in coping with cultural change (cf. David, 1969).

Kino (1973) succinctly described a situation of the mental disturbance of strangers based on psychiatric case studies of Polish men in England voluntarily admitted to mental hospitals:

> The change [toward illness] occurred with their transfer toworkshops or pits, where they found themselves isolated in aforeign environment whose language and habits were unknownto them, making every attempt at interpersonal approach verydifficult. Being accustomed at home to lively and volublecompanionship, the impossibility of making conversationand friendly contact with their new companions left thememotionally upset. Misunderstandings and misapprehensionsunavoidable in such a situation evoked their suspicion andmistrust. Harmless talks or remarks of their felloooow workersto one another were interpreted as hostile observations,though they were unable to understand the language. Gradually this morbid state of mind grew to such intensity that a rational appreciation of the environment became quite impossible. (p. 63)

As such, even the most severe forms of maladaptation and personal disintegration can be viewed as a state of individual functional misfit and ineffectual communication in a given environment. As Ruesch (1957/1972) explained, the condition that the psychiatrist labels 'psychosis' can be interpreted to be the result of the patient's misinterpretation of messages received due to a cognitive structure that lacks the ability to differentiate and selectively integrate the information received from the environment. Also, the condition commonly labeled 'neurosis' can be viewed to be a result of the unfortunate attempts of a patient to convey messages to others in social situations without success. Similarly, schizophrenic individuals can be viewed as those whose cognitive structure is incapable of discerning the multiplicity of messages.

Research findings generally available indicate a close interrelationship between strangers' personal and social communication activities and psychological well-being (cf. Church, 1982; Deutsch & Won, 1963; Y. Kim, 1976, 1977a–c, 1978a–b, 1980; Nishida, 1985; Wong-Rieger, 1984). Given the above analysis of various psychological health/disturbances from the present communication viewpoint, improved psychological health of strangers is a necessary outcome of the improved host communication competence and participation in interpersonal and mass communication processes of the host society. The improved psychological health, in turn, will facilitate subsequent personal and social communication processes.

Intercultural identity

Most strangers continually encounter situations in which symmetry between their internal reality and the external reality of the host environment is broken. Yet, every contradiction serves strangers as an occasion for refining their understanding of the host environment and of themselves. As strangers successfully overcome the multitude of stressful conditions, the internal adaptive capacity is broadened and deepened.

This stress–adaptation–growth process (described in Chapter 3) lies at the heart of strangers' experiences. As Dabrowski (1964) succinctly put it,

> Disintegration is a generally positive developmental process . . . The disintegration process, through loosening and even fragmenting the internal psychic environment, through conflict within the internal environment and with the external environment, is the ground for birth and development of a higher psychic structure. Disintegration is the basis for developmental thrusts upward, the creation of new evolutionary dynamics, and the movement of the personality to a higher level. (p. 5)

In spite of, or rather because of, the adversarial nature of the cross-cultural adaptation process, strangers grow beyond the psychological parameters of the original culture. Their increased cognitive complexity allows them to differentiate between the new and the old milieu, which in turn helps them to develop a broader perspective in dealing with the new culture and the ability to overcome cultural parochialism. This growth beyond the psychological parameters of any one culture is called in the present theory the development of *intercultural identity*.

Like 'cultural identity' (discussed in Chapter 4), intercultural identity is viewed not as a fixed psychological state, but as a continuum in which strangers vary in the degree of 'interculturalness' in their cognitive, affective, and behavioral tendencies (Y. Kim, 1985b; Y. Kim & Ruben, 1988). If cultural identity is viewed as a psychological linkage between a person and a specific cultural *group*, intercultural identity must be considered as an *intergroup* identity. As Adler (1982) described it, intercultural identity is based

> not on 'belongingness' which implies either owning or being owned by

culture, but on a style of self-consciousness that situates oneself neither totally *a part of* nor *totally apart* from a given culture. (p. 391)

The intercultural identity of strangers can be observed in terms of the development of a *third-culture perspective*, or an inclusive viewpoint that represents more than one cultural perspective — either the home culture or the host culture, but, at the same time, transcends both groups. Intercultural identity, as such, serves as a core attribute that integrates several concepts that have been variously suggested, including 'multicultural man [woman]' (Adler, 1982), 'marginality' (Lum, 1982), 'universal man [woman]' (Tagore, 1961; Walsh, 1973), and 'cultural hybrid' (Park, 1939).

In the present theory, the process of personal transformation from being a cultural person to becoming increasingly intercultural has been viewed as a form of internal growth (cf. Chapters 3 and 4). If individuals successfully overcome the multitude of challenges and frustrations and undergo the consequent alteration of their internal conditions along the way, they are likely to develop a mental, emotional and behavioral capacity that is more open, flexible and resilient than that of people who have limited exposure to the challenges of cross-cultural adaptation. Except for a small portion of individuals who are unable, or unwilling, to cope with the stress of cross-cultural encounters, most of the strangers have an impressive capacity to manage their cross-cultural stresses without damaging their overall psychological integrity.

In this process of intercultural growth, strangers are 'pushed' toward the development of a *broadened perspective* on things. In the stress–adaptation–growth process, strangers may reach a level of adaptivity in which they are capable of creatively conciliating and reconciliating seemingly contradictory characteristics of peoples and events by transforming them into complementary, interacting parts of an integral whole. This state of development is what Harris (1979) referred to as the optimal level of communication competence, or what Yoshikawa (1988) proposed as a stage of 'double-swing' or 'transcendence of binary perception of the world'. The optimal, comprehensive and inclusive identity is more than a simple combination of the host and the original cultural attributes. Instead, it is a kind of 'synergy', or 'emergence of a new self-awareness, born out of an awareness of the relative nature of values and of the universal aspect of human nature' (Yoshikawa, 1978:220).

Not all strangers may evolve this far in their adaptation process. Yet, those who do will be able to enjoy a special kind of freedom, making deliberate choices for actions in specific situations rather than simply being bound by the culturally normative courses of action. As they become increasingly functional in the host milieu and better integrated psychologically, their perspectives on cultures, peoples, and events become broadened — with a strengthened sense of selfhood that is intercultural. These outcomes of adaptive transformation, in turn, facilitate strangers' subsequent personal and social communication processes as they continue their encounter with the host milieu. Houston (1981), a Japanese-American writer, spoke of her own adaptive transformation as follows:

> Now I entertain according to how I feel that day. If my Japanese sensibility is stronger, I act accordingly and feel OK. If I feel like going all American, I can do that too and feel OK. I've come to accept the cultural hybrid of my personality and recognise it as a strength, not as a weakness. Because I am culturally neither pure Japanese nor pure American . . . does not mean that I am less of a person. It seems that I have been enriched by the heritages of both.

PART IV
THE THEORY AND
THE REALITY

10 TESTING THE THEORY: TOWARD AN INTEGRATIVE APPROACH

We shall not cease from exploration
And the end of all our exploring
Will be to arrive where we started
And know the place for the first time.
T. S. Eliot

So far in this book, the present theory has been offered as a system of description and explanation about how cross-cultural adaptation of individuals occurs and what happens to them as they adapt to the host environment. The theoretical domain was defined in Chapter 3 as inclusive of all individuals — both resettlers (immigrants and refugees) and visitors (or sojourners) — whose primary childhood enculturation was completed in a different cultural milieu. Once in the host environment, they are in continuous, prolonged first-hand contact with the milieu, and, at least minimally, dependent on the host sociocultural system for survival and for meeting their various needs. The term, stranger, has been used throughout this book to refer to everyone included in the theoretical boundary. Although the host society itself adapts to strangers as their group size increases, societal adaptation is a long-term process and is considered minor compared to the adaptation of individual strangers. The present theory, thus, has explained the adaptation of strangers only, and the adaptation of the host society is beyond the present theoretical domain.

Although numerous pieces of existing empirical evidence have been incorporated into developing the present theory, the theory and its individual theorems as a whole need to be verified through research findings. To this end, an integrative research approach is advocated in this chapter as *ideally* suited. This integrative approach essentially refers to an approach to theory-testing, maximising the conceptual correspondence with the theory as well as the methodological fit in relation to the nature of the reality that has been theorised. The approach can be applied to all phases of the research process including:

(1) designing the conceptual scheme,
(2) operationalising constructs and determining the modes of observation (or assessment), and
(3) selecting appropriate statistical methods to link the variables.

Before discussing the integrative approach, the present theoretical structure and attributes will be highlighted to show a close correspondence between the theory and the integrative research approach being advocated.

Theoretical structure and attributes

Assumptions

The theory is grounded in ten assumptions (presented in Chapter 3) that were derived from the General Systems concepts and principles. Together the assumptions explained the fundamental nature of humans as open systems interacting with and adapting to a given environment through the process of communication. They also described that human systems have the natural tendency or drive to maintain internal equilibrium, and that stress results when change in their internal conditions is necessitated by change in the environment. The resulting stress was then defined as the underlying psychological force that 'moves' individual systems to undergo adaptive transformation, which results in the systems' internal growth. In the assumptions, it was further explained that individuals are linked to their culture via communication processes, that culture defines individual communication patterns which, once acquired, serve as the mechanism to adapt and function effectively in that environment. In this process of enculturation emerges a cultural identity, a psychological linkage between the individual and the culture.

Axioms and theorems

These assumptions were taken as 'givens' in the theory, based on which ten axioms were developed in Chapter 4 as the key principles that operate in the adaptive experiences of strangers in relation to the host environment. Collectively, the axioms explain that the stress–adaptation–growth interplay lies at the center of internal fluctuation, in which strangers undergo gradual transformation. It was further explained that the personal and social communication processes of strangers with the host environment and within the ethnic community are centrally instrumental to strangers' becoming increasingly functional in an unfamiliar cultural environment. Specifically, strangers' host communication competence, and their participation in the host social (interpersonal, mass) communication activities, were identified as interactively facilitating their adaptation. Participation in the ethnic social (interpersonal, mass) communication processes was explained as initially facilitating, but eventually inhibiting, the development of host communication competence and host social (interpersonal, mass) communication, and, thus, adaptive transformation.

In addition, the differential adaptive predispositions of individual strangers and the varied receptivity and conformity pressure of the host environment were theorised as influencing the strangers' development of host communication competence and social communication processes, and thereby influencing their adaptation to the host environment indirectly. Three key outcomes from this adaptive communication processes were identified as increased functional fitness, psychological health and intercultural identity. These outcomes, in turn, are viewed to facilitate subsequent personal and social communication activities of strangers.

Based on the ten axiomatic principles, 28 theorems were explicated in Chapter 5 linking the 13 key constructs in six dimensions with one another following the relational linkages provided by the axioms. The theorems were stated in co-variational terms ('The greater A, the greater B', or 'The greater A, the lesser B'). Collectively, the theorems outline the overall structure of interrelationships among the dimensions and constructs as illustrated in Figure 6. The theorems and the model in Figure 6 are subject to empirical testing. It is by testing these theorems that the present theory (including its assumptions and axioms) can be validated.

In testing the theory, the 13 constructs need to be successfully 'operationalised' into empirically observable units so that the proposed theoretical relationships between/among them may be adequately assessed. To assist the operationalisation of constructs, Chapters 6 through 9 elaborated on each construct, identifying its specific indicators summarised below (see Table 1). Although these indicators are not exhaustive of all possible ways to assess the constructs, they have been offered as elements that bear the most direct conceptual and empirical relevance to the theory. Through these indicators, the theory is linked to the empirical realm of cross-cultural adaptation.

TABLE 1

Dimensions	Constructs	Indicators
(1) Personal communication	Host communication competence	Knowledge of host communication system Cognitive complexity Affective co-orientation Behavioral competence
(2) Host social communication	Host interpersonal communication	Size/proportion of host ties Strength of host ties
	Host mass communication	Degree of exposure Contents of exposure
(3) Ethnic social communication	Ethnic interpersonal communication	Size/proportion of ethnic ties Intimacy of ethnic ties
	Ethnic mass communication	Degree of exposure Contents of exposure
(4) Host environment	Receptivity	Openness Acceptance
	Conformity pressure	Formal language policy Informal language practice Social segregation
(5) Predisposition	Cultural/racial background	Cultural similarity Physical salience Background prestige
	Personality attribute	Openness Resilience

TABLE 1 continued

Dimensions	Constructs	Indicators
	Preparedness for change	Education Pre-entry training Prior sojourn experience Transition circumstance
(6) Adaptation outcomes	Functional Fitness	Congruent meaning system Feeling of comfort Mutuality of stranger–host perception
	Psychological Health	Absence of culture shock symptoms Absence of hostility toward host society Absence of severe stress reactions
	Intercultural Identity	Third-culture perspective Intergroup identification

Attributes of the theory

On the whole, the theory was intended to meet the central challenge currently facing the field of cross-cultural adaptation, that is, to consolidate (1) divergent and limited conceptualisations, (2) inconsistent use of key terms, and (3) less than systematic variable-oriented research activities across the human sciences. To achieve this goal required a broad conceptual framework in which the multidimensional, multifaceted phenomenon of cross-cultural adaptation could be considered simultaneously. It was also necessary to employ concepts at a high abstraction level to accommodate the concepts in existing approaches. For instance, the term, stranger, has been used to incorporate existing terms such as immigrants, refugees, sojourners and visitors. Also, the term, adaptation, has been used to incorporate existing terms such as assimilation, acculturation, integration and adjustment.

Based on these considerations, the General Systems perspective on the functioning of human organisms and its concepts — communication, homeostasis, stress, and adaptation — have been employed. The systems-theoretic emphasis on the inseparable and interactive functional relationship between an individual and the environment, and the stress–adaptation–growth fluctuation of living systems, helped the theory to integrate the elements that have been traditionally the primary research domains of psychology, social psychology, anthropology, sociology and sociolinguistics. Also, the systems-theoretic perspective on communication and adaptation enabled the present theory to include both the prevalent 'adaptation-as-problem' approach and the more recent 'adaptation-as-learning/growth' approach, as well as the ideologically-based assimilationist and pluralist views, into a single explanatory scheme.

This systems perspective has also helped emphasise the interactive nature of relationships between the strangers' adaptive predisposition, conditions of the host environment, host communication competence and social participation in host and ethnic interpersonal and mass com-munication activities. All these key dimensions then were conceptualised to directly and indirectly contribute to the adaptation outcome of strangers over time, toward increased functional and psychological facility and intercultural identity.

All in all, the present theory is an *integrative* theory with three significant features. First, it is a *comprehensive*, multidimensional, multi-faceted theory, which incorporates in its explanatory scheme psychological, social, cultural, racial, verbal, non-verbal, conscious, unconscious, sub-jective, objective, cognitive, affective and behavioral factors. Second, it is a *general* theory that potentially serves as wide a range of applicability as possible including the adaptation experiences of both short-term and long-term strangers from any cultural origin to any new destination for any voluntary or involuntary reason — since these factors are already part of the present theoretical scheme. Third, the present theory is an *interactive* theory pointing to the bidirectional (reciprocal) causal linkages be-tween/among its dimensions and constructs. The only exception to this interactive conceptualisation is the unidirectional causal linkage between adaptive predisposition (prior to migration) and the personal and social communication processes (after migration).

These three attributes of the present theory — comprehensive con-ceptual scope, broad generalisability, and interactive causal linkages between/among dimensions and constructs — necessitate an integrative research plan with comparable scope in conceptualisation, sampling, operationalisation of constructs, and modes of observation, as well as methods of data analysis accommodating the interactive nature of relationships between variables.

Comprehensive conceptual correspondence

Designing research to test the present theory presents a challenge of dealing not with one or two links at a time but with all the links simultaneously as presented in Figure 6. Limited conceptual focus in research will not be able to adequately test the overall theory. Many studies in the past with limited foci have tended to interpret their results in terms of only those variables that were regarded as important in their respective designs, often without mention of the excluded factors.

Such limited-scale research may serve the purpose of ascertaining the specific research questions raised with varying degrees of effectiveness. It cannot, however, reveal the complete empirical 'picture' of the various linkages between dimensions and constructs. A probable consequence of this limited conceptual correspondence to theory is a fragmented view of the cross-cultural adaptation phenomenon. Often, results may not be usefully integrated because of the likely methodological inconsistencies among studies. Explicit and implicit 'biases' of individual researchers are also likely to be introduced in all phases of research — including the phase of deciding which aspects of the theory should be tested, how to operationalise a given construct, what modes of observation are to be employed, how to analyse the data thus obtained, and how to interpret the findings in relation to theory. Conceptual fragmentation in research will generate fragmented information, which is precisely the opposite of the original intent of the present theory — to integrate, rather than segmentalize, the multiplicity and complexity of existing theoretical and research approaches in the field.

What is called for is a research approach that comprehensively accommodates the present conceptualisation by incorporating its total theoretical structure and elements into a single design. Researchers, of course, are well aware of the numerous difficulties and contingencies inherent in designing and implementing this research, particularly when the conceptual base is broad and complex. They face additional difficulties that stem from the usually limited time and financial resources that allow only short-term research efforts. Further, the specialised intellectual backgrounds, interests and perspectives across disciplines present additional constraints on testing a theory that incorporates elements from several disciplines. (See Blalock, 1984, for an elaboration of this point.)

Yet, it is critical that we consider the elements required for an ideal experiment for theory test, so that the limitations imposed on a given study may be more readily recognised. Once we recognise such limitations, we will be able to articulate the extent to which the research findings adequately or inadequately compare to the overall theoretical structure and attributes. Such an articulation of limitations of a given study will, in turn, help us to develop creative 'compromise plans' in which the integrity of the theory and the challenges of the research reality may be maximally balanced.

There are a number of alternative designs that allow partial testing of the theory with minimum distortion of its overall structure and attributes. Three alternatives most pertinent to the present theory are suggested here for consideration. (More systematic explanations about the logic behind these alternative designs are discussed in Campbell & Stanley, 1966; Cook & Campbell, 1979.)

Alternative 1: Randomise the excluded variables that are causally linked to the included variables. The researcher may 'control' the variables (operationalised constructs) that are being excluded from the research design when such variables are theorised as causally influencing the included variables. Take, for instance, a research focus testing only the relationship between strangers' host communication competence (Dimension 1) and their adaptive outcomes (Dimension 6). Given these two dimensions, the theory postulates that host environmental conditions (Dimension 4) and strangers' adaptive predisposition (Dimension 5) causally influence their personal and social communication activities (Dimensions 1–3). To test the focal relationship between host communication competence and adaptive outcomes, we need to control host environmental conditions (Dimension 4) and adaptive predisposition (Dimension 5). Controlling these dimensions can be done through 'randomising' pertinent variables by selecting individuals in the sample(s) who are more or less equivalent in their adaptive predisposition (Dimension 5) and who live under equivalent host environmental conditions (Dimension 4). In this example, we cannot and need not control the social communication dimensions (Dimensions 2–3) because the theory postulates that the host communication competence and ethnic and host social (interpersonal, mass) communication activities are mutually influencing and reciprocally causal.

Alternative 2: Develop a multiphased plan to test the complete theory over time. This alternative allows the researcher to maintain a single comprehensive conceptual scheme, but divide it into several phases so that only a portion of the theory may be tested at a given time until all theoretical parts are tested. In this plan, the researcher maintains control over the research throughout the phases, thus keeping the overall conceptual scheme intact while making each phase simple enough to manage. For instance, the first phase may be designed to test the relationships between predispositional factors (Dimension 5) and the personal and social communication patterns (Dimensions 1–3). This phase can then be followed by a study designed to test the relationship between host environmental conditions and the subjects' personal and social communication patterns.

In this design, however, efforts must be made to maintain the equivalence of the samples employed at different phases. This means that the same group of strangers cannot be studied repeatedly in more than one phase because their adaptation experiences are likely to have changed between research phases (as the present theory explains). One way to avoid such 'maturation' bias is to use 'cohorts', or samples drawn from equivalent populations across phases.

Alternative 3: Develop a multifaceted plan to test the complete theory in parts. In this design, the complete theory is divided into a number of manageable units to be implemented by a number of researchers simultaneously. The respective findings are then integrated for a comprehensive testing of the theory. As long as research is planned under a single, comprehensive plan, the actual implementation can be divided for efficiency, such as the testing of the relationship between predispositional and the host environmental conditions and their relationship to the development of host communication competence. Under the same design, another researcher may focus on the relationship between the host communication competence and social communication processes of strangers. Here, the same principle of equivalence across samples must be applied for the study to remain integrated.

In any of the above three compromise plans — (1) controlling the excluded causal variables through sampling, (2) developing a multiphased design testing the entire theory in equivalent samples over time, and (3) developing a multifaceted design testing the entire theory simultaneously in multiple equivalent samples — the overall conceptual integrity of the research is likely to be maximally preserved. By maintaining the systematic coherence in conceptualisation, samples, assessment methods, data analysis and interpretation of findings, these alternative research plans will allow us to test the entire theory and at the same time help make the research process more manageable.

Multiple indicators and methods

Another consideration in designing an integrative research program to test the present theory deals with employing multiple indicators and assessment methods for variables. Because most of the present theoretical constructs (such as host communication competence and environmental receptivity) are abstract and general, simple operationalisations are not likely to be sufficiently adequate to ensure the reliability and validity of the data.

Multiple indicators

In Chapters 6 through 9, a number of specific indicators for each of the present constructs were discussed, and have been reviewed earlier in this chapter. For the construct, host communication competence, for example, specific indicators were identified as: knowledge of the host communication system (language, verbal and non-verbal behavior, communication rules), cognitive complexity (differentiation, integration, flexibility), affective co-orientation (affirmative attitude, aesthetic participation), and behavioral (verbal, non-verbal, interactional) proficiency. At least some of these indicators can be combined into an index of host communication competence. Similarly, an index of host interpersonal communication can be created by combining the assessments of the heterogeneity of the interpersonal network and the intimacy levels of native ties within that network.

Multiple methods of assessment

Further, an integrative testing of the present theory further advocates multiple methods of assessment (or data collection) within a single study. Combining available assessment methods — such as 'subjective', 'objective', 'quantitative' and 'qualitative' — is likely to produce data that are more complete and reliable than using only one single method. Currently, research in cross-cultural adaptation typically relies on asking direct questions to respondents' or utilising 'paper-and-pencil' measurement scales to assess variables indirectly. The popularity of this method is due primarily to its relative simplicity, low cost, and efficiency in data collection and handling. This method allows the researcher to study a large sample speedily by distributing questionnaires or asking questions by telephone. This method can effectively assess the variables if stringent criteria are employed by the researcher in selecting questionnaire items and in checking the relevance, reliability and validity of the questions being used.

There are, however, intrinsic limitations in this subjective, quantitative assessment method. A major issue is that the information obtainable by this method is admittedly inadequate in mirroring the depth, richness, subtleties, and complexities of the real world of cross-cultural adaptation. A statistically analysed relationship, for instance, between host communication competence and functional fitness fails to describe in detail how these two variables are related in specific, concrete ways as experienced by individual strangers.

The limitations of quantitative data based on subjective responses and the statistical analyses thereof can be compensated by using qualitative, naturalistic case studies employing assessment methods of participant observation and intensive interviewing. Data thus obtained generally take the form of detailed 'idiographic' verbal accounts with additional non-verbal, visual accounts such as photographs and films in describing how things operate in the reality. (See Bellman & Jules-Rosette, 1977; Bochner, 1986; Filstead, 1970; Maanen, Dabbs & Faulkner, 1983; Whyte, 1984; Yin, 1984, for discussions on various qualitative methods and techniques.)

The potential value of employing both quantitative and qualitative methods of data collection is clear in testing the present theory that contains constructs (such as functional fitness and intercultural identity) that cannot be assessed effectively by asking simple questions. More refined and insightful qualitative assessments need to be incorporated to avoid the restrictions of statistical data. Indeed, recognition of the value of multiple modes of data is increasing. Campbell (1974) discussed the value of qualitative work in psychological research, and developed a number of specific ways such work can be done through 'quasi-experimental designs' (Campbell & Stanley, 1966; Cook & Campbell, 1979). Alderfer (1967) observed data showing that interviews and questionnaires may profitably be used in conjunction with one another. Schroder, Driver & Streufert (1967) presented considerations that objective tests may not be adequate for certain purposes, such as the assessment of cognitive complexity.

Creative integration of quantitative and qualitative methods

Frequently, however, the use of qualitative assessment methods involves a complicated and time-consuming process. Also, the very flexibility and unstructured nature of qualitative assessments attract the charges that such work is impressionistic and biased. The researcher needs to find creative ways to integrate qualitative assessment with conventional quantitative assessment with maximum efficiency. To this end, a number of 'hybrid' methods of assessments have been developed. Moos' (1974) review of such attempts identify various techniques illustrating how rich, complex observational and interview data may be effectively quantified and the resulting data utilised in elaborate statistical analyses. Techniques described by Moos include:

(1) Q-technique used in interviews allowing factor analysis;
(2) focused semistructured interview allowing rank-order data for statistical analysis; and
(3) the use of diaries, autobiographic essays, sentence-completion and responses to short story and problem situations analysed statistically through content analysis or factor analysis.

As Moos pointed out, recent developments in automated content analyses of written materials will make these techniques even more useful (Krippendorff, 1980; Stone et al., 1966). In this connection, McLaughlin (1966) and Gordon (1969) have provided systems for the analysis of 'who am I' information for use with the General Inquirer approach to computer-aided content analysis.

In addition to employing the combined assessment methods such as the ones discussed above, the goal of maximising the benefits of both quantitative and qualitative approaches and minimising their shortcomings can be achieved by conducting a large-scale quantitative assessment of variables, to be followed by smaller scale in-depth interviews and participant observation of individuals selected from the original sample (Dyal & Dyal, 1981:320). The sequence may be reversed: one may begin with smaller-scale in-depth interviews and then proceed with a large-scale quantitative assessment.

Whatever integrative method is used will result in some form of compromise. The methods discussed above are some of the promising forms of compromise between the relatively real, yet less than rigorous and involving, features of qualitative approaches and the efficient and rigorous but less than in-depth feature of quantitative approaches.

Linking variables in data analysis

The present theory has generated 28 predictive theorems that assert co-variational relationships between constructs, based on the interactive mutually-causal nature of relationships between most of the the key constructs. For this interactive theory to be adequately tested statistically, research data using statistical tools that reflect bidirectional, multiple causality is required.

Bidirectional, multiple causality

It is clear that the frequently employed unidirectional methods of linking data, such as multiple regression analysis and path analysis, would not adequately test the present theory. The only unidirectional causal linkage postulated is the influence of pre-migration adaptive predisposition (Dimension 4) on host communication competence (Dimension 1) and on social communication (Dimensions 2 and 3). For all other theorems, causal links are bidirectional. For instance, the relationship between host communication competence, host interpersonal communication, and host mass communication are theorised as mutually influencing. Collectively, these three processes of communication are postulated to influence, as well as to be influenced by, host environmental conditions.

To test such bidirectional, multiple causality postulated in the present theory, statistical tools for testing unidirectional causality (with a clearly definable set of 'independent' and 'dependent' variables) cannot be used. More appropriate statistical methods for them would be correlational methods, including 'canonical analysis' and 'factor comparison' (Levine, 1977), 'cluster analysis' (Tryon & Bailey, 1970), and structural equation models (Duncan, 1975). These analyses allow the testing of the relationships between sets of variables without assuming unidirectional causal influence. (See Olmedo, 1980, for a discussion of statistical models in relation to assessments of psychological acculturation.)

Trend analysis

Although testing of the present theory does not necessitate repeated assessments of variables, longitudinal research data would add a significant insight to the data obtained at one point in time. By 'following through' a 'panel' sample (consisting of the same individuals) over a period of time — such as throughout the entire duration of a sojourn or throughout the initial ten years of immigration — the research will be able to ascertain insights into adaptive experiences as well as changes that are postulated to take place in internal conditions (functional fitness, psychological health and intercultural identity).

Simple time-series analysis (Ostrom, 1978) can be employed on data from repeated assessments over time to test the linearity in the trend of change in each key construct of the present theory. (See Y. Kim, 1976, for an application of this analysis based on cross-sectional data.) Other newer and more refined statistical tools such as stochastic analysis (Buckley, 1968) and dynamic modeling (Huckfeldt, Kohfeld & Likens, 1982) treat change in the 'interaction matrix' (e.g., the observed interrelationships among the present theoretical dimensions and constructs) as a succession of states described in terms of transition probabilities. These system-based statistical analyses of change need to be closely examined for their applicability to testing the present theory.

In sum, we have examined in this chapter the overall structure, the key dimensions and constructs, and the comprehensive, multidimensional, interactive nature of the present theory. Based on these considerations, three basic issues have been emphasised as important to an integrative research designed to test the present theory:

(1) comprehensive conceptual correspondence between the theory and the research,
(2) use of multiple indicators, multiple methods of data collection combining and integrating quantitative and qualitative approaches, and
(3) use of statistics that allow testing of relationships between variables for bidirectional and multiple causality.

These basic considerations have been presented as elements that ensure maximum validity and reliability in testing the present theory.

11 PRACTICAL CONSIDERATIONS

When the skies grow dark, the stars begin to shine.
Charles Beard

A theory finds its ultimate utility in its potential contribution to improving the conditions of those involved in the phenomenon being theorised. Because a theory is by nature about uniformity and regularity, its concepts and principles are abstract. Yet the substance of its construction is solely the concrete human experiences under observation. Once a theory is constructed, it must be brought back 'home' where the phenomenon theorised by it 'lives'.

In the case of the present theory, its reality is found in virtually every corner of the world where countless individuals are faced with the challenges of life in an alien cultural milieu. For them, the theory offers practical ideas that help individuals understand and manage the complex and often confusing process of cross-cultural adaptation. The theory also suggests implications for the host societies that, after all, are inseparable partners of strangers in this process. The following discussion deals with some of the more general implications for the strangers and the host society derived from this theory.

1. Everyone adapts, but at a different rate

One of the most fundamental assumptions of the present theory is that cross-cultural adaptation occurs naturally and necessarily regardless of the intentions of individuals *as long as* they continuously engage in communication with the host environment and are in some way functionally dependent on it. Immigrants who make their livelihood side by side with the host nationals, or students who carry out their academic work overseas, are in such situations of functional dependence on the host society. For the immigrants, students, and others who are similarly situated, adaptation is an inevitable occurrence over time. Except during the initial phase, adaptive changes are generally so gradual and subtle that they may not be recognised by the strangers themselves. Particularly if a sojourn lasts only a month or so, changes that have taken place may be too minute to be noticeable even to a trained researcher. This tendency still does not negate the present theoretical assertion that all strangers adapt and change as long as they are continuously interfaced with a new cultural environment through communication.

The theory further suggests that, given an equal length of residence in the host society, adaptation rates of strangers would vary depending on factors of the host environmental conditions (receptivity, conformity pressure), the conditions of strangers' own predisposition (cultural/racial background, personality, and preparedness for change), their host communication competence (knowledge of the host communication systems, cognitive complexity, adaptive motivation, affirmative attitude, aesthetic appreciation and behavioral capability), interpersonal communication relationship patterns with host nationals and with fellow ethnic strangers (heterogeneity of relational network, strength of ties with host nationals, ethnic support network during the initial phase), and participation in the mass communication processes of the host society (use of host mass media, use of ethnic mass media during the initial phase). Because each of these factors will be present in individual strangers differently, their adaptation experiences will be varied for everyone. Conversely, one can influence the adaptation process by 'playing up' or 'playing down' these factors according to their individual goals and aspirations.

2. Personal and societal ideologies influence cross-cultural adaptation

The apparent dilemma arising from the assimilation–pluralism ideological controversy is a non-theoretical issue. It is an issue of value and choice only between those who believe in preserving ethnicity and those who believe in assimilation as a desirable personal and social goal. In the reality of the adaptation process as viewed from the present theoretical perspective, both ethnicity and acculturation are simultaneously present in strangers in their process of adaptation. In adapting to the host environment, some 'loss' of original cultural attributes inevitably occurs, while some 'gain' of new cultural attributes is made. The issue facing the strangers is not so much having to choose either culture as understanding that they cannot adapt to a new cultural milieu successfully and at the same time remain rigidly ethnic.

Given this fundamental principle of human adaptation *vis-à-vis* changed environmental conditions, either ideological preference loses its theoretical significance. Distinction must be made between an ideology (willful value position concerning what *ought to be* a personal or societal goal) and a theory (a system of interrelated generalisable propositions that describe and explain *what is*). Of course, the prevailing ideologies of individual strangers are likely to influence their adaptation process as a factor for their adaptative motivation (as was explained in Chapter 6). The present theory helps clarify that, when viewed from the systems perspective, the question of whether assimilation (or ethnicity) is good or bad, functional or dysfunctional, useful or not, must be answered based not on *how it feels* so much as on *how it serves* a system's (individual, societal) adaptive ends. Such adaptive ends are ultimately in the domain of individual and societal decision, not of the theory.

3. Cross-cultural adaptation is both challenging and rewarding

The theory, based on the systems perspective and its principles, argues that all stranger–host interaction occurs through communication, and that it is through communication activities that individuals adapt to their host environment. In this process, individuals undergo internal transformation through the dynamic interplay of stress–adaptation–growth in the direction of greater functional fitness, psychological health and intercultural identity.

The theory, thus, argues that stressful experiences of cross-cultural adaptation need not be regarded only as 'problems' to be avoided or minimised, as they have been in many previous approaches, but as a phenomenon naturally occurring in all situations of change to which individuals must adapt. Stress, as such, is an essential and integral part of the dynamics that helps 'mobilise' individuals for adaptive change and growth beyond the parameters of the original culture. Further, the theory suggests that stressful experiences are most intense in the initial phase of the adaptation process, and that, as strangers become increasing functional in the host environment, their cross-cultural stress will be eased.

4. Individuals' adaptation potential can be assessed prior to migration

The theory identifies a number of factors that will help future strangers assess their adaptive potential in a given host society by asking themselves questions such as: How similar or compatible are my cultural patterns to those of the host culture? Is my home country in a friendly relationship with the host country? How does my cultural and racial (physical) background 'fare' in the minds of the host nationals at large? How well am I prepared for the move psychologically and informationally? How old and how educated am

I? Do I have prior overseas experience? Am I moving from a cosmopolitan environment to a similarly cosmopolitan environment?

These predispositional factors can be seriously taken into account in estimating the enormity of challenges individual strangers are likely to face once they move to the host culture. For immigrants, such factors may be considered in selecting a country to which they plan to migrate or in deciding whether they should be taking the risk of a potentially strenuous start in the host society. In addition, understanding these predispositional factors helps individuals identify ways to prepare themselves for a smoother adaptation in the host society. They may, for instance, study the 'culture at a distance' and familiarise themselves with the host communication systems, particularly its language.

In addition, strangers may take into consideration the personality factors — openness and resilience — identified in the present theory as crucial to adaptation. Related to these factors are such characteristics as gregariousness, non-defensiveness, relaxedness, flexibility, tolerance for ambiguity, persistence, self-confidence and affirmative orientation toward self and others in general. Someone who is intolerant of uncertainty and difficulty, shy, closed-minded, and hypersensitive is likely to have greater difficulty in withstanding the challenges of cross-cultural adaptation, and, therefore, may attempt to improve on their own psychological orientations. Strangers may further consider that the difficulties they encounter are at least partly their own responsibilities to manage rather than placing the 'blame' exclusively on others and the host society.

5. Host communication competence is essentially to cross-cultural adaptation

Once strangers set foot in the host society, the subsequent adaptation process starts moving forward. In the present theory, a centrally critical factor in this process is viewed as the strangers' host communication competence. To facilitate adaptation, then, strangers need to develop their ability to communicate effectively and efficiently according to the systems of language, non-verbal behavior, and communication rules prevalent in the host society. They also need to equip themselves with a set of affective orientations, particularly a strong willingness to participate in the host environment, an accepting and affirmative attitude toward themselves and the environment, and a serious appreciation for the emotional and aesthetic sensibilities of the natives. In addition, strangers need to cultivate a sufficient repertoire of behavioral skills to prepare themselves to perform successfully in various social encounters with host nationals.

Host language competence, in particular, has been pointed out as a primary instrument for strangers in promoting their social power and credibility, and its lack an individual deprivation. A person speaks not only to be understood but also to be believed, respected and distinguished. Hence the full benefit of acquiring host language competence is to gain access to the right of the fuller benefit that native speakers enjoy. Exceptions to this observation can be found if the language minority becomes large and powerful enough to claim special language rights, ranging from local tolerance for limited purposes to universal and equal status for all purposes under the jurisdiction of the state. Afrikaans in Africa, Flemish in Belgium, French in Canada, and more recently, Basque and Catalan in Spain are examples of languages whose speakers have obtained official status within bilingual states (Mackey, 1979). Except for these special circumstances of multilingual nations, strangers' acquisition of the host language is critical to their becoming functional and to gaining fuller opportunity for participation in the host society.

Indeed, one cannot over-emphasise the paramount importance of developing host communication competence, should adaptation be an important goal. Being able to communicate well means being able to understand and experience the people, events and issues that are taking place in the host society, to manage life activities with proficiency, and to increase the chances to meet various social needs successfully.

6. Participation in the interpersonal communication and mass communication processes of the host society facilitates cross-cultural adaptation

Along with developing host communication competence, strangers may attempt to to maximise their social participation by developing interpersonal relationships with host nationals and utilising the mass communication channels of the host society. More-than-casual encounters with host nationals provide strangers with important feedback — approval or rejection — mirrored in the faces, gestures, words and silences of host nationals. Although it is easy to misinterpret such reactions, they provide some commentary on the stranger's efforts at successive approximation.

In a sense, serious strangers can be considered as conducting continuous experiments in which they try in various attempts to check their host communication competence, and make further attempts to make it more successful. Through active communication participation, they learn to communicate better — just as one learns to swim better by actually being in the water and swimming. Arrangements such as enrolling in an academic program of a local university would provide intensive interpersonal contact situations that will offer a challenging environment for strangers to cultivate their host communication competence. What is critical to the success of this trial-and-error process of developing host communication competence is that strangers see the process instructively as a learning process rather than defensively. Failures, when they are not devastating, are often far more informative than successes.

7. **If the host society pursues the goal of maintaining and reinforcing its cultural coherence and integrity, it is in its interest to provide opportunities for strangers to participate in its communication processes**

As described in the present theory, the process of adaptation is an interactive process of 'push and pull' between individual strangers and the host environment. In this partnership, the host society needs to do what it can to facilitate the adaptation of strangers, particularly to promote the overall public receptiveness toward strangers, making them feel welcomed and encouraged to become an active part of the society.

Every person whom strangers encounter in the course of daily life activities contributes to the process of adaptation in some way. Through openness and receptivity, the natives can express their acceptance and support for strangers, motivate them to acquire host communication competence, and encourage them to participate in the development of supportive interpersonal relationships with the natives. The natives must realise that it is in the collective interest of the host society, and thus of themselves, to accept strangers as fellow members of the society and as unique opportunities for them to understand people in general, rather than to regard them as 'foreigners'. Without genuine acceptance of and regard for strangers, the natives are likely to send out subtle, non-verbal messages of apathy and denial, if not of outright aloofness, hostility, or apathy. These negative messages can be a serious source of discouragement to immigrants already experiencing a great deal of stress in trying to overcome their communication barriers. In some cases, such negative cues may trigger an extreme defensiveness and hostility in strangers that further reinforces their inclination to be defensive of their own backgrounds and hostile to the host society.

Not only will an affirmative milieu enhance the supportive communication climate providing strangers with a needed environmental 'pull', it will affect the host nationals as well. As host nationals encounter individuals from varied cultural backgrounds, they will also have opportunities to develop their own competence to communicate, only this time, interculturally. Through such opportunities, they are able to increase their understanding of different cultural patterns and human conditions.

Experiences of dealing with differences potentially challenge their ordinary, culturally-limited internal conditions and facilitate their growth beyond their own cultural parameters — just as strangers become increasingly intercultural through their communication experiences in the host society.

As such, the host society benefits from recognising the potential value of educating its citizens in the concept of intercultural communication. Recognising the need for its citizens to be able to manage and relate effectively across cultural differences, the host society may design policies to help minimise prejudices and ethnocentrism and maximise the awareness, attitude, and skill to communicate effectively interculturally. Two of the most powerful means for achieving this goal are education and mass media communication. These two institutions are potentially the most effective agents available to carry out a task of projecting and cultivating a new direction of public character formation. By utilising the educational and mass media systems, the host society can help its citizens and their children to replace existing national, racial, ethnic and territorial biases and replace them with ways of thinking that are more adaptive to the closely-knit intercultural reality.

The issue, then, is not necessarily one of assimilating immigrants into an already established culture and people, but rather one of trying to develop, in conjunction with strangers, a diverse and yet integrated society. The task of the host society should not be to 'eliminate' differences that strangers bring because it is realistically not possible, but instead to accept them and encourage them to develop necessary host communication competence. At the same time, it should facilitate among the natives the intercultural awareness, attitudes, and skills to deal with cultural differences effectively. As both strangers and host nationals are better able to communicate with each other, the host society will see an increased common base for social integration and integrity.

The host society can actively encourage strangers' adaptation through specific educational and training programs. Such programs' primary objectives need to be focused on improving host communication competence, particularly language competence, as the present theory suggests. Traditionally in the United States, teachers of English-as-a-second-language (ESL) have concerned themselves exclusively with linguistic questions such as grammar, pedagogical problems, and correct usage of English. Recently, more ESL teachers have recognised the significance of adding the training of broader aspects of host communication competence including the teaching of host cultural rules, aesthetic orientations and history.

A good example of a comprehensive training program that a host society may offer to strangers to facilitate their host communication competence has been offered by the Bureau for Refugee Programs of the United States Department of State (U. S. Committee for Refugees, 1984:34–35). The program consists of such components as ESL, cultural orientation, and Pre-Employment Training, designed specifically for the Southeast Asian refugees in refugee camps as well as the refugees in the United States since 1976. The ESL curriculum in this program provides not only English instruction but also emphasises listening and speaking conversational skills. The curriculum is organised around topics such as housing, clothing, food, health, transportation, employment and banking, thus providing refugees with information about the American society.

The cross-cultural adaptation processes of strangers are indeed a co-operative effort between the strangers themselves and the host society. At the heart of this interactive process lies various communication activities linked together into an inseparable network of adaptation. The importance of communication clearly lies in its role to make the adaptation network operate smoothly to maximise benefits for all. Acquisition of communication competence by strangers is instrumental to all other aspects of their functioning in the host society. It is equally instrumental to the host society as well if it is to effectively accommodate diverse elements and maintain its necessary unity and strength. As long as common channels of communication remain strong, consensus and patterns of concerted action will persist in the host society. As Mendelsohn (1964) stated, communication makes it possible to bring divergent ethnic groups into one cohesive social organisation of common ideas and values.

8. The host society benefits from working with ethnic communities to facilitate the initial adaptation of new arrivals

Although prolonged involvement in an ethnic community may ultimately delay the adaptation process, the ethnic community can play a significant adaptation-facilitating function for new strangers in their early stages of adaptation. Ethnic communities possess 'natural' support systems to assist new arrivals in coping with the acute stresses and initial uncertainties and can guide them toward effective adaptation. Particularly, those ethnic individuals who have become successfully adapted in the host society may play the invaluable role of a 'cultural middleman [woman]' or 'liaison' providing the vital linkage between the host society and the new arrivals.

Increasing attention has been given to developing effective

mechanisms for utilising such individuals in delivery of services in ethnic communities. A number of researchers who have participated in studies of various social service programs for immigrants have pointed out the importance of utilising the natural ethnic support system. As Herbert (1980) and Keefe, Padilla & Carlos (1978) pointed out, public and community provisions of physical and mental health services of host societies need to closely link with the existing ethnic support system. Consistent with this view, some innovative mechanisms have been implemented in the United States to rework the patterns of service within and between agencies to include more effective use of ethnic resources combined with native professionals. Cohon (1978, cited in Deusen, 1982), for example, utilised Southeast Asian paraprofessional trainees working under the clinical supervision of a native psychologist in providing mental health services in a special San Francisco area project. The project's emphasis on linking native professional and ethnic paraprofessional personnel was proven to be useful in crisis prevention in the community.

The emphasis on combined ethnic–host team social service delivery recognises the interactive nature of the process of cross-cultural adaptation. A bond cannot be one-sided because one-sided communication is dysfunctional to the eventual adaptation of strangers. Although much of the adaptation task must be carried out by the immigrants themselves, their efforts alone cannot be fully effective unless the host environment participates in the process with receptivity and acceptance. The social and cultural integration of strangers into the mainstream must be a conscious and visible part of the philosophy of the host society. The merging of ethnic and host team social service delivery is an approach that is sensitive to the cultural and communication barriers of the strangers, as well as facilitative of their adaptation and integration.

9. In time, strangers will become increasingly proficient in managing their life activities in the host society

As the present theory postulates, most strangers, although at different rates, will become increasingly capable of functioning effectively in the host environment. A small proportion of strangers may give up their will to adapt and return to their home country prematurely, or may be subject to severe mental illnesses, being unable to cope with the challenges of cross-cultural adaptation. Yet most strangers will adapt, and have adapted, according to the systems principles explained in the present theory, and knowing this should serve as a guiding thought for them to 'embrace' at least some of their short-term stresses with willingness and resolve. Commitment to this notion is based on not blind faith but a 'foresight' understanding of fundamental nature of human systems and their evolution in the face of environmental change. Right at this moment, numerous individuals in virtually every part of the world, even those under hardships, are demonstrating that they are managing to survive and make their new milieu a home.

Relatedly, the present theory suggests that, to resist change by avoiding the accompanying stress would be like the fly who likes the sweetness of honey but not its stickiness. To be tested is often good for the individual system and the challenged life projects its light further and farther into the future. Strangers who are strangers by choice may place their stress reactions into the principle of the stress–adaptation–growth dynamics offered in the present theory. By doing so, they may develop an orientation that simultaneously accommodates contradiction and reconciliation, conflict and synthesis, the old and the new.

This understanding carries with it an awakening of hope, and thereby reinforces the emotional strength of strangers who may find their cross-cultural situation overwhelming at times. As much as their experiences present serious symptoms of culture shock, including even physical illnesses, it helps to 'know' that such reactions are temporary if accepted and managed, and that, in the end, they will come out with a regained sense of control and efficacy. It further helps to realise that, to this end, strangers need to continue to develop their host communication competence and actively participate in the social processes of the host society. In time, the acuteness of their stressful experiences will be eased and the opportunities for fulfilling their aspirations will grow.

10. Adaptation comes most naturally when strangers stop 'fighting' and remain open and relaxed instead

Whether it be the Vietnamese refugees in France or a British missionary in Ghana, most strangers manage to cope with the uncertainties and difficulties of dealing with the host environment. Among those who are particularly successful, however, special personal qualities are observed. In the present theory, two basic personality traits — openness and resilience — have been identified as the essential ingredients of individual personality that help 'make' adaptation experiences smoother and less troublesome.

Openness and resilience, we have noted, are manifested in many specific ways — particularly in an affirmative outlook on life, self and people in general. Individuals with openness and resilience are fully engaged in the present moment with an inner posture of being ready to cease to 'fight' for or against the process of change, and are willing to 'let go' some of the existing inner conditions, with an understanding perhaps that 'pain', and the effort to be separate from pain, are in essence the same thing. This psychological orientation of letting-go, in turn, strengthens the resilience of an individual, just as in the situation in which we sink when we try to stay on the surface of the water, but float when we let our body go. Instead of resisting, resilient individuals 'ride with' what comes their way with a spirit of exploration. Temporarily, they are able to suspend their preconceived notions about the way things ought to be, and thus are able to experience the sight, sound, smell and rhythm of the place as if for the first time. This psychological posture understands that our mind has the power of 'give' and can absorb so much, and that 'giving away' to change is not at all the same as 'running way' from the present, denying the past, or clinging to the present.

The story of Mohm, a young Cambodian girl, told by Gail Sheehy in *Spirit of Survival* (1986), adds concrete reality to what has been discussed above. Mohm had lived through the genocidal regime of Pol Pot. Her entire family, with the possible exception of a brother, was wiped out. She arrived in the United States as a refugee at the age of 12 and became the author's daughter. Although her tribulations were staggering, her story offers a lesson that the human spirit has resources to prevail over tremendous adversity, to heal itself, and to emerge strengthened. A series of events had taken place leading to the moment of Mohm's healing when her past was finally put in her mind's resting place, and when she was able to affirm herself and her new world for the first time.

As such, adaptive individuals find sooner or later that, in the most frustrating moments of change arises new awareness and growth. The darker the frustration, the more shining the realisation of the opening of 'the third eye' with a newly emerging formation of self that transcends both old and new contingencies, and deeper and more acute sensibilities for understanding and participating in the ever-changing experiences of life.

Indeed, the history of the world presents us with ample cases of successful immigrants and sojourners who have demonstrated extraordinary openness and resilience. They have also shown us that their experiences of going through many adaptive challenges bring about a special privilege and freedom — to think, feel, and behave beyond the parameters of any single culture and beyond the 'either–or' way of categorisation. From this angle is revealed an understanding of 'both–and' and an increased depth to participate in the aesthetic and emotional experiences of people around them.

The cross-cultural adaptation of strangers examined through the present theory reminds us all of an extraordinary human capacity to incorporate varied, new elements of life and form a new identity. In this understanding, our strength lies no longer in rigidly insisting on who we were in the past and who we are at the moment, but in affirming what we may yet become and in committing our 'uncommitted potentiality for change' (Bateson, 1951/1972:497). In moments of inner calm, our victorious personality may spring forward accompanying altered perceptions and flashes of creative insights, and help us reinvent ourselves toward inter-cultural evolution. And such evolution may just be what all of us need in the years ahead.

BIBLIOGRAPHY

ABADAN-UNAT, NERMIN (1977, Spring). Implications of migration on emancipation of Turkish women. *International Migration Review* 11(1), 31–57.

ABBINK, J. (1984, October). The changing identity of Ethiopian immigrants (Falashas) in Israel. *Anthropological Quarterly* 57(4), 139–53.

ABOUD, FRANCES E. (1976, September). Self-evaluation, information seeking strategies for interethnic social comparisons. *Journal of Cross-cultural Psychology*, 7(3), 289–300.

——(1984, March). The development of ethnic attitudes. *Journal of Cross-cultural Psychology*, 15(1), 3–34.

ABRAM, H. S. (ed.) (1970). *Psychological Aspects of Stress*. Springfield, IL: Charles C. Thomas.

ADAMS, B. (1971). *The American Family: A Sociological Interpretation*. Chicago: Markham.

ADAMS, B. & WEIRATH, T. (1971). *Readings on the Sociology of the Family*. Chicago: Markham.

ADAMS, ROMANZO (1937/1969). *Interracial Marriage in Hawaii*. New York: Macmillan.

ADLER, N. (1981, September). Reentry: Managing cross-cultural transitions. *Groups and Organizational Studies*, 6(3), 341–56.

ADLER, PETER S. (1972/1987). Culture shock and the cross-cultural learning experience. In LOUISE F. LUCE & ELISE C. SMITH (eds), *Toward Internationalism*. Cambridge, MA: Newbury, 24–35.

——(1975, Fall). The transition experience: An alternative view of culture shock. *Journal of Humanistic Psychology*, 15(4), 13–23.

——(1976). Beyond cultural identity: Reflections on cultural and multicultural man. In L. A. SAMOVAR & R. E. PORTER (eds), *Intercultural Communication: A Reader*. Belmont, CA: Wadsworth, 389–408.

——(1982). Beyond cultural identity: Reflections on cultural and multicultural man. In LARRY A. SAMOVAR & RICHARD E. PORTER (eds), *Intercultural Communication: A Reader* (3rd ed.). Belmont, CA:

Wadsworth.

AGAR, MICHAEL H. (1986). *Speaking of Ethnography*. Beverly Hills, CA: Sage.

AITKEN, THOMAS (1973). *The Multinational Man: The Role of the Manager Abroad*. New York: Wiley.

ALBA, RICHARD D. (1976, December). Social assimilation among American Catholic national origin groups. *American Sociological Review* 41(6), 1030–46.

——(1978, Spring). Ethnic networks and tolerant attitudes. *Public Opinion Quarterly* 42(1), 1–16.

ALBA, RICHARD D. & CHAMLIN, MITCHELL B. (1983). A preliminary examination of ethnic identification among whites. *American Sociological Review*, 48(2), 240–7.

ALBRECHT, TERRANCE L. & ADELMAN, MARA B. (1984, Fall). Social support and life stress: New directions for communication research. *Human Communication Research*, 11(1), 3–32.

——(eds). (1987). *Communicating Social Support*. Newbury Park, CA: Sage.

ALDERFER, C. (1967). Convergent and discriminant validation of satisfaction and desire measures by interviews and questionnaires. *Journal of Applied Psychology*, 51, 509–20.

AL-KHEDAIRE, KHEDAIR SAUD (1978, August). Cultural perception and attitudinal differences among Saudi Arabian male college students in the United States. *Dissertation Abstracts International*, 39, #7813906, 1–296.

ALLEN, CAROL & LAMBERT, W. E. (1972). Ethnic identification and personality adjustments of Canadian adolescents of mixed English–French parentage. In J. W. BERRY & G. J. S. WILDE (eds), *Social Psychology: The Canadian Context*, Toronto: McClelland and Stewart, 173–92.

ALLEN, RICHARD (1981, February). Influence of life events on psychosocial functioning. *Journal of Social Psychology*, 113, 95–100.

ALLERS, RUDOLF (1973). Psychogenic disturbances in a linguistically strange environment. In CHARLES ZWINGMANN & MARIA PFISTER-AMMENDE (eds), *Uprooting and after . . . .* New York: Springer-Verlag, 50–1.

ALLPORT, GORDON W. (1955). *Becoming: Basic Consideration for a Psychology of Personality*. New Haven, CT: Yale University Press.

ALTMAN, IRWIN & CHEMER, M. M. (1980). Cultural aspects of environment-behavior relationship. In H. C. TRIANDIS & R. W. BRISLIN (eds), *Handbook of Cross-cultural Psychology: Social Psychology* vol. 5, Boston: Allyn & Bacon, 335–93.

ALTMAN, IRWIN & TAYLOR, DALMAS (1973). *Social Penetration: The Develop-*

ment of Interpersonal Relationships. New York: Holt, Rinehart & Winston.

AMARANTO, ERNESTO A. (1978). *Mental Health Study of Filipino Immigrants in the New York Metropolitan Area.* (Report No. 13). Scholar-in-residence Program, Asian American Mental Health Research Center.

AMATO, PAUL R. & COOK, JAMES (1981). Urban-rural differences in helping: Behavior in Australia and the United States. *Journal of Social Psychology*, Queensland, Australia: University of North.

AMERSFOORT, HANS VAN (1972/1984). *Immigration and the Formation of Minority Groups: The Dutch Experience 1945–1975.* (ROBERT LYNG, Trans.). New York: Cambridge University Press.

AMIR, YEHUDA (1969, May). Contact hypothesis in ethnic relations. *Psychological Bulletin*, 7(5), 319–42.

AMIR, YEHUDA & CHANA, GARTI (1977, Summer). Personal influence on attitude change following ethnic contact. *International Journal of Intercultural Relations*, 1(2), 58–75.

AN, ROSARIO (1979). *Korean immigrants in Atlanta.* (Report No. 12). Scholar-in-residence Program. Asian American Mental Health Research Center.

ANDERSON, C. A. (1975). Equality of opportunity in a pluralistic society. *International Review*, 21(3), 287–300.

ANDERSON, GRACE M. & CHRISTIE, T. LAIRD (1978, Fall). Ethnic networks: North American perspectives. *Connections*, 2(1), 25–34.

ANDERSON, KURT (1985, July 8). New York: Final destination. *Time*, 43–6.

ANDERSON, N. & BUTZIN, C. (1974). Performance = motivation × ability. *Journal of Personality and Social Psychology*, 30(5), 598–604.

ANGYAL, A. (1956). A theoretical model for personality studies. In C. E. MOUSTAKAS (ed.), *The Self.* New York: Harper & Brothers.

ANTUNES, G. & GAITZ, C. (1975). Ethnicity and participation: A study of Mexican-Americans, Blacks, and Whites. *American Journal of Sociology*, 80(5), 1192–9.

APPLEGATE, JAMES L. (1981). *The Implicit Cultural Communication Theories on Social Cognitive and Communication Development: A Constructivist Analysis.* University of Kentucky.

APPLEGATE, JAMES L. & LEICHTY, GREGORY B. (1984). Managing interpersonal relationships: Social cognitive and strategic determinants of competence. In ROBERT N. BOSTROM (ed.), *Competence in Communication: A Multidisciplinary Approach.* Beverly Hills, CA: Sage, 33–55.

APPLEGATE, JAMES L. & SYPHER, HOWARD E. (1988). A constructivist theory of communication and culture. In YOUNG YUN KIM & WILLIAM B. GUDYKUNST (eds), *Theories of Intercultural Communication.* Newbury

Park, CA: Sage.

ARANALDE, M. D., KURTINE, W., SCOPETTA, M. & SZAPOCZNIK, J. (eds) (1978). Theory and measurement of acculturation. *InterAmerican Journal of Psychology*, 12(2), 113–30.

ARGYLE, MICHAEL (1982). Inter-cultural communication. In STEPHEN BOCHNER (ed.), *Cultures in Contact: Studies in Cross-cultural Communication*. New York: Pergamon.

ARNBERG, LENORE (1987). *Raising Children Bilingually: The Pre-school Years*. Clevedon, England: Multilingual Matters.

ARRENDONDO-HOLDEN, JOSEPHINE (1979, May). La Salud Mental De La Raza: Curanderas and mental health centers in two Mexican-American communities. *Dissertation Abstracts International*, 39, 11-B, 5532–3.

ASHTON, G. (1972). The differential adaptation of two slum subcultures to a Colombian housing project. *Urban Anthropology*, 1(2), 176–94.

ASTHANA, H. S. (1974, March). A procedure for achieving equivalence of communication in cross-cultural research. *Journal of Social and Economic Studies*, 2(1), 87–94.

ASTROFF, ROBERTA (1985). Language and power in multilingual societies: A cultural studies approach. Paper presented at the annual meeting of the International Communication Association Annual Conference, Honolulu, HI.

ATKENSON, P. (1970). Building communication in intercultural marriage. *Psychiatry*, 33, 396–408.

AUSTIN, CLYDE N. (ed.) (1986). *Cross-cultural Reentry: A Book of Readings*. Abilene, TX: Abilene Christian University.

BACK, ROBERT L., GORDON, LINDA W., HAINES, DAVID W. & HOWELL, DAVID R. (1984). Geographic variations in the economic adjustment of Southeast Asian refugees in the United States. In U.S. Committee for Refugees, *World Refugee Report*, 7–8.

BAGLEY, CHRISTOPHER (1971, October). Mental illness in immigrant minorities in London. *Journal of Biosocial Science*, 3, 449–59.

——(1971, Spring). Immigrant minorities in the Netherlands: Integration and assimilation. *International Migration Review*, 5, 18–35.

——(1979). Self-esteem as a pivotal concept in race and ethnic relations. In CORA BAGLEY MARRETT and CHERYL LEGGON (eds), *Research in Race and Ethnic Relations* vol. 1. Greenwich, CT: Jai Press, 127–67.

BAKER, REGINALD P. & NORTH, DAVID S. (1984). *The 1975 Refugees: Their First Five Years in America*. Washington, DC: Center for Labor and Migration Studies.

BALDASSINI, JOSE G. & FLAHERTY, VINCENT F. (1982). Acculturation process of Colombian immigrants into the American culture in Bergen County,

New Jersey. *International Journal of Intercultural Relations*, 6(2), 127–35.

BANCROFT, GEORGE W. (1975). Teacher education for the multicultural reality. In AARON WOLFGANG (ed.), *Education of Immigrant Students: Issues and Answers*. Toronto: Ontario Institute for Studies in Education, 164–83.

BANTON, MICHAEL (1961). The restructuring of social relationships. In A. W. SOUTHALL (ed.), *Social Change in Modern Africa*. London: Oxford University Press, 113–25.

BARNA, LeRAY M. (1976). How culture shock affects communication. *Communication Journal of the Communication Association of the Pacific*, 4(23), Honolulu, HI: University of Hawaii Press.

——(1983). The stress factor in intercultural relations. In DAN LANDIS & RICHARD W. BRISLIN (eds), *Handbook for Intercultural Training: Issues in Training Methodology* vol. 11. New York: Pergamon, 19–49.

BARNETT, L. D. (1963). Research on international and interracial marriages. *Marriage and Family Living*, 25(1), 105–7.

BARNLUND, DEAN C. & NOMURA, NAOKI (1985). Decentering, convergence, and cross-cultural understanding. In LARRY A. SAMOVAR & RICHARD E. PORTER (eds), *Intercultural Communication: A Reader* 4th ed. Belmont, CA: Wadsworth, 347–66.

BAR-YOSEF, R. W. (1968). Desocialization and resocialization: The adjustment process of immigrants. *International Migration Review*, 2, 27–42.

BATES, BENJAMIN J. (1984, May). Conceptualizing the information society: The search for a definition of social attributes. Paper presented at the annual meeting of the International Communication Association, San Francisco, CA.

BATESON, GREGORY (1951/1972). Communication and human relations: An interdisciplinary approach. In JURGEN RUESCH & GREGORY BATESON (eds), *Communication: The Social Matrix of Psychiatry*. New York: W. W. Norton, 21–49.

——(1972). *Steps to an Ecology of Mind*. New York: Ballantine.

BATY, R. M. & DOLD, E. (1977, Spring). Cross-cultural homestays: An analysis of college students responses after living in an unfamiliar culture. *International Journal of Intercultural Relations*, 1(1), 62–76.

BEARDSMORE, HUGO BAETENS (1986). *Bilingualism: Basic Principles* (2nd ed.). Clevedon, England: Multilingual Matters.

BECK, CLIVE (1975). Is immigrant education only for immigrants? In AARON WOLFGANG (ed.), *Education of Immigrant Students: Issues and Answers*. Toronto: Ontario Institute for Studies in Education, 5–18.

BECKER, T. (1968). Patterns of attitudinal changes among foreign students. *American Journal of Sociology*, 73(4), 431–42.

BELLMAN, BERYL L. & JULES-ROSETTE, BENNETTA (1977). *A Paradigm for Looking: Cross-cultural Research with Visual Media*. Norwood, NJ: Ablex.

BENNETT, J. W. (1976). *The Ecological Transition: Cultural Anthropology and Human Adaptation*. New York: Pergamon.

BENNETT, JANET (1977, December). Transition shock: Putting culture shock in perspective. In NEMI JAIN (ed.), *International Intercultural Communication Annual* vol. 4, 45–52.

BENNETT, JANET W., PASSIN, J. & McKNIGHT, R. (1958). *In Search of Identity: Japanese Overseas Scholars in the United States*. Minneapolis: University of Minnesota Press.

BENNETT, SPENCER & BOWERS, DAVID (1976). *An Introduction to Multivariate Techniques for Social and Behavioral Sciences*. New York: John Wiley & Sons.

BENSON, PHILIP G. (1978, Spring). Measuring cross-cultural adjustment: The problem of criteria. *International Journal of Intercultural Relations*, 2(1), 21–37.

BENTLEY, G. CARTER (1981). *Ethnicity and Nationality: A Bibliographic Guide*. Seattle, WA: University of Washington Press.

BERGER, CHARLES R. (1979). Beyond initial interaction: Uncertainty, understanding, and the development of interpersonal relationships. In HOWARD GILES & ROBERT N. ST. CLAIR (eds), *Language and Social Psychology*. Baltimore: University Park Press, 122–44.

BERGER, CHARLES R. & BRADAC, JAMES J. (1982). *Language and Social Knowledge*. London: Edward Arnold.

BERGER, CHARLES R. & CALABRESE, RICHARD (1975). Some explorations in initial interactions and beyond. *Human Communication Research*, 1, 99–112.

BERGER, CHARLES R. & GUDYKUNST, WILLIAM B. (in press). Uncertainty and communication. Prepared for B. DERVIN (ed.), *Progress in Communication Sciences*. Norwood, NJ: Ablex.

BERGER, CHARLES R. & KELLNER, H. (1970). Marriage and construction of reality. In H. DREITZEL (ed.), *Recent Sociology, No. 2: Patterns of Communication Behavior*. New York: Macmillan.

BERGER, MONROE, THEODORE, ABEL & PAGE, CHARLES H. (eds) (1954). *Freedom and Control in Modern Society*. New York: Macmillan.

BERGER, PETER L. & LUCKMANN, THOMAS (1967). *The Social Construction of Reality: A Treatise in the Sociology of Knowledge*. Garden City, NY: Anchor Books.

BERGER, W. K. (1977, August). Culture change and psychological adjustment. *American Ethnologist*, 4(3), 471–95.

BERGHAHN, MARION (1984). *German-Jewish Refugees in England*. New

York: St. Martins.

BERRY, JOHN W. (1970). Marginality, stress & ethnic identification in an acculturated aboriginal community. *Journal of Cross-cultural Psychology*, 1, 239–52.

——(1972). Psychological research in the north. In JOHN W. BERRY and G. J. S. WILDE (eds), *Social Psychology: The Canadian Context*. Toronto: McClelland and Stewart Limited, 230–43.

——(1975). Ecology, cultural adaptation, and psychological differentiation: Traditional patterning and acculturative stress. In RICHARD W. BRISLIN, STEPHEN BOCHNER & W. L. LONNER (eds), *Cross-cultural Perspectives on Learning*. New York: Sage, 207–28.

——(1976). *Human Ecology and Cognitive Style: Comparative Studies in Cultural and Psychological Adaptation*. New York: Halstead Press.

——(1980). Acculturation as varieties of adaptation. In AMADO M. PADILLA (ed.), *Acculturation: Theory, Models and Some New Findings*. Washington, DC: Westview Press, 9–25.

——(1984). Cultural relations in plural societies: Alternatives to segregation and their sociopsychological implications. In NORMAN MILLER & MARILYNN B. BREWER (eds), *Groups in Contact: The Psychology of Desegregation*. New York: Academic Press, 11–27.

BERRY, JOHN W. & ANNIS, R. C. (1974, December). Acculturative stress: The role of ecology, culture, and differentiation. *Journal of Cross-cultural Psychology*, 5(4), 382–406.

BERRY, JOHN W., KALIN, RUDOLF & TAYLOR, DONALD M. (1976). *Multiculturalism and Ethnic Attitudes in Canada*. Ottawa, Canada: Minister of State for Multiculturalism.

BERRY, JOHN W. & KALIN, R. (1979, Spring). Reciprocity of inter-ethnic attitudes in a multicultural society. *International Journal of Intercultural Relations*, 3(1), 99–112.

BERRY, JOHN W., KIM, UICHOL & BOSKI, PAWEL (1987). Psychological acculturation of immigrants. In YOUNG YUN KIM & WILLIAM B. GUDYKUNST (eds), *Cross-cultural Adaptation: Current Theory and Research*. Newbury Park, CA: Sage.

BERRY, JOHN W., TRIMBLE, JOSEPH E. & OLMEDO, ESTEBAN L. (1986). Assessment of acculturation. In WALTER J. LONNER & JOHN W. BERRY (eds), *Field Methods in Cross-cultural Research*. Newbury Park, CA: Sage, 291–324.

BERTALANFFY, LUDWIG VON (1956). General systems theory. *General Systems*, 1, 1–2.

——(1967). *Robots, Men, and Minds*. New York: Braziller.

BESHERS, JAMES M. & LAUMAN, E. O. (1967). Social distance: A network approach. *American Sociological Review*, 32, 225–36.

BHARATI, AGEHANANDA (1972). *The Asians in East Africa*. Chicago: Nelson-Hall.

BIEGEL, DAVID E., McCARDLE, ELLEN & MENDELSON, SUSAN (1985). *Social Networks and Mental Health: An Annotated Bibliography*. Beverly Hills, CA: Sage.

BLALOCK, HUBERT M., Jr. (1969). *Theory Construction: From Verbal to Mathematical Formulations*. Englewood Cliffs, NJ: Prentice-Hall.

——(1982). *Race and Ethnic Relations*. Englewood Cliffs, NJ: Prentice-Hall.

——(1984). *Basic Dilemmas in the Social Sciences*. Beverly Hills, CA: Sage.

BLAU, PETER M. & SCHWARTZ, JOSEPH E. (1984). *Crosscutting Social Circles*. Orlando, FL: Academic.

BLAU, P. M. (1970, May). A theory of social integration. *The American Journal of Sociology*, 65(6), 545–56.

BLOCK, HARRIET (1976, January). Changing domestic roles among Polish immigrant women. *Anthropological Quarterly*, 49(1), 3–10.

BLOOM, B. S. (1966). *Stability and Changes in Human Characteristics*. New York: Wiley.

BOCHNER, STEPHEN (1973). The mediating man and cultural diversity. In RICHARD BRISLIN (ed.), *Topics in Culture Learning* vol. 3. Honolulu, HI: East-West Center, 23–7.

——(1977). Friendship patterns of overseas students: A functional model. *International Journal of Psychology*, 12(4), 277–94.

——(ed.), (1982). *Cultures in Contact: Studies in Cross-cultural Interaction*. New York: Pergamon.

——(1986). Observational methods. In WALTER J. LONNER & JOHN W. BERRY (eds), *Field Methods in Cross-cultural Research*. Newbury Park, CA: Sage, 165–201.

BOCHNER, STEPHEN & WICKS, P. (eds). (1972). *Overseas Students in Australia*. Sydney, Australia: University of New South Wales Press.

BOND, MICHAEL H. & YANG, K. (1982, June). Ethnic affirmation versus cross-cultural accommodation. *Journal of Cross-cultural Psychology*, 13(2), 169–85.

BOND, MICHAEL H. & CHEUNG, M. K. (1984). Experimental language choice and ethnic affirmation by Chinese trilinguals in Hong Kong. *International Journal of Intercultural Relations*, 8(4), 347–56.

BONNHEIM, MALCOLM (1978, June). Family interaction and acculturation among Mexican-American inhalant users. (Doctoral dissertation, University of Texas). *Dissertation Abstracts International*, 38, 12-B, 6136.

BOSCH, JAMES (1966). Measurement of acculturation level in the Guttman scale. (Doctoral dissertation, Stanford University). *Dissertation Univ-*

versity Microfilms, Ann Arbor, MI.

BOULDING, K. E. (1956/1977). *The Image: Knowledge in Life and Society*. Ann Arbor: The University of Michigan.

BOURDIEU, P. (1979). The economics of linguistic exchanges. *Social Science Information*, 16(6).

BOURHIS, RICHARD Y. (1979). Language in ethnic interaction: A social psychological approach. In HOWARD GILES & B. SAINT-JACQUES (eds), *Language and Ethnic Relations*. New York: Pergamon, 117–42.

BOURHIS, RICHARD Y., GILES, HOWARD, LEYENS, JACQUES P. & TAJFEL, HENRI (1979). Psychological distinctiveness: Language divergence in Belgium. In HOWARD GILES & ROBERT N. ST. CLAIR (eds), *Language and Social Psychology*. Baltimore, MD: University Park Press, 158–85.

BOUSCAREN, ANTHONY T. (1963). *International Migrations Since 1945*. New York: Frederick A. Praeger.

BRADBURN, N. (1969). *The Structure of Psychological Wellbeing*. Chicago: Aldine.

BRAND, E. S., RUIZ, R. A. & PADILLA, A. M. (1974). Ethnic identification and preference: A review. *Psychological Bulletin*, 81(11), 860–90.

BREED, W. (1958, December). Mass communication and socio-cultural integration. *Social Forces*, 37(2), 109–16.

BREIN, MICHAEL & DAVID, KENNETH H. (1971). Intercultural communication and the adjustment of the sojourner. *Psychological Bulletin*, 76(3), 215–30.

BRENT, S. (1978). Individual specialization, collective adaptation and rate of environmental change. *Human Development*, 21(1), 21–33.

BRETON, RAYMOND (1964). Institutional completeness of ethnic communities and the personal relations of immigrants. *American Journal of Sociology*, 70(2), 193–205.

——(1979). Ethnic stratification viewed from three theoretical perspectives. In JAMES CURTIS & WILLIAM SCOTT (eds), *Social Stratifications: Canada* 2nd ed., Scarborough, Ontario: Prentice-Hall, 270–94.

BREWER, MARILYNN B. (1979). The role of ethnocentrism in intergroup conflict. In WILLIAM G. AUSTIN & STEPHEN WORCHEL (eds), *The Social Psychology of Intergroup Relations*. Monterey, CA: Brooks/Cole, 71–84.

BREWER, MARILYNN B. & CAMPBELL, DONALD T. (1976). *Ethnocentrism and Intergroup Attitudes*. New York: John Wiley & Sons.

BREWER, MARILYNN B. & MILLER, NORMAN (1984). Beyond the contact hypothesis: Theoretical perspectives on desegregation. In NORMAN MILLER & MARILYNN B. BREWER (eds), *Groups in Contact*. Orlando, FL: Academic, 281–302.

BRIGGS, NANCY E. & HARWOOD, GLENN R. (1982). Training personnel in multinational business. *International Journal of Intercultural Relations*, 6(4), 341–54.

BRISLIN, RICHARD W. (ed.). (1976). *Translation: Applications and Research*. New York: John Wiley/Halsted.

——(1981). *Cross-cultural Encounters*. Elmsford, NY: Pergamon.

——(1986). The wording and translation of research instruments. In WALTER J. LONNER & JOHN W. BERRY (eds), *Field Methods in Cross-cultural Research*. Newbury Park, CA: Sage, 137–63.

BRISLIN, RICHARD W., LANDIS, DAN & BRANDT, MARY E. (1983). Conceptualizations of intercultural behavior and training. In DAN LANDIS & RICHARD W. BRISLIN (eds), *Handbook of Intercultural Training* vol. 1. *Issues in Theory and Design*. New York: Pergamon, 1–35.

BRISLIN, RICHARD W., LONNER, W. J. & THORNDIKE, R. M. (1973). *Cross-cultural Research Methods*. New York: John Wiley & Sons.

BRISLIN, RICHARD W. & PEDERSEN, P. (1976). *Cross-cultural Orientation Programs*. New York: Gardner Press.

BRODY, E. B. (1969). Migration and adaptation: The nature of the problem. In E. B. BRODY (ed.), *Behavior in new environments: Adaptation of Migrant Populations*. Beverly Hills, CA: Sage, 13–21.

BRONSON, WANDA C. (1979). Competence and personality. In KEVIN CONNOLLY & JEROME BRUNER (eds), *The Growth of Competence*. New York: Academic Press, 241–64.

BROOM, L. & KITSUSE, J. I. (1955, February). The validation of acculturation: A condition to ethnic assimilation. *American Anthropologist*, 62, 44–8.

BROWER, I. C. (1980). Counseling Vietnamese. *Personal Guidance Journal*, 58(10), 646–52.

BUCHIGNANI, NORMAN (1979). South Asian Canadians and the ethnic mosaic: An overview. *Canadian Ethnic Studies*, 11(1), 48–68.

——(1979, March/April). Immigration, adaptation, and the management of ethnic identity: An examination of Fijian East Indians in British Columbia. (Doctoral dissertation, Simon Fraser University, Canada). *Dissertation Abstracts International*, 39, 7906521.

BUCK, ROSS (1984). *The Communication of Emotion*. New York: The Guilford Press.

BUCKLEY, WALTER (1968). Society as a complex adaptive system. In WALTER BUCKLEY (ed.), *Modern Systems Research for the Behavioral Scientist*. Chicago: Aldine.

BURGESS, M. ELAINE (1978, July). The resurgence of ethnicity: Myth or reality? *Ethnic and Racial Studies*, 1(3), 265–85.

BURKE, KENNETH (1974). Communication and the human condition. In *Communication* vol. 1, United Kingdom: Gordon and Breach Science

Publishers, Ltd, 135–52.

Burke, K. (1935). *Permanence and Change*. New York: The New Republic.

Burns, G. Leonard & Farina, Amerigo (1984). Social competence and adjustment. *Journal of Social and Personal Relationships*, 1(1), 99–113.

Burt, Ronald S. & Schott, Thomas (1985). Relation contents in multiple networks. *Social Science Research*, 14(4), 287–308.

Busch, Ronald J. (1976). Ethnic assimilation versus cultural pluralism: Some political implications. In Daniel E. Weinberg (ed.), *Ethnicity: A Conceptual Approach*. Cleveland, OH: Cleveland Ethnic Heritage Studies, Cleveland State University.

Buxbaum, E. C. (1967). *The Greek-American Group of Tarpon Springs, Florida: A Study of Ethnic Identification and Acculturation*. Unpublished doctoral dissertation, University of Pennsylvania.

Cach, Robert (1979, March/April). Mexican workers in the United States: A study of migration and social change. (Doctoral dissertation, Duke University). *Dissertation Abstracts International*, 39.

Campbell, Donald T. (1964). Distinguishing differences of perception from failures of communication in cross-cultural studies. In F. S. C. Northrup & H. H. Livingston (eds), *Cross-cultural Understanding: Epistemology in Anthropology*. New York: Harper & Row, 308–36.

——(1967). Stereotypes and the perception of group differences. *American Psychologist*, 22(10), 817–29.

——(1974). Qualitative knowing in action research. Kurt Lewin Award Address presented at the annual meeting of the American Psychological Association, New York.

Campbell, Donald T. & LeVine, R. A. (1970). Convergent and discriminant validation by the multitrait–multimethod matrix. *Psychological Bulletin*, 56, 81–105.

Campbell, Donald T. & Stanley, J. C. (1966). *Experimental and Quasi-experimental Designs for Research*. Chicago: Rand McNally.

Campfens, H. (1980, May 13–15). Ethnicity as an organizing principal of social policy and practice in the modern welfare state: Some theoretical observations and international illustrations. In *Symposium Papers: Helping Networks and the Welfare State, Community and State* vol. 2, University of Toronto, 96–128.

Caplan, R. D. (1979). Social support, person-environment fit, and coping. In L. A. Ferman & J. P. Gordus (eds), *Mental Health and the Economy*. Kalamazoo, MI: W.E. Upjohn Institute for Employment Research, 89–137.

Capra, Fritjof (1982). *The Turning Point*. New York: Bantam Books.

Cartwright, Dorwin *et al.* (1971). *Psychological Adjustment: Behavior and the Inner World*. Chicago: Rand McNally.

CATTELL, R. B. (1973). The measurement of the healthy personality and the healthy society. *The Counseling Psychologist*, 4, 13–18.

CHANCE, NORMAN A. (1965, April). Acculturation, self-identification, and personality adjustment. *American Anthropologist*, 67, 373–93.

CHANG, WON H. (1972). *Communication and Acculturation: A Case Study of Korean Ethnic Groups in Los Angeles*. Unpublished doctoral dissertation, University of Iowa.

——(1974). Mass communication and acculturation. Paper presented at the annual meeting of the Association of Education & Journalism, San Diego, CA.

CHOMSKY, NOAM (1972). *Language and Mind*. New York: Harcourt Brace Jovanovich.

CHRISTIE, T. LAIRD (1976). Reserve colonialism and sociocultural change: A case study. Unpublished doctoral dissertation, University of Toronto.

CHURCH, AUSTIN T. (1982). Sojourner adjustment. *Psychological Bulletin*, 91(3), 540–72.

CHURCHMAN, C. WEST (1968). *The Systems Approach*. New York: Dell.

CLEMENT, RICHARD (1980). Ethnicity, contact, and communicative competence in a second language. In HOWARD GILES, W. PETER ROBINSON & PHILIP M. SMITH (eds), *Language: Social Psychological Perspectives*. New York: Pergamon, 147–54.

COCHRAN, RAYMOND (1979). A comparative study of the adjustment of Irish, Indian and Pakistani immigrants to England. *The Mahesh Desai Memorial Lecture: British Psychological Society*.

——(1979, February). Psychological & behavioral disturbances in West Indians, Indians and Pakistanis in Britain. *British Journal of Psychiatry*, 134, 201–10.

COELHO, GEORGE V. (1958). *Changing Images of America: A Study of Indian Students Perceptions*. New York: Free Press.

——(ed.) (1962). Impacts of studying abroad. *Journal of Social Issues*, 18(1).

COELHO, GEORGE V. & ADAMS, JOHN E. (1974). Introduction. In GEORGE V. COELHO, DAVID A. HAMBURG & JOHN E. ADAMS (eds), *Coping and Adaptation*. New York: Basic Books, 15–25.

COHEN, E. (1977). Expatriate communities. *Current Sociology*, 24, 5–133.

COHN, S. & WOOD, R. E. (1982). Peace Corps volunteers and host country nationals: Determinants of variations in social interaction. *The Journal of Developing Areas*, 16(4), 543–60.

COLLETT, P. (1971). Training Englishmen in the non-verbal behaviour of Arabs. *International Journal of Psychology*, 6, 209–15.

COMEAU, L. R. & DRIEDGER, L. (1978). Ethnic opening and closing in an open system: A Canadian example. *Social Forces*, 57(2), 600–20.

CONROY, HILARY & MIYAWAKA, T. SCOTT (eds) (1972). *East across the Pacific: Historical and Sociological Studies of Japanese Immigration and Assimilation*. Santa Barbara, CA: American Bibliographical Center - Clio Press.

COOK, S. W. (1962). The systematic analysis of socially significant events: A strategy for social research. *Journal of Social Issues*, 18(2), 66–84.

COOK, T. D. & CAMPBELL, DONALD T. (1979). *Quasi-experimentation: Design and Analysis for Field Settings*. Chicago: Rand McNally.

COOLEY, C. H. (1909). *Social Organization: A Study of the Larger Mind*. New York: Charles Scribner's Sons, 61.

COOMBS, GARY (1977, February). Opportunities, information networks and the migration-distance relationship. *Social Networks*, 1(3), 257–76.

CORT, D. A. & KING, M. (1979). Some correlates of culture shock among American tourists in Africa. *The Journal of Intercultural Relations*, 3, 211–25.

CRAVEN, PAUL & WELLMAN, BARRY (1973). The network city. *Sociological Inquiry*, 43, 57–88.

CROCKETT, W. (1965). Cognitive complexity and impression formation. In B. A. MAHER (ed.), *Progress in Experimental Personality Research* vol. 1. New York: Academic Press.

CRONEN, VERNON E., CHEN, VICTORIA & PEARCE, W. BARNETT (1988). Coordinated management of meaning: A critical theory. In YOUNG YUN KIM & WILLIAM B. GUDYKUNST (eds), *Theories of Intercultural Communication*. Newbury Park, CA: Sage.

DABROWSKI, KAZIMIERZ (1964). *Positive Disintegration*. Boston: Little, Brown & Co.

——(1968). *Theory of Positive Disintegration*. (Transcription of audio-record of lecture). Big Sur Recordings 1120.

DANCE, FRANK E. & LARSON, CARL E. (1976). *The Function of Human Communication: A Theoretical Approach*. New York: Holt, Rinehart & Winston.

DANSEN, JOHN M. VAN (1982). Health/mental health studies of Indochinese refugees: A critical overview. *Medical Anthropology*, 6(4), 231–52.

DAVID, HENRY P. (1969). Involuntary international migration: Adaptation of refugees. In EUGENE B. BRODY (ed.), *Behavior in New Environments: Adaptation of Migrant Populations*. Beverly Hills, CA: Sage, 73–95.

DAVID, K. (1971). Culture shock and the development of self-awareness. *Journal of Contemporary Psychotherapy*, 4, 44–8.

DEAMICIS, JAN JOSEPH (1977). It just happens: American migration to Australia. Unpublished doctoral dissertation, University of

Massachusetts.

DeCocq, G. A. (1976). European and North American self-help movements: Some contrasts. In A. H. Katz & E. C. Bender (eds), *The Strength in us: Self-help Groups in the Modern World*. New York: New Viewpoint Books, 202–8.

DeFleur, M. L. & Cho, C. S. (1957, January). Assimilation of Japanese-born women in an American city. *Social Problems*, 4, 244–57.

Detweiler, R. (1980). Intercultural interaction and the categorization process. *International Journal of Intercultural Relations*, 4, 275–93.

Deusen, J. M. V. (1982). Health/mental health studies of Indochinese refugees. *Medical Anthropology*, 6, 231–52.

Deutsch, Steve E. & Won, George Y. M. (1963). Some factors in the adjustment of foreign nationals in the United States. *Journal of Social Issues*, 19(3), 115–22.

Dewey, John (1916). *Democracy and Education*. New York: Macmillan.

Diez, Mary E. (1984). Communicative competence: An interactive approach. In Robert N. Bostrom (ed.), *Communication Yearbook* 8. Beverly Hills, CA: Sage, 56–79.

Dinges, Norman (1983). Intercultural competence. In Dan Landis & Richard W. Brislin (eds), *Handbook of Intercultural Training: Issues in Theory and Design* vol. 1, New York: Pergamon, 176–202.

Dobzhansky, T. (1962). *Mankind Evolving: The Evolution of the Human Species*. New Haven, CT: Yale University Press.

Dosman, Edgar J. (1972). *Indians: The Urban Dilemma*. Toronto: McClelland & Stewart.

Dubin, Robert (1969). *Theory Building*. New York: The Free Press.

Dubos, Rene (1965). *Man Adapting*. New Haven, CT: Yale University Press.

Duncan, H. D. (1967). The search for social theory in communication in American sociology. In Frank E. Dance (ed.), *Human Communication Theory: Original Essays*. New York: Holt, Rinehart & Winston.

Duncan, O. D. (1975). *Introduction to Structural Equation Models*. New York: Academic Press.

Dyal, James A. & Dyal, Ruth T. (1981). Acculturation, stress and coping. *International Journal of Intercultural Relations*, 5(4), 301–28.

Eames, Edwin & Schwab, William (1964). Urban migration in India and Africa. *Human Organization*, 23, 24–7.

Eaton, W. W. & Lasry, J. C. (1978). Mental health and occupational mobility in a group of immigrants. *Science and Medicine*, 12, 53–8.

Eisenstadt, S. N. (1954/1966). *The Absorption of Immigrants*. London: Routledge & Kegan Paul.

——(1966). Communication processes among immigrants in Israel. In *Culture and Communication*. New York: Holt, Rinehart & Winston, 576–87.

EKMAN, P. & FRIESEN, W. (1971). Constants across cultures in the face and emotion. *Journal of Personality and Social Psychology*, 17, 124–9.

ENDO, RUSSEL & HIROKAWA, DALE (1984, July/October). Japanese American intermarriage. *P/AAMHRC Research Review*, 3(3/4), 1–2.

ERICKSON, E. (1963). The problem of ego identity. In M. STEIN and A. VIDICH (eds), *Identity and Anxiety Survival of the Person in Mass Society*. Glencoe, IL: The Free Press of Glencoe, 38–87.

ERIKSON, ERIK HOMBURGER (1964). *Insight and Responsibility*. New York: Norton.

EVERNHAM, LORRAINE & MARETZKI, THOMAS W. (1982, May 1–5). Anthropological and psychiatric issues in ethnic social support systems. Paper presented at the annual meeting of the International Communication Association, Boston, MA.

FABREGA, H. Jr. (1969, July). Social psychiatric aspects of acculturation and migration: A general statement. *Comprehensive Psychiatry*, 10(4), 314–26.

FANTINI, A. E. (1985). *Language Acquisition of a Bilingual Child: A Sociolinguistic Perspective (to age ten)*. Clevedon, England: Multilingual Matters, 219–61.

FATHI, A. (1973). Mass media and a Moslem immigrant community in Canada. *Anthropologica*, 15, 201–3.

FEAGIN, JOE R. (ed.) (1984). *Racial and Ethnic Relations* (2nd ed.). Englewood Cliffs, NJ: Prentice-Hall.

FERGUSON, CHARLES A. & HEATH, SHIRLEY BRICE (eds). (1981). *Language in the U.S.A.* New York: Cambridge University Press.

FERNANDEZ-BARILLAS, H.J. & MORRISON, T. L. (1984, December). Cultural affiliations and adjustments among male Mexican-American college students. *Psychological Reports*, 55(3), 855–60.

FIELDING, NIGEL C. & FIELDING, JANE L. (1986). *Linking Data*. Beverly Hills, CA: Sage.

FILSTEAD, WILLIAM J. (1970). *Qualitative Methodology: Firsthand Involvement with the Social World*. Chicago: Markham.

FINDLAY, PETER C. (1975). Multiculturalism in Canada: Ethnic pluralism and social policies. In AARON WOLFGANG (ed.), *Education of Immigrant Students: Issues and Answers*. Toronto: Ontario Institute for Studies in Education, 215–24.

FISCHER, CLAUDE S. (1982). *To Dwell Among Friends: Personal Networks in Town and City*. Chicago: The University of Chicago Press.

FISHMAN, J. A. *et al.* (1966). *Language Loyalty in the United States*. The Hague: Mouton.

FISKE, D. & MADDI, S. (eds) (1961). *Functions of Varied Experience.* Homewood, IL: Dorsey Press.

FITZPATRICK, J. P. (1976). The importance of community in the process of immigrant assimilation. In D. E. WEINBERG (ed.), *Ethnicity: A Conceptual Approach.* Cleveland, OH: Cleveland Ethnic Heritage Studies, Cleveland State University, 81–90.

FOA, U. (1967). Differentiation in cross-cultural communication. In L. THAYER (ed.), *Communication: Concepts and Perspectives.* Washington, DC: Spartan Books, 135–51.

FOGEL, DANIEL S. (1979, November). Human development and communication competencies. Paper presented at the annual Speech Communication Association meeting, San Antonio, TX.

FOSTER, LOIS & STOCKLEY, DAVID (1984). *Multiculturalism: The Changing Australian Paradigm.* Clevedon, England: Multilingual Matters.

FRAD, S. (1982, Summer). Bilingualism, cognitive growth and divergent skills. *Educational Forum*, 46(4), 469–74.

FRANK, LAWRENCE K. (1975). Cultural organization. In BRENT D. RUBEN & JOHN Y. KIM (eds), *General Systems Theory and Human Communication.* Rochelle Park, NJ: Hayden Books, 128–35.

FRENCH, JOHN R. P., Jr., RODGER, WILLARD L. & COBB, SIDNEY (1974). Adjustment as person environment fit. In GEORGE V. COELHO, DAVID A. HAMBURG & JOHN E. ADAMS (eds), *Coping and Adaptation.* New York: Basic, 316–33.

FRIEDRICH, OTTO (1985, July 8). The changing faces of America. TIME, 26–33.

FURNHAM, ADRIAN (1984). Tourism and culture shock. *Annals of Tourism Research*, 11(1), 41–57.

FURNHAM, ADRIAN & BOCHNER, STEPHEN (1982). Social difficulty in a foreign culture: An empirical analysis of culture shock. In A. FURNHAM & S. BOCHNER (eds.), *Cultures in Contact.* Elmsford, NY: Pergamon, 161–98.

——(1986). *Culture Shock: Psychological Reactions to Unfamiliar Environments.* London: Mathuen.

GAL, SUSAN (1978). Variation and change in patterns of speaking: Language shift in Austria. In DAVID SANKOFF (ed.), *Linguistic Variation: Models and Methods.* New York: Academic Press, 227–38.

GALAN, FERNANDO JARVIER (1979, February). Alcohol use among Chicanos and Anglos: A cross-cultural study. (Doctoral dissertation, Brandeis University), *Dissertation Abstracts International*, 39, 7821699.

GALLO, P. J. (1974). *Ethnic Alienation: The Italian Americans.* Cranbury, NJ: Fairleigh Dickinson University Press.

GALLOIS, CINDY, FRANKLYN-STOKES, ARLENE, GILES, HOWARD & COUPLAND, NIKOLAS (1988). Communication accommodation in intercultural encounters. In YOUNG YUN KIM & WILLIAM B. GUDYKUNST (eds), *Theories of Intercultural Communication*. Newbury Park, CA: Sage.

GAMA, ELIZABETH M. P. & PEDERSEN, PAUL (1977, Winter). Readjustment problems of Brazilian returnees from graduate studies in the United States. *International Journal of Intercultural Communication*, 1(4), 46–59.

GANS, HERBERT J. (1962). *The Urban Villagers*. New York: The Free Press.

GARDNER, R. C. & LAMBERT, W. E. (1972). Motivational variables in second-language acquisition. In J. W. BERRY & G. J. S. WILDE (eds), *Social Psychology: The Canadian Context*. Toronto: McClelland and Stewart Ltd, 113–22.

GENDLIN, E. T. (1962). *Experiencing and the Creation of Meaning*. New York: The Free Press.

——(1978). *Focusing*. New York: Everest House.

GEYER, R. FELIX (1980). *Alienation Theories: A General Systems Approach*. New York: Pergamon.

GIFFIN, KIM (1970, December). Social alienation by communication denial. *Quarterly Journal of Speech*, 56(4), 347–57.

GILES, HOWARD W. (ed.) (1977). *Language, Ethnicity, and Intergroup Relations*. London: Academic.

GILES, HOWARD W., BOURHIS, R. & TAYLOR, D. (1977). Towards a theory of language in ethnic group relations. In HOWARD GILES (ed.), *Language, Ethnicity, and Intergroup Relations*. London: Academic.

GILES, HOWARD W. & JOHNSON, PATRICIA (1981). Language in ethnic group relations. In JOHN C. TURNER & HOWARD GILES (Eds.), *Intergroup Behavior*. Chicago: The University of Chicago Press, 199–243.

——(1986). Perceived threat, ethnic commitment, and interethnic language behavior. In YOUNG YUN KIM (ed.), *Interethnic Communication: Current Research*. Newbury Park, CA: Sage.

GILES, HOWARD W., ROBINSON, P. & SMITH, P. M. (eds) (1980) *Language Social Psychological Perspectives*. New York: Pergamon.

GILES, HOWARD W. & RYAN, ELLEN BOUCHARD (1982). Prolegomena for developing a social psychological theory of language attitudes. In ELLEN BOUCHARD-RYAN & HOWARD GILES (eds), *Attitudes Towards Language Variation: Social and Applied Contexts*. London: Edward Arnold, 208–23.

GILES, HOWARD W. & SMITH, PHILIP (1979). Accommodation theory: Optimal levels of convergence. In HOWARD GILES & ROBERT N. ST. CLAIR (eds.), *Language and Social Psychology*. Baltimore, MD: University Park Press, 45–65.

GINSBERG, A. & GIOIELLI, M. (1979). A comparative study of acculturation & adaptation of descendants of Japanese born in Brazil compared with

Japanese and Brazilians. *Human Development*, 22(51), 340–57.

GIORDANO, JOSEPH (1973). *Ethnicity and Mental Health: Research and Recommendations*. New York: Institute on Pluralism and Group Identity.

GIORDANO, JOSEPH & GIORDANO, GRACE PINEIRO (1977). *The Ethno-cultural Factor in Mental Health*. New York: The Institute on Pluralism & Group Identity.

GLAZER, NATHAN (1954). Ethnic groups in America: From national culture to ideology. In M. BERGER, T. ABEL & C. H. PAGE (eds), *Freedom and Control in Modern Society*. New York: D. Van Nostrand.

GLAZER, NATHAN & MOYNIHAN, DANIEL PATRICK (1963). *Beyond the Melting Pot*. Cambridge, MA: MIT Press.

——(1975). *Ethnicity: Theory and Experience*. Cambridge, MA: Harvard University Press.

GLEESON, P. & WAKEFIELD, N. (1968). *Language and Culture*. Columbus, OH: Charles E. Merrill.

GLENN, NORVAL D. (1977). *Cohort Analysis*. Beverly Hills, CA: Sage.

GLICK, CLARENCE E. (1980). *Sojourners and Settlers: Chinese Migrants in Hawaii*. Honolulu, HI: University Press of Hawaii.

GOLDLUST, J. & RICHMOND, A. H. (1974). A multivariate model of immigrant adaptation. *International Migration Review*, 8, 193–225.

GORDON, C. (1969). Self-conceptions methodologies. *Journal of Nervous and Mental Disease*, 148, 328–64.

GORDON, MILTON M. (1964). *Assimilation in American Life: The Role of Race, Religion, and National Origins*. New York: Oxford University Press.

——(1973). Assimilation in America: Theory and reality. In P. I. ROSE (ed.), *The Study of Society*. New York: Random House, 350–65.

GORDON, T. F. (1974, August). Mass media and minority socialization: conceptualizing the process. Paper presented at the annual meeting of the Association for Education in Journalism, San Diego, CA.

GRANOVETTER, MARK S. (1973). The strength of weak ties. *American Journal of Sociology*, 78(6), 1360–80.

GRAVES, T. D. (1967, June/August). Acculturation, access, and alcohol in a tri-ethnic community. *American Anthropologist*, 69, 306–21.

GREELEY, ANDREW M. (1974). *Ethnicity in the United States: A Preliminary Reconnaissance*. New York: Wiley.

GROVE, CORNELIUS LEE & TORBIORN, INGEMAR (1985). A new conceptualization of intercultural adjustment and the goals of training. *International Journal of Intercultural Relations*, 9(2), 205–33.

GUDYKUNST, WILLIAM B. (1983). Toward a typology of stranger host relationships. *International Journal of Intercultural Relations*, 7(4),

401–13.

——(1983, Fall). Similarities and differences in perceptions of initial intracultural and intercultural encounters: An exploratory investigation. *The Southern Speech Communication Journal*, 49(1), 49–65.

——(1985). The influence of cultural similarity, type of relationship, and self-monitoring on uncertainty reduction processes. *Communication Monographs*, 52, 203–17.

——(1986). Ethnicity, types of relationship, and interethnic uncertainty reduction. In YOUNG YUN KIM (ed.), *Interethnic Communication: Current Research*. Beverly Hills, CA: Sage, 201–24.

——(1988). Uncertainty and anxiety. In YOUNG YUN KIM & WILLIAM B. GUDYKUNST (eds), *Theories of Intercultural Communication*. Beverly Hills, CA: Sage.

GUDYKUNST, WILLIAM B., HAMMER, M. & WISEMAN, R. (1977, Summer). An analysis of an integrated approach to cross-cultural training. *International Journal of Intercultural Relations*, 1(2), 99–110.

GUDYKUNST, WILLIAM B. & KIM, YOUNG YUN (1984). *Communicating with Strangers: An Approach to Intercultural Communication*. New York: Random House.

GUDYKUNST, WILLIAM B., WISEMAN, R. L. & HAMMER, M. (1977). Determinants of the sojourner's attitudinal satisfaction: A path model. In BRENT D. RUBEN (ed.), *Communication Yearbook I*. Brunswick, NJ: Transaction Books, 415–25.

GULLAHORN, J. T. & GULLAHORN, J. E. (1963). An extension of the U-curve hypothesis. *Journal of Social Issues*, 19(3), 33–47.

GUMPERZ, JOHN J. (1978). The conversational analysis of interethnic communication. In E. LAMAR ROSS (ed.), *Interethnic Communication*. Athens, GA: The University of Georgia Press, 13–31.

GUMPERZ, JOHN J. & COOK-GUMPERZ, JENNY (1982). Introduction: Language and the communication of social identity. In JOHN J. GUMPERZ (ed.), *Language and Social Identity*. Cambridge, England: Cambridge University Press, 1–21.

GUTHRIE, GEORGE M. & ZEKTICK, I. M. (1967). Predicting performance in the Peace Corps. *Journal of Social Psychology*, 71, 11–21.

HAGGARD, ERNEST A. (1974). A theory of adaptation and the risk of trauma. In E. JAMES ANTHONY & CYRILLE KOUPERNIK (eds), *The Child in his Family*. New York: John Wiley & Sons, 47–60.

HALE, C. L. (1980, November). Cognitive complexity-simplicity as a determinant of communication effectiveness. *Communication Monographs*, 47(4), 304–11.

HALL, A. D. & FAGEN, R. E. (1975). Definition of system. In BRENT D. RUBEN & JOHN Y. KIM (eds), *General Systems Theory and Human*

Communication. Rochelle Park, NJ: Hayden Books, 52–65.

HALL, EDWARD T. (1976). *Beyond Culture*. Garden City, NY: Anchor.

——(1983). *The Dance of Life*. New York: Doubleday.

HAMBURG, DAVID A., COELHO, GEORGE V. & ADAMS, JOHN E. (1974). Coping and adaptation: Steps toward a synthesis of biological and social perspectives. In GEORGE V. COELHO, DAVID A. HAMBURG & JOHN E. ADAMS (eds), *Coping and Adaptation*. New York: Basic Books, 403–40.

HAMMER, MITCHELL R., GUDYKUNST, WILLIAM B. & WISEMAN, R. L. (1978, Winter). Dimensions of intercultural effectiveness: An exploratory study. *International Journal of Intercultural Relations*, 2(4), 382–93.

HANDLIN, O. (1951). *The Uprooted*. Boston, MA: Little, Brown.

HARRIS, LINDA M. (1979, May). Communication competence: An argument for a systemic view. Paper presented at the annual meeting of the International Communication Association, Philadelphia, PA.

HARTMANN, HEINS (1939). *Ego Psychology and the Problem of Adaptation*. New York: International Universities Press.

HARVEY, O. J. (1966). *Experience, Structure, and Adaptability*. New York: Springer-Verlag.

HAWES, FRANK & KEALEY, DANIEL J. (1981). An empirical study of Canadian technical assistance. *International Journal of Intercultural Relations*, 5(3), 239–58.

HEATH, DOUGLAS H. (1977). *Maturity and Competence: A Transcultural View*. New York: Gardner Press.

HEISLER, MARTIN O. (ed.). (1977). Ethnic conflict in the world today. *Annuals of the American Academy of Political and Social Science*, 433.

HERBERT, DOROTHY C. (1980). Multicultural workers' network: Taking ethno-culture seriously. In *Helping Networks and the Welfare State: A Symposium: Volume II: Community & State*. Toronto, Canada: University of Toronto.

HERSKOVITS, M. J. (1958). *Acculturation: The Study of Culture Contact*. Gloucester, MA: Peter Smith.

HICKS, D. & ALPERT, G. (1978, June). Patterns of change & adaptation in prisons. *Social Science Quarterly*, 59(1), 37–50.

HINNENKAMP, VOLKER (1980). The refusal of second language learning in inter-ethnic context. In HOWARD GILES, W. PETER ROBINSON & PHILIP M. SMITH (eds), *Language: Social Psychological Perspectives*. New York: Pergamon, 179–84.

HIRSCH, BARTON J. (1981). Social networks and the coping process: Creating personal communities. In BENJAMIN H. GOTTLIEB (ed.), *Social Networks and Social Support*. Beverly Hills, CA: Sage, 149–70.

HOFMAN, J. & FISHERMAN, H. (1971). Language shift and maintenance in Israel. *International Migration Review*, 5(2), 204–26.

HOIJER, HARRY (1982). The Sapir–Whorf hypothesis. In LARRY SAMOVAR & RICHARD E. PORTER (eds.), *Intercultural Communication: A Reader* 3rd ed., Belmont, CA: Wadsworth Publishing, 210–22.

HOLMES, THOMAS H. & RAHE, RICHARD H. (1967). The social readjustment rating scale. *Journal of Psychometric Research*, 11, 213–8.

HOMAN, G. C. (1961). *Social Behavior: Its Elementary Forms*. New York: Harcourt, Brace.

HONG, KI SUN (1980). The interest level and exposure to informational contents of mass media: A study of Korean immigrants in the United States. In *Shin-Moon-Hak-Bo* (Journal of Mass Communication). Korean Association of Mass Communication, Seoul, Korea.

HONG, L. (1976, Winter). Recent immigrants in the Chinese-American community: Issues of adaptations and impacts. *International Migration Review*, 10(4), 509–14.

HOUSTON, JEANNE WAKATSUKI (1981, May 14). *Beyond Mansamar: A personal view on the Asian-American womanhood*. Audio recording of lecture given to Governors State University. University Park, IL.

HSU, F. L. K. (1971). *The Challenge of the American dream: The Chinese in the United States*. Belmont, CA: Wadsworth Publishing.

HUCKFELDT, R. ROBERT, KOHFELD, C. W. & LIKENS, THOMAS W. (1982). *Dynamic Modeling: An Introduction*. Beverly Hills, CA: Sage.

HUNTER, E. (1960). *In Many Voices: Our Fabulous Foreign-language Press*. Norman Park, GA: Norman College.

HUR, K. KYOON (1981, May 22–26). Asian American media and audiences: An institutional and audience analysis. Paper presented at the annual meeting of the International Communication Association, Minneapolis, MN.

HURH, WON M., KIM, HEI C. & KIM, KWANG C. (1987). *Assimilation Patterns of Immigrants in the United States: A Case Study of Korean Residents in the Chicago Area*. Washington, DC: University Press of America.

HYMES, DELL (1972). On communicative competence. In J. B. PRIDE & J. HOLMES (eds), *Sociolinguistics*. New York: Pergamon, 269–93.

INGLIS, MARGARET & GUDYKUNST, WILLIAM B. (1982). Institutional completeness and communications acculturation: A comparison of Korean immigrants in Chicago and Hartford. *International Journal of Intercultural Relations*, 6(3), 251–72.

IVEY, A. E. & HURST, J. C. (1971, September). Communication as adaptation. *The Journal of Communication*, 21, 199–207.

JAEGER, STEFAN & SANDU, HARPREET (1985, September). *Southest Asian refugees: English language development and acculturation*. Rosslyn, VA: National Clearinghouse for Bilingual Education.

JAMES, B. J. (1961). Social-psychological dimensions of Ojibwa acculturation. *American Anthropologist*, 63, 721–46.

JANTSCH, ERICH (1980). *The Self-organizing Universe: Scientific and Human Implications of the Emerging Paradigm of Evolution*. New York: Pergamon.

JEFFRES, LEO W. & HUR, K. KYOON (1981). Communication channels within ethnic groups. *International Journal of Intercultural Relations*, 5(2), 115–32.

JOHNSTON, R. (1963). A new approach to the meaning of assimilation. *Human Relations*, 16(3), 295–8.

JOURARD, SYDNEY (1974). Growing awareness and the awareness of growth. In B. PATTON & K. GIFFIN (eds), *Interpersonal Communication*. New York: Harper & Row.

JUSTICE, B. *et al.* (1980). *Stress: In the Eye of the Beholder the Key to Competent Coping*. Sacramento, CA: Jalmar Press.

KALIN, RUDOLF, RAYKO, DONALD S. & LOVE, NORAH (1980). The perception and evaluation of job candidates with four different ethnic accents. In HOWARD GILES, W. PETER ROBINSON & PHILIP M. SMITH (eds), *Language: Social Psychological Perspectives*. New York: Pergamon, 197–202.

KANG, MYUNG KOO (1984). Conflict and consensus on new international information order: A q-technique analysis. Paper presented at the annual meeting of the International Communication Association, San Francisco, CA.

KANG, TAI S. (ed.) (1976). Ethnic relations in Asia. *Journal of Asian Affairs*, 1(2).

KAPOOR, SURAJ & WILLIAMS, WENMOUTH, Jr. (1979, May). Acculturation of foreign students by television: A q methodology approach. Paper presented at the annual meeting of the International Communication Association, Philadelphia, PA.

KEALEY, DANIEL & RUBEN, BRENT D. (1983). Cross-cultural personnel selection criteria, issues and methods. In DAN LANDIS & RICHARD W. BRISLIN (eds), *Handbook of Intercultural Training: Vol. I. Issues in Theory and Design*. New York: Pergamon, 155–75.

KEEFE, SUSAN EMLEY (1980). Acculturation and the extended family among urban Mexican Americans. In AMADO M. PADILLA (ed.), *Acculturation: Theory, Research and Some New Findings*. AAAS Selected Symposium. Washington, DC: Westview Press, 85–110.

KEIFER, C. W. (1974). *Changing Cultures, Changing Lives*. San Francisco, CA: Jossey-Bass.

KELLY, JAMES (1985, July 8). To the land of free speech. *Time*, pp. 95–7.

KELMAN, H. & EZEKIAL, R. (1970). *Cross-national Encounters*. San Francisco, CA: Hossey-Bass.

KERPIN, KAREN S. (1984). Services to refugees: Political dimensions.

Migration Today, 12(1), 11.

KIKIMURA, AKEMI (1979). The life history of an Issei woman: Conflicts and strain in the process of acculturation. Unpublished doctoral dissertation, University of California, Berkeley, CA.

KIM, JIN KEON (1980, August). Explaining acculturation in a communication framework: An empirical test. *Communication Monographs*, 47(3), 155–79.

KIM, JIN KEON, LEE, BYUNG-HYO & JEONG, WON JO (1982, July 25-9). Uses of mass media in acculturation: Dependency, information preference, and gratifications. Paper presented at the annual meeting of the Association for Education in Journalism, Athens, Ohio.

KIM, YOUNG YUN (1976). Communication patterns of foreign immigrants in the process of acculturation: A survey among the Korean population in Chicago. Unpublished doctoral dissertation, Northwestern University, Evanston, IL.

——(1977a). Communication patterns of foreign immigrants in the process of acculturation. *Human Communication Research*, 4(1), 66–77.

——(1977b). Inter-ethnic and intra-ethnic communication: A study of Korean immigrants in Chicago. *International and Intercultural Communication Annual*, 4, 53–68.

——(1977c, March). Communication patterns of Mexican-Americans in the Chicago area. Paper presented at the Third World Conference, Chicago, IL.

——(1978a). A communication approach to acculturation processes: Korean immigrants in Chicago. *International Journal of Intercultural Relations*, 2(2), 197–224.

——(1978b, November). Acculturation and patterns of interpersonal communication relationships: A study of Japanese, Mexican, and Korean communities in the Chicago area. Paper presented at the Speech Communication Association Conference, Minneapolis, MN.

——(1979a). Toward an interactive theory of communication-acculturation. In BRENT D. RUBEN (ed.), *Communication Yearbook III*. New Brunswick, NJ: Transaction Books, 435–53.

——(1979b, May). Mass media and acculturation: Toward development of an interactive theory. Paper presented at the Eastern Communication Association Conference, Philadelphia, PA.

——(1979c, September). Need for a unified theory of acculturation. Paper presented at the American Psychological Association Conference, New York, NY.

——(1979d, November). Dynamics of intrapersonal and interpersonal communication: A study of Indochinese refugees in the initial phase of acculturation. Paper presented at the Speech Communication

Association Conference, San Antonio, TX.

—— (1980). *Research project report on Indochinese refugees in Illinois: Vol. 1. Introduction, summary and recommendations. Vol. 2. Methods and procedures. Vol. 3. Population characteristics and service needs. Vol. 4. Psychological, social and cultural adjustment of Indochinese refugees. Vol. 5. Survey of agencies serving Indochinese refugees.* (Based on a grant from the Department of Health, Education and Welfare Region V). Chicago: Travelers Aid Society, 95–549.

—— (1982). Communication and acculturation. In LARRY A. SAMOVAR & RICHARD E. PORTER (eds), *Intercultural Communication: A Reader* 3rd ed. (359–68). Also in 4th ed. (1983, 379–88). Belmont, CA: Wadsworth.

—— (1984). Searching for creative integration. In WILLIAM B. GUDYKUNST & YOUNG YUN KIM (eds), *Methods for Intercultural Communication Research*. Beverly Hills, CA: Sage, 13–30.

—— (1985a). Communication, information, and behavior. In BRENT D. RUBEN (ed.), *Information and Behavior* vol. 1. New Brunswick, NJ: Transaction Books, 324–40.

—— (1985b). Intercultural personhood: An integration of Eastern and Western perspectives. In LARRY A. SAMOVAR & RICHARD E. PORTER (eds), *Intercultural Communication: A Reader* 4th ed. . Belmont, CA: Wadsworth, 400–10.

—— (1986a). Understanding the social context of intergroup communication: A personal network approach. In WILLIAM B. GUDYKUNST (ed.), *Intergroup Communication*. London: Edward Arnold, 86–95.

—— (1986b). Introduction: A communication approach to interethnic relations. In YOUNG YUN KIM (ed.), *Interethnic Communication: Current Research*. Newbury Park, CA: Sage, 9–18.

—— (1987). Facilitating immigrant adaptation: The role of communication and interpersonal ties. In TERRANCE C. ALBRECHT and MARA B. ADELMAN (eds), *Communicating Social Support: Process in Context*. Newbury Park, CA: Sage.

KIM, YOUNG YUN & GUDYKUNST, WILLIAM B. (eds). (1987). *Cross-cultural Adaptation*. Newbury Park, CA: Sage.

KIM, YOUNG YUN & RUBEN, BRENT D. (1988). Intercultural transformation: A systems theory. In YOUNG YUN KIM & WILLIAM B. GUDYKUNST (eds), *Theories of Intercultural Communication*. Newbury Park, CA: Sage.

KINCAID, D. LARRY (1988). The convergence theory and intercultural communication. In YOUNG YUN KIM & WILLIAM B. GUDYKUNST (eds), *Theories of Intercultural Communication*. Newbury Park, CA: Sage.

KING, SARAH SANDERSON (1984, June). *Natural Helping Networks Among Ethnic Groups in Hawaii: Yearbook II. Help Seeking Behavior Survey*.

Washington, DC: National Institute of Mental Health.

KINLOCH, GRAHAM (1974). *The Dynamics of Race Relations: A Sociological Analysis*. New York: McGraw-Hill.

KINO, F. F. (1973). Aliens' paranoid reacton. In CHARLES ZWINGMANN & MARIA PFISTER-AMMENDE (eds), *Uprooting and After. . . .* New York: Springer-Verlag, 60–6.

KINZIE, J. D., TRAN, K. A., BRECKENRIDGE, A. & BLOOM, J. L. (1980). An Indochinese refugee psychiatric clinic: Culturally accepted treatment approaches. *American Journal of Psychiatry*, 137, 1429–32.

KIRKPATRICK, JOHN (1987). Ethnic antagonism and innovation in Hawaii. In JERRY BOUCHER, DAN LANDIS & KAREN A. CLARK (eds), *Ethnic Conflict: International Perspectives*. Newbury Park, CA: Sage.

KLINEBERG, OTTO & HULL, W. FRANK IV (1979). *At a Foreign University: An International Study of Adaptation and Coping*. New York: Praeger.

KOESTLER, Arthur (1967). *The Ghost in the Machine*. New York: Macmillan.

KRAMARAE, CHERIS, SCHULZ, MURIEL & O'BARR, WILLIAM M. (1984). Introduction: Toward an understanding of language and power. In CHERIS KRAMARAE, MURIEL SCHULZ & WILLIAM M. O'BARR (eds), *Language and Power*. Beverly Hills, CA: Sage, 9–22.

KRASHEN, STEPHEN D. (1981). *Second Language Acquisition and Second Language Learning*. New York: Pergamon.

KRAUSE, C. A. (1978). Urbanization without breakdown: Italian, Jewish and Slavic immigrant women in Pittsburg, 1900–1945. *Journal of Urban History*, 4(3), 291–306.

KRIPPENDORF, KLAUS (1975). The systems approach to communication. In BRENT D. RUBEN & J. Y. KIM (eds), *General Systems Theory and Human Communication*. Rochelle Park, NJ: Hayden Book Co., 138–63.

——(1980). *Content Analysis*. Beverly Hills, CA: Sage.

KUHN, ALFRED (1975). Social organization. In BRENT D. RUBEN & J. Y. KIM (eds), *General Systems Theory and Human Communication*. Rochelle Park, NJ: Hayden, 114–27.

KUO, WEN (1976, June). Theories of migration and mental health: An empirical testing on Chinese-Americans. *Social Science and Medicine*. 10(6), 297–306.

KURTZ, NORMAN (1970). Gatekeepers in the process of acculturation. Unpublished doctoral dissertation. University of Colorado.

LAMBERT, R. & BRESSLER, M. (1956). *Indian Students on an American Campus*. Minneapolis, MN: University of Minnesota Press.

LAMBERT, WALLACE E. (1979). Language as a factor in inter-group relations. In HOWARD GILES & ROBERT N. ST. CLAIR (eds), *Language and Social Psychology*. Baltimore, MD: University Park Press, 186–92.

LANDIS, DAN & BRISLIN, RICHARD W. (eds). (1983). *Handbook of Inter-*

Cultural Training vols. I–III. New York: Pergamon.

LASSWELL, HAROLD D. (1948/1964). The structure and function of communication in society. In LYMAN BRYSON (ed.), *The Communication of Ideas*. New York: Cooper Systems, 37–51.

LASZLO, ERVIN (1972). *The Systems View of the World*. New York: George Braziller.

——(1975). Basic constructs of systems philosophy. In BRENT D. RUBEN & J. Y. KIM (eds), *General Systems Theory and Human Communication*. Rochelle Park, NJ: Hayden Books, 66–77.

LAUMANN, E. O. (1973). *Bonds of Pluralism: The Form and Substance of Urban Social Networks*. New York: John Wiley & Sons.

LAZARSFELD, PAUL F. & MERTON, ROBERT K. (1954). Friendship as a social process: A substantive and methodological analysis. In MORRIE BERGER, THEODORE ABEL & CHARLES H. PAGE (eds), *Freedom and Control in Modern Society*. New York: D. Van Nostrand, 18–66.

LAZARUS, RICHARD S. (1966). *Psychological Stress and the Coping Process*. St. Louis, MO: McGraw-Hill.

LAZARUS, RICHARD S., AVERILL, JAMES R. & OPTON, EDWARD M., Jr. (1974). The psychology of coping: Issues of research and assessment. In GEORGE V. COELHO, DAVID A. HAMBURG & JOHN E. ADAMS (eds), *Coping and Adaptation*. New York: Basic Books, 249–315.

LAZERWITZ, B. (1954). Some factors in Jewish identification. *Jewish Social Studies*, 15, 3–24.

LAZSLO, J. A. (1972). *A Systems View of the World*. New York: Braziller.

LEFCOURT, HERBERT M. (1984). Locus of control and stressful life events. In B. S. DOHRENWEND & B. P. DOHRENWEND (eds), *Series in Psychosocial Epidemiology: Stressful Life Events and their Contexts* vol. 2. New Brunswick, NJ: Rutgers University Press, 157–66.

LEVINE, DONALD N. (1979). Simmel at a distance: On the history and systematics of the sociology of the stranger. In WILLIAM A. SHACK & ELLIOTT P. SKINNER (eds), *Strangers in African Societies*. Berkeley, CA: University of California Press, 21–36.

LEVINE, MARK S. (1977). *Canonical Analysis and Factor Comparison*. Beverly Hills, CA: Sage.

LEVINE, ROBERT A. & CAMPBELL, D. T. (1972). *Ethnocentrism: Theories of Conflict, Ethnic Attitudes and Group Behavior*. New York: Wiley.

LI, PETER S. (1974). Kinship as a source of information among Chinese immigrants. Paper presented at the annual meeting of the International Sociological Association, Toronto, Canada.

LIEBERSON, STANLEY (1961, December). A societal theory of race and ethnic relations. *American Sociological Review*, 26(6), 902–10.

——(1981). Linguistic and ethnic segregation in Montreal. In STANLEY

LIEBERSON (ed.), *Language Diversity and Language Contact*. Stanford, CA: Stanford University Press.

LINTON, R. (1940). *Acculturation in Seven American Indian Tribes*. New York: Appleton-Century.

LITTLE, KENNETH (1957). The role of voluntary associations in West African urbanization. *American Anthropologist*, 59, 579–96.

LOEVINGER, JANE (1976). *Ego Development*. San Fransicso, CA: Jossey-Bass.

LONNER, WALTER J. & BERRY, JOHN W. (Eds.). (1986). *Field Methods in Cross-cultural Research*. Beverly Hills, CA: Sage.

LUCE, LOUISE F. & SMITH, ELISE C. (1987). Cross-cultural literacy: A national priority. In LOUISE F. LUCE & ELISE C. SMITH (eds), *Toward Internationalism*. Cambridge, MA: Newbury, 3–9.

LUM, J. (1982). Marginality and multiculturalism. In LARRY A. SAMOVAR and RICHARD E. PORTER (eds), *Intercultural Communication: A Reader* (3rd ed.). Belmont, CA: Wadsworth.

LUTZKER, D. (1960). Internationalism as a predictor of cooperative behavior. *Journal of Conflict Resolution*, 4(4), 426–30.

LYSGAARD, SVERRE (1955). Adjustment in a foreign society: Norwegian Fulbright grantees visiting the United States. *International Social Science Bulletin*, 7(1), 45–51.

MAANEN, JOHN VAN, DABBS, JAMES M., Jr. & FAULKNER, ROBERT R. (1983). *Varieties of Qualitative Research*. Beverly Hills, CA: Sage.

MCCALLISTER, Lynne & FISHER, CLAUDE S. (1978, November). A procedure for surveying personal networks. *Sociological Methods and Research*, 7(2), 131–48.

MCDERMOTT, VIRGINIA ANNE (1980). Interpersonal communication networks: An approach through the understanding of self-concept, significant others, and the social influence process. *Communication Quarterly*, 28(4), 13–25.

MACKEY, WILLIAM F. (1979, Spring). Language policy and language planning. *Journal of Communication*, 29(2), 48–53.

MACKINNON, D. W. (1978). *In Search of Human Effectiveness*. Buffalo, NY: Creative Education Foundation.

MCLAUGHLIN, B. (1966). The Who Am I dictionary and self-perceived identity in college students. In P. J. STONE *et al.* (eds), *The General Inquirer: A Computer Approach to Content Analysis*. Cambridge, MA: MIT Press.

MALPASS, ROY S. & POORTINGA, YPE H. (1986). Strategies for design and analysis. In WALTER J. LONNER & JOHN W. BERRY (eds), *Field Methods in Cross-cultural Research*. Beverly Hills, CA: Sage.

MANGIN, WILLIAM (1960). *Mental Health and Migration to Cities: A Peruvian*

Case. New York: Academy of Sciences.

MANSELL, MAUREEN (1981, April). Transcultural experience and expressive response. *Communication Education*, 30, 93–108.

MARDEN, C. F. & Meyer, G. (1968). *Minorities in America* 3rd ed. New York: Van Nostrand Reinhold.

MARMOT, M. G. & SYME, S. L. (1976). Acculturation and coronary heart disease in Japanese-Americans. *American Journal of Epidemiology*, 104(3), 225–47.

MARRETT, CORA BAGLEY & LEGGON, CHERYL B. (1979). Introduction. In CORA BAGLEY MARRETT & CHERYL B. LEGGON (eds), *Research in Race and Ethnic Relations: A Research Annual* vol. 1. Greenwich, CT: Jai Press, 9–19.

MARSDEN, PETER V. & CAMPBELL, KAREN E. (1983, August 31–September 4). Measuring tie strength. Paper presented at the annual meeting of the American Sociological Association, Detroit, MI.

MARTIN, JUDITH N. (1984). The intercultural reentry: Conceptualization and directions for future research. *International Journal of Intercultural Relations*, 8(2), 115–34.

——(1985, May). Patterns of communication in three types of reentry relationships. Paper presented at the annual meeting of the International Communication Association, Honolulu, HI.

MARZOLF, M. T. (1979). *The Danish-language Press in America*. New York: Arno Press.

MASLOW, ABRAHAM H. (1970). *Motivation and Personality* 2nd ed. New York: Harper & Row.

——(1971). *The Further Reaches of Human Nature*. New York: Viking Press.

MASON, PHILIP (1970). *Patterns of Dominance*. London: Oxford University Press.

MATSUMOTO, GARY M., MEREDITH, GERALD M. & MASUDA, MINORU (1973). Ethnic identity: Honolulu and Seattle Japanese-Americans. In STANLEY SUE & NATHANIEL N. WAGNER (eds), *Asian-Americans: Psychological Perspectives*. Palo Alto, CA: Science & Behavior Books, 65–74.

MECHANIC, DAVID (1974). Social structure and personal adaptation: Some neglected dimensions. In GEORGE V. COELHO, DAVID A. HAMBURG & JOHN E. ADAMS (eds), *Coping and Adaptation*. New York: Basic Books, 32–44.

MENDELSOHN, HAROLD (1964). Sociological perspective on the study of mass communication. In LEWIS A. DEXTER & DAVID M. WHITE (eds), *People, Society, and Mass Communication*. New York: The Free Press.

MERCER, N., MEAD E. & MEARS, R. (1979). Linguistic and cultural affiliation among young Asian people in Leicester. In HOWARD GILES & B. ST

JACQUES (eds), *Language and Ethnic Relations*. Oxford: Pergamon.

MEZNARIC, SILVA (1984). Sociology of migration in Yugoslavia. *Current Sociology*, 32(2), 41–59.

MILLER, S. (1979). Controllability and human stress: Method, evidence and theory. *Behavior Research and Therapy*, 17(4), 287–304.

MILROY, LESLIE (1980). *Language and Social Networks*. Baltimore, MD: University Park Press.

——(1982). Social network and linguistic focusing. In SUZANNE ROMAINE (ed.), *Sociolinguistic Variation in Speech Communities*. London: Edward Arnold, 141–52.

MINDLER, M. & BILLER, R. (1979). Role shock: A tool for conceptualizing stresses accompanying disruptive role transitions. *Human Relations*, 32(2), 125–40.

MIRANDA, M. R. & CASTRO, F. G. (1977). Culture distance and success in psychotherapy with Spanish speaking clients. In J. L. MARTINEZ Jr. (ed.), *Chicano Psychology*. New York: Academic, 249–62.

MIROWSKY, JOHN & ROSS, CATHERINE E. (1983, August 31–September 4). Language networks and social status among Mexican Americans. Paper presented at the annual meeting of the American Sociological Association, Detroit, MI.

MOOS, RUDOLF H. (1974). Psychological techniques in the assessment of adaptive behavior. In GEORGE V. COELHO, DAVID A. HAMBURG & JOHN E. ADAMS (eds), *Coping and Adaptation*. New York: Basic Books, 334–99.

——(ed.). (1976). *Human Adaptation: Coping With Life Crisis*. Lexington, MA: Heath.

MOOS, RUDOLF H. & MITCHELL, R. (1982). Social network resources and adaptation: A conceptual framework. In THOMAS WILLS (ed.), *Basic Processes in Helping Relationships*. New York: Academic, 213–32.

MOOS, RUDOLF H. & TSU, VIVIEN DAVIS (1976). Human competence and coping. In RUDOLF H. MOOS (ed.), *Human Adaptation: Coping With Life Crisis*. Lexington, MA: Heath, 3–16.

MOREK, E. (1972). The acculturation of the Mexican American minority to the Anglo-American Society in the United States. *Journal of Human Relations*, 20(3), 317–25.

MORRIS, RICHARD T. (1960). *The Two-way Mirror*. Minneapolis, MN: University of Minnesota Press.

MORROW, LANCE (1985, July 8). Immigrants. *Time*, pp. 4–25.

MORTLAND, CAROL A. & LEDGERWOOD, JUDY (1987). Refugee resource acquisition: The invisible system. In YOUNG YUN KIM & WILLIAM B. GUDYKUNST (eds), *Cross-cultural Adaptation: Current Theory and Research*. Newbury Park, CA: Sage.

MURPHY, H. B. M. (1973). Migration and major mental disorders - A reappraisal. In CHARLES ZWINGMANN & MARIA PFISTER-AMMENDE (eds), *Uprooting and after . . . .* New York: Springer-Verlag, 204–20.

MURRAY, H. A. (1938). *Explorations in Personality.* New York: Oxford University Press.

NAGATA, GIYOSHI (1969). A statistical approach to the study of acculturation of an ethnic group based on communication oriented variables: The case of Japanese Americans in Chicago. Unpublished dissertation, University of Illinois at Urbana-Champaign.

NISHIDA, HIROKO (1985). Japanese intercultural communication competence and cross-cultural adjustment. *International Journal of Intercultural Relations,* 9(3), 247–69.

NOESJIRWAN, JENNIFER (1978). A rule-based analysis of cultural differences in social behavior: Indonesia and Australia. *International Journal of Psychology,* 13(4), 305–16.

NOVAK, MICHAEL (1971). *The Rise of the Unmeltable Ethnics.* New York: MacMillan.

——(1973). New ethnicity. *The Humanist,* May/June, 18–21.

OBERG, KALVERO (1960). Cultural shock: Adjustment to new cultural environments. *Practical Anthropology,* 7, 170–9.

OFFICE OF REFUGEE RESETTLEMENT (1982, January). *Refugee Resettlement Program: Report to the Congress.* Washington, DC: U.S. Department of Health & Human Services.

——(1984). *A Study of English Language Training for Refugees in the United States.* Washington, DC: U.S. Department of Health & Human Services.

OLMEDO, ESTEBAN L. (1980). Quantitative models of acculturation: An overview. In AMADO M. PADILLA (ed.), *Acculturation: Theory, Models and Some New Findings.* Boulder, CO: Westview, 27–45.

OLSEN, MARVIN E. (1968). *The Process of Social Organization.* New York: Holt, Rinehart & Winston.

ORBACH, MICHAEL K. & BECKWITH, JANESE (1982, July). Indochinese adaptation and local government policy: An example from Monterey. *Anthropological Quarterly,* 55(3), 135–45.

OSSENBORG, R. J. (1964). The social integration and adjustment of post-war immigrants in Montreal and Toronto. *Canadian Review of Sociology and Anthropology I,* 204–14.

OSTROM, CHARLES W., Jr. (1978). *Time Series Analysis.* Beverly Hills, CA: Sage.

PADILLA, AMADO M. (ed.). (1980). *Acculturation: Theory, Models and some New Findings.* Washington, DC: Westview.

PADILLA, AMADO, WAGATSUMA, YURIA & LINDHOLM, KATHRYN J. (1985,

October). *Acculturation and Personality as Predictors of Stress in Japanese and Japanese-Americans*. Los Angeles, CA: Department of Psychology, University of California.

PARENTI, M. (1967). Ethnic politics and the persistence of ethnic voting identification. *American Political Science Review*, 67, 717–26.

PARK, ROBERT E. (1939). Reflections on communication and culture. *The American Journal of Sociology*, 44, 191-205.

PARRILLO, VINCENT N. (1966). *Strangers to These Shores: Race and Ethnic Relations in the United States*. Boston, MA: Houghton Mifflin.

PEARCE, W. BARNETT & STAMM, KEITH R. (1973). Communication behavior and coorientation relations. In P. CLARKE (ed.), *New Models for Mass Communication Research*. Beverly Hills, CA: Sage, 177–203.

PEDONE, R. J. (1980). *The Retention of Minority Language in the United States*. Washington, DC: National Center for Education Status.

PERES, Y. & SCHRIFT, R. (1978, October). Intermarriage and interethnic relations: A comparative study. *Ethnic and Racial Studies*, 1, 428–51.

PERVIN, L. A. (1968). Performance and satisfaction as a function of individual environment fit. *Psychological Bulletin*, 69, 56–68.

PETERSON, THEODORE, JENSEN, JAY W. & RIVERS, WILLIAM L. (1965). *The Mass Media and Modern Society*. New York: Holt, Rinehart & Winston.

PETTIGREW, THOMAS F. (1978). Three issues in ethnicity: Boundaries, deprivations, and perceptions. In J. MILTON YINGER & STEPHEN J. CUTLER (eds), *Major Social Issues: A Multidisciplinary View*. New York: The Free Press, 25–49.

PFISTER-AMMENDE, MARIA (1973). The problem of uprooting. In CHARLES ZWINGMAN & MARIA PFISTER-AMMENDE (eds), *Uprooting and After. . .* New York: Springer-Verlag, 7–18.

PHINNEY, JEAN S. & ROTHERAM, MARY JANE (1987). *Children's Ethnic Socialization: Pluralism and Development*. Newbury Park, CA: Sage.

PHIZACKLEA, ANNIE (1984, Winter). A sociology of migration or 'race relations?' A view from Britain. *Current Sociology*, 32(3), 199–209.

PIAGET, J. (1977). Problems of equilibration. In M. APPEL & L. GOLDBERG (eds), *Topics in Cognitive Development*. New York: Plenum.

POOL, ITHIEL DE SOLA (1965). Effects of cross-national contact on national and international images. In HERBERT C. KELMAN (ed.), *International Behavior: A Social-psychological Analysis*. New York: Holt, Rinehart & Winston, 106–29.

POSTIGLIONE, GERARD A. (1983). *Ethnicity and American Social Theory: Toward Critical Pluralism*. Lanham, MD: University Press of America.

PRICE, J. A. (1968, Summer). The migration and adaptation of American Indians to Los Angeles. *Human Organization*, 27(2), 168–75.

PRUITT, F. J. (1978, Spring). The adaptation of African students to

American society. *International Journal of Intercultural Relations*, 2(1), 90-118.

PUNETHA, DEEPA, GILES, HOWARD & YOUNG, LOUIS (1987). Interethnic perceptions and relative deprivation: British data. In YOUNG YUN KIM & WILLIAM B. GUDYKUNST (eds), *Cross-cultural Adaptation: Current Theory and Research*. Newbury Park, CA: Sage.

QUISUMBING, MARIA S. R. (1982). Life events, social support and personality: Their impact upon Filipino & psychological adjustment. Unpublished doctoral dissertation, University of Chicago.

REDFIELD, R., LINTON, R. & HERSKOVITS, M. J. (1936). Outline for the study of acculturation. *American Anthropologist*, 38, 149–52.

RELLA, P. & VADALA, T. (1984). Sociological literature on migration in Italy. *Current Sociology*, 32(2), 143–51.

RICHMOND, ANTHONY H. (1967). *Post-war Immigration in Canada*. Toronto: University of Toronto Press.

ROGERS, CARL R. (1961). *On Becoming a Person*. Boston: Houghton Mifflin.

ROGERS, EVERETT M. & KINCAID, D. LAWRENCE (1981). *Communication Networks: A New Paradigm for Research*. New York: Free Press.

ROLLO, M. (1963). Centrality of the problem in our day. In M. STEIN & A. VIDICH (eds), *Identity and Anxiety Survival of the Person in Mass Society II*. Glencoe, IL: The Free Press of Glencoe, 120–8.

ROSS, E. LAMAR (1978). Interethnic communication: An overview. In E. LAMAR ROSS (ed.), *Interethnic Communication*. Athens, GA: The University of Georgia Press, 1–12.

RUBEN, BRENT D. (1975). Intrapersonal, interpersonal, and mass communication processes in individual and multi-person systems. In BRENT D. RUBEN & JOHN Y. KIM (eds), *General Systems Theory and Human Communication*. Rochelle Park, NJ: Hayden, 164–90.

——(1976, September). Assessing communication competency for intercultural adaptation. *Group and Organization Studies*, 1(3), 334–54.

——(1980, March). Culture shock: The skull and the lady — Reflections on cultural adjustment and stress. Paper presented at the annual conference of the Society for Intercultural Education, Training, and Research, Mount Pocono, PA.

——(1983). A system-theoretic view. In WILLIAM B. GUDYKUNST (ed.), *International and Intercultural Communication Annual: Intercultural Communication Theory* vol. 12. Beverly Hills, CA: Sage, 131–45.

——(1985). Human communication and cross-cultural effectiveness. In LARRY A. SAMOVAR & RICHARD E. PORTER (eds), *Intercultural Communication: A Reader* 4th ed. Belmont, CA: Wadsworth, 338–46.

——(1987). Guidelines for cross-cultural communication effectiveness. In LOUISE F. LUCE & ELISE C. SMITH (eds), *Toward Internationalism*.

Cambridge, MA: Newbury, 36–46.

RUBEN, BRENT D., ASKLING, LAWRENCE R. & KEALEY, DANIEL J. (1977). Cross-cultural effectiveness: An overview. In DAVID S. HOOPES, PAUL B. PEDERSEN & GEORGE W. RENWICK (eds), *Overview of Intercultural Education, Training and Research: Volume I: Theory*. LaGrange Park, IL: Intercultural Network, Inc., 89–102.

RUBEN, BRENT D. & KEALEY, DANIEL J. (1979, Spring). Behavioral assessment of communication competency and the prediction of cross-cultural adaptation. *International Journal of Intercultural Relations*, 3(1), 15–47.

RUBEN, BRENT D. & KIM, JOHN Y. (eds). (1975). *General Systems Theory and Human Communication*. Rochelle Park, NJ: Hayden.

RUESCH, JURGEN (1951/1968). Communication and human relations: An interdisciplinary approach. In JURGEN RUESCH & GREGORY BATESON (eds), *Communication: The Social Matrix of Psychiatry*. New York: Norton, 21–49.

——(1972/1957). *Disturbed Communication*. New York: Norton.

RUESCH, JURGEN & BATESON, GREGORY (1951/1968). *Communication: The Social Matrix of Psychiatry*. New York: W. W. Norton.

RYAN, ELLEN BOUCHARD (1979). Why do low-prestige language varieties persist? In HOWARD GILES & ROBERT N. ST. CLAIR (eds), *Language and Social Psychology*. Baltimore, MD: University Park Press, 145–57.

RYU, JUNG SHIG (1976, November). Neo-socialization function of mass media working among foreign students. Paper presented at the annual meeting of the Mass Communication Association, San Francisco, CA.

——(1980, August). Media functions among minorities: A comparative analysis of media uses. Paper presented at the annual meeting of the Association for Education in Journalism, Boston, MA.

SAPIR, EDWARDS (1931). Communication. *Encyclopedia of the Social Sciences*, 4, 78-80.

SCHNEIDER, MICHAEL J. (1979, December). Cross-cultural communication and the acquisition of communicative competence. Unpublished doctoral dissertation, University of Iowa.

SCHRODER, HAROLD M., DRIVER, MICHAEL J. & STREUFERT, SIEGFRIED (1967). *Human Information Processing*. New York: Holt, Rinehart and Winston.

——(1975). Intrapersonal organizaton. In BRENT D. RUBEN & JOHN Y. KIM (eds), *General Systems Theory and Human Communication*. Rochelle Park, NJ: Hayden, 96–113.

SCHUETZ, A. (1944). The homecomer. *American Journal of Sociology*, 50, 369–76.

——(1944/1963). The stranger. *American Journal of Sociology*, 49,

499–507. Reprinted in M. Stein & A. Vidich, (eds), *Identity and Anxiety*. Glencoe, IL: Free Press.

——(1964). Making music together. *Collected Papers II*. The Hague: Nijhoff, 159–78.

Sechrest, Lee, Fay, Todd L. & Zaidi, S. M. (1982). Problems of translation in cross-cultural communication. In Larry A. Samovar & Richard E. Porter (eds), *Intercultural Communication: A Reader* 3rd ed. Belmont, CA: Wadsworth, 223–33.

Seelye, H. Ned & Wasilewski, Jacqueline Howell (1981, March). *Social competency development in multicultural children, aged 6–13. Final report of exploratory research on Hispanic-background children*. Pursuant to National Institute of Education Contract No. 400-80-0003. LaGrange, IL: International Resource Development, Inc.

Seeman, Julius (1983). *Personality Integration: Studies and Reflections*. New York: Human Sciences Press.

Segalowitz, Norman & Catbonton, Elizabeth (1977). Studies of the non-fluent bilingual. In Peter A. Hornby (ed.), *Bilingualism: Psychological, Social, and Educational Implications*. New York: Academic Press, 77–89.

Selltiz, Claire, Christ, June R., Havel, Joan & Cook, Stuart W. (1963). *Attitudes and Social Relations of Foreign Students in the United States*. Minneapolis, MN: University of Minnesota Press.

Selltiz, Claire & Cook, Stuart W. (1962). Factors influencing attitudes of foreign students toward the host country. *Journal of Social Issues*, 18(1), 7–23.

Sewell, William H. & Davidsen, Oluf M. (1961). *Scandinavian Students on an American Campus*. Minneapolis, MN: University of Minnesota Press.

Sheehy, Gail (1986). *Spirit of Survival*. New York: Bantam Books.

Shibutani, Tamotsu & Kwan, Kian M. (1965). *Ethnic Stratification: A Comparative Approach*. New York: Macmillan.

Shostrum, E. L. (1976). *Actualizing Therapy*. San Diego: Edits.

Shuval, Judith T. (1963). *Immigrants on the Threshold*. New York: Atherton Press.

Silverman, Marsha L. (1979, October 24–28). Vietnamese in Denver: Cultural conflicts in health care. Paper presented at the annual meeting of the Conference on Indochinese Refugees, Fairfax, VA.

Simard, Lise M. (1981). Cross-cultural interaction: Potential invisible barriers. *Journal of Social Psychology*, 113, 171–92.

Simmel, George (1950). The stranger. In K. Wolff (ed. and trans.), *The Sociology of George Simmel*. New York: Free Press.

——(1955). The web of group affiliation. (R. Bendix, trans.). *In Conflict and the Web of Group Affiliation*. Glencoe, IL: The Free Press of Glencoe, 125–95.

SMITH, M. ESTELLIE (1976, January). Networks and migration resettlement: Cherchez la femme. *Anthropological Quarterly*, 49(1), 20–27.

SNYDER, PETER A. (1976). Neighborhood gatekeepers in the process of urban adaptation: Cross-ethnic commonalities. *Urban Anthropology*, 5(1), 35–52.

SOCIAL SCIENCE RESEARCH COUNCIL SUMMER SEMINAR ON ACCULTURATION (1954, December). Acculturation: An exploratory formation. *American Anthropologist*, *LVI*, 973–1002.

SOUTHALL, AIDAN W. (1961). Kinship, friendship and the network of relations in Kisengi, Kampala. In A. W. SOUTHALL (ed.), *Social Change in Modern Africa*. London: Oxford University Press, 217–29.

SPICER, E. H. (1968). Acculturation. In D. L. SILLS (ed.), *International Encyclopedia of the Social Sciences*. New York: Macmillan, 21–27.

SPINDLER, G. C. & GOLDSCHMIDT, W. (1952, Spring). Experimental design in the study of culture change. *Southwestern Journal of Anthropology*, 8, 68–83.

SPINDLER, GEORGE D. (1955). *Sociocultural and Psychological Processes in Menomini Acculturation*. Berkeley, CA: University of California Press.

SPIRO, M. E. (1955). The acculturation of American ethnic groups. *American Anthropologist*, 57, 1240–52.

SPITZBERG, BRIAN H. & CUPACH, WILLIAM R. (1984). *Interpersonal Communication Competence*. Beverly Hills, CA: Sage.

STANDING, GUY (1984). *Population Mobility and Productive Relations*. World Bank Staff Working papers #695. Washington, DC: The World Bank.

STENING, B. W. (1979). Problems in cross-cultural contact: A literature review. *International Journal of Intercultural Relations*, 3(3), 269–313.

STONE, P., DUNPHY, D., SMITH, M. & OGILVIE, D. (eds). (1966). *The General Inquirer: A Computer Approach to Content Analysis*. Cambridge, MA: MIT Press.

STONEQUIST, E. V. (1964). The marginal man: A study in personality and culture conflict. In ERNEST W. BURGESS & DONALD J. BOGUE (eds), *Contributions to Urban Sociology*. Chicago: The University of Chicago Press, 327–45.

STREET, RICHARD L. JR. & GILES, HOWARD (1982). Speech accommodation theory: A social cognitive approach to language and speech behavior. In MICHAEL E. ROLOFF & CHARLES R. BERGER (eds), *Social Cognition and Communication*. Beverly Hills, CA: Sage, 193–226.

SUBERVI-VELEZ, FEDERICO A. (1986). The mass media and ethnic assimilation and pluralism. *Communication Research*, 13(1), 71–96.

SzALAY, LORAND B. & INN, ANDRES (1987). Cross-cultural adaptation and diversity: Hispanic Americans. In YOUNG YUN KIM & WILLIAM B. GUDYKUNST (eds), *Cross-cultural Adaptation*. Newbury Park, CA: Sage.

SzAPOCZNIK, JOSE & HERRERA, MARIA CHRISTINA (1978). *Cuban Americans: Acculturation, Adjustment & the Family*. Washington, DC: National Coalition of Hispanic Mental Health and Human Service Organizations, 9–62.

TAFT, RONALD (1957). A psychological model for the study of social assimilation. *Human Relations*, 10(2), 141–56.

——(1966). *From Stranger to Citizen*. London: Tavistock.

——(1977). Coping with unfamiliar cultures. In NEIL WARREN (ed.), *Studies in Cross-cultural Psychology: Volume I*. London: Academic Press, 121–53.

TAGORE, R. (1961). *Toward Universal Man*. New York: Asia Publishing House.

TAJFEL, HENRI (1978a). *Differentiation Between Social Groups*. London: Academic Press.

——(1978b). Social categorization, social identity and social comparison. In HENRI TAJFEL (ed.), *Differentiation Between Social Groups*. London: Academic Press, 61–76.

TAJFEL, HENRI & TURNER, JOHN C. (1979). An integrative theory of intergroup conflict. In WILLIAM G. AUSTIN & STEPHEN WORCHEL (eds), *The Social Psychology of Intergroup Relations*. Monterey, CA: Brooks/Cole, 33–47.

TAYLOR, D. M. & SIMARD, L. M. (1975). Social interaction in a bilingual setting. *Canadian Psychological Review*, 16(4), 240–54.

TESKE, R. H. C. & NELSON, B. H. (1974). Acculturation and assimilation: A clarification. *American Anthropologist*, 1, 351–67.

THAYER, LEE (1968). *Communication and Communication Systems*. Homewood, IL: Richard D. Irwin.

——(1975). Knowledge, order, and communication. In BRENT D. RUBEN & JOHN Y. KIM (eds), *General Systems Theory and Human Communication*. Rochelle Park, NJ: Hayden, 237–45.

TING-TOOMEY, STELLA (1981). Ethnic identity and close friendship in Chinese-American college students. *Journal of Intercultural Relations*, 5(4), 383–406.

TINKER, J. N. (1973). Intermarriage and ethnic boundaries: The Japanese American case. *Journal of Social Issues*, 29(2), 49–66.

TOFFLER, ALVIN (1970). *Future Shock*. New York: Bantam Books.

——(1980). *The Third Wave*. New York: Bantam Books.

TORBIORN, INGEMAR (1982). *Living Abroad: Personal Adjustment and*

Personnel Policy in the Overseas Setting. New York: John Wiley & Sons.

——(1987). Cultural barriers as a social psychological construct: An empirical validation. In YOUNG YUN KIM & WILLIAM B. GUDYKUNST (eds), *Cross-cultural Adaptation: Current Theory and Research*. Newbury Park, CA: Sage.

TRIFONOVITCH, G. (1977). Culture learning/culture teaching. *Educational Perspectives*, 16(4), 18–22.

TRYON, R. C. & BAILEY, D. E. (1970). *Cluster Analysis*. New York: McGraw-Hill.

TURNER, JOHN C. (1987). *Rediscovering the Social Group: A Self-categorizing Theory*. London: Basil Blackwell.

TURNER, JOHN C. & GILES, HOWARD (1981). *Introduction. Intergroup Behavior*. Chicago: University of Chicago Press, 1–32.

U.S. COMMITTEE FOR REFUGEES (1984). *World Refugee Survey*. New York: U. S. Committee for Refugees.

USEEM, JOHN (1963). The community of man: A study of the third culture. *The Centennial Review*, 7, 481–98.

USEEM, JOHN, USEEM, RUTH HILL & DONOGHUE, J. D. (1963). Men in the middle of the third culture: The roles of American and non-western people in cross-cultural administration. *Human Organization*, 22(3), 169–79.

VALDEZ, AVELARDO (1979). The social and occupational integration among Mexican and Puerto Rican ethnics in an urban industrial society. Unpublished doctoral dissertation, University of California, Los Angeles.

VAN DEN BERGHE, PIERRE L. (1967). Language and nationalism in South Africa. *Race*, 9, 36–46.

VAN MAANEN, JOHN, DABBS, JAMES M., Jr. & FAULKNER, ROBERT R. (1982). *Varieties of Qualitative Research*. Beverly Hills, CA: Sage.

WALSH, ANTHONY (1979, April). The relation of blood levels to the assimilation of immigrants and intolerence of ambiguity. *Journal of Social Psychology*, 107(29), 257–65.

WALSH, J. E. (1973). *Intercultural Education in the Community of Man*. Honolulu, HI: University of Hawaii Press.

WARHEIT, GEORGE et al. (1982, October). Interpersonal coping networks and mental health problems among four race-ethnic groups. *Journal of Community Psychology*, 10(4), 312–24.

WARSHAUER, M. E. (1966). Foreign language broadcasting. In J. FISHMAN et al. (eds), *Language Loyalty in the United States*. The Hague: Mouton.

WASHINGTON, BENNETTA (1951). Background factors and adjustment: A

Dissertation. Washington: Catholic University of America Press.

WATSON, O. M. & GRAVES, T. D. (1966). Quantitative research in proxemic behavior. *American Anthropologist*, 68, 971–85.

WATZLAWICK, PAUL, BEAVIN, JANET HELMICK & JACKSON, DON D. (1967). *Pragmatics of Human Communication*. New York: Norton.

WEBB, EUGENE J., CAMPBELL, DONALD T., SCHWARTZ, RICHARD D. & SECHREST, LEE (1966). *Unobtrusive Measures: Nonreactive Research in the Social Sciences*. Chicago: Rand McNally.

WEIMANN, GABRIEL (1983, September). The strength of weak conversational ties in the flow of information and influence. *Social Networks*, 5(3), 245–67.

WEINBERG, ABRAHAM A. (1973). Mental health aspects of voluntary migration. In CHARLES ZWINGMANN & MARIA PFISTER-AMMENDE (eds), *Uprooting and after.* . . . New York: Springer-Verlag, 110–20.

WEINSTOCK, ALEXANDER (1964). Some factors that retard or accelerate the rate of acculturation. *Human Relations, XVII*, 321–40.

WELLMAN, BARRY (1982). Studying personal communities. In PETER V. MARSDEN & NAN LIN (eds), *Social Structure and Network Analysis*. Beverly Hills, CA: Sage, 61–80.

—(1983). Network analysis: From method and metaphor to theory and substance. *Sociological Theory I*. San Francisco: Jossey-Bass.

WEN, K. (1976). Theories of migration and mental health. *Social Science and Medicine*, 10, 297–306.

WERNER, OSWALD & SCHOEPFLE, G. MARK (1987). *Systematic Fieldwork: Foundations of Ethnography and Interviewing*. Newbury Park, CA: Sage.

WHYTE, WILLIAM FOOTE (1984). *Learning from the Field*. Beverly Hills, CA: Sage.

WIEMANN, JOHN M. & BACKLUND, PHILIP (1980, Spring). Current theory and research in communicative competence. *Review of Educational Research*, 50(1), 185–99.

WILLIAMS, CAROLYN L. & WESTMEYER, JOSEPH (1986, July/October). Psychiatric problems among adolescent Southeast Asian refugees: A descriptive study. *Pacific/Asian American Mental Health Research Center Newsletter*, 4(3/4), 22–4.

WINCH, R. F. & SPANIER, G. B. (1974). *Selected Studies in Marriage and the Family* 4th ed. New York: Holt, Rinehart & Winston.

WITKIN, H. A. & BERRY, J. W. (1975). Psychological differentiation in cross-cultural perspectives. *Journal of Cross-Cultural Psychology*, 5, 4-87.

WOLFINGER, R. (1965). The development and persistence of ethnic voting. *American Political Science Review*, 59, 896–908.

WONG-RIEGER, Durhane (1984). Testing a model of emotional and coping responses to problems in adaptation: Foreign students at a Canadian university. *International Journal of Intercultural Relations*, 8(2), 153–184.

YIN, ROBERT K. (1984). *Case Study Research*. Beverly Hills, CA: Sage.

YOSHIKAWA, MUNEO J. (1978). Some Japanese and American cultural characteristics. In MICHAEL H. PROSSER, *The Cultural Dialogue: An Introduction to Inter-cultural Communication*. Boston, MA: Houghton Mifflin, 220–39.

——(1988). Cross-cultural adaptation and perceptual development. In YOUNG YUN KIM & WILLIAM B. GUDYKUNST (eds), *Cross-cultural Adaptation: Current Approaches*. Newbury Park, CA: Sage.

YUM, JUNE OCK (1982). Communication patterns and information acquisition among Korean immigrants in Hawaii. *Human Communication Research*, 8(2), 154–69.

——(1983). Social network patterns of five ethnic groups in Hawaii. In ROBERT BOSTROM (ed.), *Communication Yearbook 7*. New Brunswick, NJ: Transaction, 574–91.

——(1984). Network analysis. In WILLIAM B. GUDYKUNST & YOUNG YUN KIM (eds), *Methods for Intercultural Communication Research*. Beverly Hills, CA: Sage, 95–116.

——(1987). Locus of control and communication patterns of immigrants. In YOUNG YUN KIM & WILLIAM B. GUDYKUNST (eds), *Cross-cultural Adaptation*. Newbury Park, CA: Sage.

——(1988). Network theory in intercultural communication. In YOUNG YUN KIM & WILLIAM B. GUDYKUNST (eds), *Theories of Intercultural Communication*. Newbury Park, CA: Sage.

ZAJONC, ROBERT B. (1952). Aggressive attitude of the 'stranger' as a function of conformity pressures. *Human Relations*, 5, 205–16.

ZENNER, W. P. (1970). International networks in a migrant ethnic group. In R. F. SPENCER (ed.), *Migration and Anthropology*. Seattle, WA: University of Washington Press, 36–48.

ZONGREN, LIU (1984). *Two Years in the Melting Pot*. San Francisco, CA: China Books.

ZUBRZYCKI, J. (1958). The role of the foreign language press in immigrant integration. *Population Studies*, 12, 73–82.

ZURCHER, LOUIS A. Jr. (1977). *The Mutable Self: A Self Concept for Social Change*. Beverly Hills, CA: Sage.

ZWINGMANN, CHARLES & PFISTER-AMMENDE, MARIA (1973). Uprooting and after: General review. In CHARLES ZWINGMANN & MARIA PFISTER-AMMENDE (eds), *Uprooting and After. . . .* New York: Springer-Verlag, 1–3.

About the author

Young Yun Kim received her B. A. degree in 1969 from Seoul National University in Korea, and moved to the United States in 1970. She completed her M. A. degree in Speech Communication at the University of Hawaii in 1972 under the sponsorship of the East–West Center, and Ph. D. degree in Communication Studies at Northwestern University in 1976. Currently, she is Professor of Communication at Governors State University (University Park, Illinois), teaching graduate-level courses in communication theory, research methodology, intercultural communication, nonverbal communication, and communication training. Her primary research focus has been on the role of communication in cross-cultural adaptation. She has directed a number of research projects in Asian and Hispanic communities including a federally-funded two-year study of Indochinese refugees' psychological, social, and economic adaptation patterns. Her recent publications include: Communicating with strangers (Random House, 1984), Methods for intercultural communication research (Sage, 1984), Interethnic communication (Sage, 1986), Cross-cultural adaptation (Sage, 1987), and Theories of intercultural communication (Sage, 1988).

INDEX OF NAMES

INDEX OF SUBJECTS